KF
9625
.G64

Goldkamp, John S.

Two classes of
accused

DATE			

© THE BAKER & TAYLOR CO

Two Classes
of Accused

Two Classes of Accused

A Study of Bail and Detention in American Justice

John S. Goldkamp
Department of Criminal Justice
Temple University

Ballinger Publishing Company ● Cambridge, Massachusetts
A Subsidiary of Harper & Row, Publishers, Inc.

International Standard Book Number: 0-88410-802-3

Library of Congress Catalog Card Number: 79-13042

Printed in the United States of America

Library of Congress Cataloging in Publication Data

Goldkamp, John S
 Two classes of accused.

 Bibliography: p.
 Includes index.
 1. Arrest—United States. 2. Bail—United States. 3. Arrest—Pennsylvania—Philadelphia. 4. Bail—Pennsylvania—Philadelphia. I. Title.
KF9625.G64   345'.73'072   79-13042
ISBN 0-88410-802-3

Dedication

To Mary, Otto, and the entire clan
with deep appreciation
—and to S.M. Cristina

Contents

List of Figures and Tables   xi

Foreword   *Michael J. Hindelang*   xv

Acknowledgments   xvii

Part I
Understanding Bail and Detention   1

Chapter 1
Introduction   3

Bail, Detention, and Reform: Background   4
Bail Decisionmaking and the Determination of Pretrial
   Custody   6
The Format of the Inquiry   9
Equal Protection and the Preadjudicatory Classification
   of Defendants   11
Notes   13

Chapter 2
Making Sense of Bail Decisionmaking:
A Search for Legal Policy   15

The Eighth Amendment of the Constitution of the United
   States and the Right to Bail   15

Pretrial Flight and Danger: The Juxtaposition of Two Bail
   Decision Functions in Court Cases (1951–1965)   18
The Federal Bail Reform Act of 1966   23
The Use of Decision Criteria in Court Cases Since the Bail
   Reform Act   25
Notes   31

Chapter 3
Other Sources of Bail Policy: A Chronology   39

The Standards of the American Bar Association (1968)   39
The Preventive Detention Code of the District of Columbia
   (1970)   41
The Standards of the National Advisory Commission on
   Criminal Justice Standards and Goals (1973)   43
The Uniform Rules of Criminal Procedure (1974)   45
The Standards of the National Association of Pretrial
   Services Agencies (1978)   46
Conclusion: Detention Under the Various Models   49
Notes   51

Chapter 4
State Bail Guidelines   55

Provisions in State Bail Guidelines   55
Decision Criteria Recommended in State Bail Guidelines   62
Summary: Bail Decisionmaking and Pretrial Detention
   According to Present Legal Guidelines   70
Notes   73

Chapter 5
Lessons From Previous Research: Findings and Issues   77

Descriptive Studies   78
Community Ties, ROR, and Flight   88
The Predictive Validity of Criteria Employed in the
   Bail Decision   92
Crime on Pretrial Release and Preventive Detention   95
Conclusion: The Present State of Knowledge   101
Notes   104

Part II
Bail and Detention in Philadelphia 109

Chapter 6
Philadelphia as a Case Study: The Site and Method 111

Overview of Criminal Processing in Philadelphia 112
Guidelines Governing Bail in Philadelphia 115
The Sample and Data 122
Characteristics of Philadelphia Defendants 126
Notes 133

Chapter 7
Bail Decisionmaking in Philadelphia:
An Empirical Analysis 139

Bail Decisions in Philadelphia: An Overview 139
Bailsetting as a Trifurcated Decision Process: An
  Analytic Model 143
Granting ROR: Step One 145
Detention Without Bail: Step Two 151
Cash Bail: Step Three 151
Conclusion 157
Notes 158

Chapter 8
Release or Detention Before Trial: An Analysis of the
Determination of Pretrial Custody in Philadelphia 163

Custody Status Twenty-Four Hours After First Appearance 165
Multivariate Analysis of Pretrial Custody 169
Developing a Defendant Typology to Predict Pretrial
  Detention 174
Notes 182

Chapter 9
Pretrial Custody and Later Judicial Outcomes 185

Interpretations of the Relationship and Their Implications 185
The Philadelphia Data 188
Adjudication and Pretrial Custody 189

Pretrial Custody and the Sentencing of Philadelphia
   Defendants   199
The Effects of Detention: The Verdict in Philadelphia
   and Its Implications   209
Notes   211

Part III
Conclusion   215

Chapter 10
Bail and Detention in American Justice:
Unresolved Issues   217

The Search for Bail Policy   217
Lessons from Previous Research   220
Bail and Detention in Philadelphia: The Charge Standard   222
The Effect of Community Ties on Pretrial Custody   224
The Effects of Detention Question   225
Two Classes of Accused: An Equal Protection Assessment
   of the Findings   226
Disparity in Bail and Detention   229
Conclusion: More Questions   230
Notes   231

Appendix A
Directory of State Bail and Pretrial Release Guidelines   233

Appendix B
Pennsylvania Rules of Criminal Procedure—4001,4003,4004   237

Appendix C
List of Variables in the Philadelphia Data   241

Appendix D
Coding of Charge in the Philadelphia Study   245

References   249

Index   257

About the Author   261

List of Figures and Tables

FIGURES

1-1 Bail Decisionmaking and the Determination of Pretrial
     Custody: Overview   8
4-1 The Evolution of the Appearance and Danger Views
     of Bail Decisionmaking   71
6-1 Simplified Schematic of Criminal Processing in
     Philadelphia   113
6-2 Definition of the Philadelphia Sample   124
7-1 The Bail Decision as a Trifurcated Decision Process   144
8-1 Predictive Attribute Analysis of Rate of Detention
     Among Philadelphia Defendants   177
9-1 Models Explaining the Relationship Between
     Pretrial Custody and Disposition   187
9-2 The Adjudication of Defendants' Cases Viewed as
     a Trifurcated Decision Process   192
9-3 Sentencing of Philadelphia Defendants Viewed as
     a Bifurcated Decision Process   201

TABLES

4-1 Provisions Included in State Bail and Release
     Guidelines, by State: December, 1978   56
4-2 State Bail and Pretrial Release Guidelines:
     Prescriptive Decision Criteria, by State:
     December, 1978   64

4-3	Bail Decision Criteria: Number of Criteria, by State: 1978	66
6-1	ROR Interview Dimensions and Scoring Criteria	120
6-2	Estimated Number of Defendants Appearing for Preliminary Arraignment, by Number of Prior Arrests, Number of Prior Convictions, and Most Serious Prior Conviction, Philadelphia: August to November, 1975	128
6-3	Estimated Number of Defendants Appearing for Preliminary Arraignment, by ROR Points Scored, Philadelphia: August to November, 1975	129
6-4	Estimated Number of Defendants Appearing at Preliminary Arraignment, by Final Community-Ties Rating (good risk/poor risk), by Age, Race, Sex, Employment, and Income, Philadelphia: August to November, 1975	132
7-1	Estimated Number of Defendants Appearing at Preliminary Arraignment, by Bailsetting Outcomes, by Age, Race, Sex, Marital Status, Employment, Income, Prior Criminal Record, and Criminal Charge, Philadelphia: August to November, 1975	140
7-2	Multiple Regression of ROR Outcomes of Groups of Independent Variables for Defendants Appearing at Preliminary Arraignment, Philadelphia: August to November, 1975	146
7-3	Multiple Regression of ROR Outcomes on All Independent Variables (Eight Variables Entering First in Free, Stepwise Regression Solution) for Defendants Appearing at Preliminary Arraignment, Philadelphia: August to November, 1975	149
7-4	Estimated Number of Defendants with Cash Bail Set at Preliminary Arraignment, by Median Amount of Ten Percent Bail, by Selected Attributes, Philadelphia: August to November, 1975	152
7-5	Multiple Regression of Amount of Cash Bail on Groups of Independent Variables for Defendants Appearing at Preliminary Arraignment, Philadelphia: August to November, 1975	154
7-6	Multiple Regression of Amount of Cash Bail on All Independent Variables (Five Variables Entering First in a Free, Stepwise Solution) for Defendants Appearing at Preliminary Arraignment, Philadelphia: August to November, 1975	155

7-7   Evaluation of First-Order Interaction Effects of the
        Five First-Entering Independent Variables on the
        Amount of Cash Bail Using a Group-Stepwise Regres-
        sion Procedure, for Defendants Appearing at Pre-
        liminary Arraignment, Philadelphia: August to
        November, 1975   156
8-1   Estimated Number of Defendants with Cash Bail
        Set at Preliminary Arraignment, by Amount of Cash
        Bail and Pretrial Custody Status, Philadelphia:
        August to November, 1975   164
8-2   Estimated Number of Defendants Appearing at
        Preliminary Arraignment, by Custody Status, by
        Selected Attributes, Philadelphia: August to
        November, 1975   166
8-3   Multiple Regression of Pretrial Custody on Groups
        of Independent Variables for Defendants Appearing
        at Preliminary Arraignment, Philadelphia: August to
        November, 1975   170
8-4   Multiple Regression of Pretrial Custody on All Inde-
        pendent Variables (Nine Variables Entering First in
        a Free, Stepwise Solution) for Defendants Appearing
        at Preliminary Arraignment, Philadelphia: August to
        November, 1975   173
8-5   Defendant Classes Using Predictive Attribute Analysis,
        by Rates of Detention   180
9-1   Estimated Number of Defendants Appearing at
        Preliminary Arraignment, by Final Case Disposition,
        by Pretrial Custody, Philadelphia: August to
        November, 1975   190
9-2   Product Moment Correlations Between Pretrial
        Custody Vectors and Six Control Variables with
        Diversion Outcomes for Philadelphia Defendants
        with Step Two Dispositions   195
9-3   Testing the Relationship Between Pretrial Custody
        and Diversion Outcomes: Multiple Regression of
        Diversion Outcomes on Six Control Variables
        (Entered on First Step) and Vectors Representing
        Pretrial Custody (Entered on Last Step) for
        Philadelphia Defendants with Step Two Dispositions   196
9-4   Product Moment Correlations Between Pretrial
        Custody Vectors and Six Control Variables with
        Subsequent Adjudication for Philadelphia Defen-
        dants with Step Three Dispositions   197

9-5   Testing the Relationship Between Pretrial Custody
       and Adjudication: Multiple Regression of Formal
       Adjudication on Six Control Variables (Entered
       First Step) and Vectors Representing Pretrial Custody
       (Entered on Last Step) for Philadelphia Defendants
       with Step Three Dispositions   198
9-6   Estimated Number of Defendants Appearing at
       Preliminary Arraignment, by Sentencing Outcomes,
       by Pretrial Custody, Philadelphia: August to
       November, 1975   200
9-7   Step One Sentencing Outcomes for Convicted
       Philadelphia Defendants: The Relationship
       Between Pretrial Custody and Nonincarceration/
       Incarceration   202
9-8   Product Moment Correlations Between Pretrial
       Custody Vectors and Six Control Variables with
       Nonincarceration/Incarceration Sentencing
       Outcomes for Convicted Philadelphia Defendants   203
9-9   Testing the Relationship Between Pretrial Custody
       and Sentencing: Multiple Regression of Nonincar-
       ceration/Incarceration on Six Control Variables
       (Entered on First Step) and Vectors Representing
       Pretrial Custody (Entered on Last Step) for
       Convicted Philadelphia Defendants   204
9-10   Step Two Sentencing Outcomes for Convicted
       Philadelphia Defendants Sentenced to Incarcera-
       tion: the Relationship Between Pretrial Custody
       and Length of Incarceration   206
9-11   Product Moment Correlations Between Pretrial
       Custody Vectors and Six Control Variables with
       Length of Sentences for Convicted Philadelphia
       Defendants Sentenced to Incarceration   207
9-12   Testing the Relationship Between Pretrial Custody
       and Sentence Length: Multiple Regression of
       Sentence Length on Six Control Variables (Entered
       on First Step) and Vectors Representing Pretrial
       Custody (Entered on Last Step) for Convicted
       Philadelphia Defendants Sentenced to Incarceration   208

Foreword

The institution of bail is among the oldest and yet the least studied aspects of criminal justice processing in Anglo-American law. From a jurisprudential point of view it represents a cruel irony: bail, a concept designed to be compatible with a presumption of innocence through a grant of freedom pending trial, requires balancing this freedom against the potential social costs of the released defendant's committing pretrial crimes and/or failing to appear for a determination of guilt at trial. The more defendants who are released on bail, the greater the likelihood of pretrial crime and failure to appear. Hence, if some balance or equilibrium is not maintained, the very existence of pretrial release could be threatened as too costly from a societal point of view. At the same time a restrictive pretrial release policy has associated with it the financial and nonfinancial costs of confining large numbers of defendants in jail before trial. From a practical point of view the decision whether to grant bail—a decision that has dramatic impact on individual defendants at least with respect to the emotional and economic trauma of confinement—has typically been made with limited (and sometimes conflicting) legislative guidance, with only scant information about the defendant and the alleged offense, after only a brief period of deliberation by the decisionmakers, and with limited (if any) feedback to the decisionmakers regarding appearance for trial and pretrial offending. To complicate matters further, the precarious balance struck between potential costs to defendants and to society is highly sensitive to diverse political pressures—witness the constitutional amendment passed by Michigan voters in 1978 authorizing preventive detention. The result is that the institution of bail has often fared better in theory than in practice.

Because questions concerning a "right to bail" are so fundamental, and particularly because they are so inextricably bound up with the cornerstone of Anglo-American law, presumption of innocence, it is perhaps surprising that bail has received relatively little systematic attention. Foote, Thomas, and others have made important contributions to the study of bail, but not until the emergence of this volume have the key pieces been assimilated in such a thorough fashion. To my mind, the contributions of this effort derive from the analysis of the relevant legal and empirical materials, and, to the extent possible, a synthesis of the two.

In the legal realm, the Constitution, the case law, and the statutory law at the state and federal levels are examined to discover what light they can shed on the ideological origins of current practices surrounding the use of bail and to learn, quite simply, how bail "ought" to be decided from a legal point of view. In the empirical realm, the tangled web of previous research is dissected in order to distill the current state of empirical knowledge regarding bail in practice. In the original empirical research, conducted in Philadelphia as a case study, an impressively thorough quantitative assessment goes to the key questions that are at the heart of the matter: how many are detained without bail, released on their own recognizance, or have cash bail set? To what extent do these decisions flow from apparently relevant legal considerations as distinct from personal considerations such as the defendant's race, social class, or ties to the community? What factors seem to dominate the use of pretrial detention? And, to what extent does pretrial detention affect the likelihood of conviction and the severity of judicial sanction?

The answers to all of the questions are important in practical and in theoretical terms. Certainly any attempt to improve bail as it currently operates requires some comprehensive assessment of just how it does operate. It is because of its comprehensive scope, its in-depth analyses, its well-conceptualized approach, and its overall quality that John Goldkamp's efforts in this volume represent a solid and an important contribution to our understanding of bail—how it is supposed to work and how, for example, it works in Philadelphia, a model reform jurisdiction.

Perhaps the most important implication of this work is that serious questions that have been obscured by nearly a decade and a half of bail reform are raised about the institution of bail and pretrial detention. This research opens the door to a re-examination of bail and detention issues and provides a firm grounding for future efforts.

Michael J. Hindelang

Acknowledgments

My thanks are due to the many people who helped in different ways to move this book from inception to completion. First and foremost, I would like to express my deepest gratitude to Michael Hindelang, whose support, advice, and special abilities as an educator served as the foundation for this undertaking. I am especially grateful for the criticism, encouragement, and friendship of Marguerite Warren, and for the helpful comments and enthusiasm of Donald Newman.

A major debt is also owed my colleagues and friends at the Criminal Justice Research Center, Albany, New York. In the early stages, the typing of Mary Ann Hammond and Susanne Freeman was indispensable. For help in the later stages, I am very grateful for the typing of Sharleen Saxe, Susan Durant, Suzette Geary, and Lucy Siegal—and for the proofing and other clerical labor of Maria Casapini, Marjorie Jones, and Connie Rowe. Without the programming skills of Dan Papenfuss, the components of the Philadelphia data might never have been successfully merged and made suitable for analysis; he has my sincere thanks. Ann Pastore and Mary Lee (Lou) Newell should also know that I am grateful for their help and friendship. I was especially fortunate to have the typing services of Lois Kirby Davies in the final "final" stage of the manuscript; she set a pace that was hard to match. Her diligence has done much to improve the integrity of the final product.

Needless to say, a major part of this study would not have been possible without the cooperation of the officials of the Philadelphia court system. It was due mainly to the interest and openness of

Dewaine L. Gedney, Jr., that the study was carried out in Philadelphia—although he should in no way bear responsibility for its results. Thanks to Nick Gedney and his especially tolerant staff at the Pretrial Services Division of the Court of Common Pleas and Muncipal Court of Philadelphia, many potential obstacles to the research were easily overcome. By reviewing and critiquing this work at various stages of development, Nick has contributed valuable insight that has improved its content. Where I have chosen not to heed his advice, he may be assured that it is no reflection of my appreciation or esteem. Forewarned, however, I am prepared to accept the consequences for positions I have taken and interpretations I have made.

I am also greatly indebted to Mary Picado of the Data Processing Unit of the Court of Common Pleas. It was Ms. Picado who listened to my particular request for court data and who set about devising ways to respond to it. Without her special competence, I never would have been able to obtain the data I sought. It is through the efforts and cooperation of Mary Picado and Dewaine Gedney that the collection of data in Philadelphia was so successful.

I'd like to thank two sisters—Gail Goldkamp Bagley and Carole Goldkamp—for their considerable help during the hot Philadelphia, data-gathering summer of 1976. The former sister I exploited shamelessly for food and shelter; the latter for labor. Their love and companionship made bearable an often tedious task. I'm not sure what I would have done without them. Similarly, Dr. Dan Butterworth and his peculiar stringed affliction have, without doubt, helped to keep this research in its proper perspective.

Indirectly, John Vesely and Paul Davallou, my first teachers in criminal justice, had much to do with this work. They have my gratitude and admiration.

The final version of this text has incorporated comments and criticism from a number of persons. First and foremost, I am indebted to Nicolette Parisi for her eye for detail and her practical comments. She helped me over many a hurdle. For constructive criticism (and other kinds of abuse), I am especially grateful to Michael Gottfredson and Michael Hindelang. Michael Kirby's incisive comments were also invaluable (and certainly expressive!), especially when counterbalanced by those of D. Alan Henry. Robert Waller deserves special mention—for making the last stretch in the road bumpy, when it had looked quite smooth. For his legal dentistry (though not of the painless variety), he has my thanks.

The research reported in this book was supported in part by a grant from LEAA to the Criminal Justice Research Center, Albany, New York. The opinions expressed and conclusions drawn are the sole responsibility of the author, and not of any of the sponsoring or participating agencies.

Taken from the county jail
  by a set of curious chances;
Liberated then on bail,
  on my own recognizances.

W.S. Gilbert
The Mikado, I (1885)

There was an old Justice named Percival,
Who said, "I suppose you'll get worse if I
  Send you to jail,
    So I'll put you on bail."
Now wasn't Judge Percival merciful?

Old English Limmerick

✳ *Part I*

Understanding Bail and Detention

Chapter 1

Introduction

It appears that each and everyone of us has been denied some basic constitutional right and we stand before the public at large guilty until we can prove ourselves innocent . . . .

> From grievances of defendants
> detained in the Tombs,
> August 11, 1970.

The due process precept that persons accused of crimes are "innocent until proven guilty" is central to the constitutional framework governing the administration of justice in the United States. Problematically, pretrial detention—the practice of locking people in jail prior to trial—treats certain defendants who are presumed innocent as if they were guilty. For the nearly fifty thousand defendants detained in the nation's jails on a given day, the implications of this contradiction are substantial, both in terms of the hardships that accompany confinement and the possible negative effects on the outcomes of their cases. For jailed defendants in the United States today, the presumption of innocence is more a myth than a legal reality. This book investigates, on both theoretical and empirical grounds, the role of pretrial detention in the American criminal justice system. Many questions must be answered. What is the purpose of pretrial detention? Who is typically detained? How is release or detention before trial determined? What are the consequences of detention for defendants? What are the consequences for the state?

Logically, study of bail decisionmaking holds the key to understanding the role of pretrial detention, for it is the bail decision that serves as the gatekeeping mechanism for detention. It creates two classes of accused—those who are detained and those who are released—at their first appearance before a judge. The role of pretrial detention can only be understood by considering the decision process that juxtaposes detention with release and by comparing those who are granted pretrial liberty with those who await adjudication in jail.

This chapter prepares the reader for the inquiry into bail and pretrial detention that follows. First, the origin and evolution of bail and detention are briefly highlighted, and the bail decision as it occurs presently in the United States is described. In addition, Chapter 1 provides an overview of the various components of the investigation that form the content of this book. Finally, a discussion of the possible constitutional implications of the process that divides defendants into two pretrial groups is included to serve as a backdrop against which the results of this study may be meaningfully viewed.

BAIL, DETENTION, AND
REFORM: BACKGROUND

Bail and detention are features of the American criminal justice system that have their origins in ancient history.[1] Detention and a form of bailed release were mentioned, for example, by Plato in *The Laws* (Plato, 1960:261). More recognizable precursors of the American forms of these practices existed in the Middle Ages. Proliferation of places of detention occurred, in particular, under the reign of Henry II in twelfth-century England (Barnes and Teeters, 1951; Burns, 1971; Mattick, 1975). During times of economic crisis in the late sixteenth and seventeenth centuries in England and France, jails, along with houses of correction and debtors' prisons, flourished (Foucault, 1965: 38–64).

With the growth of population centers in the United States during the eighteenth and nineteenth centuries and a simultaneous shift in philosophy away from corporal retribution and toward institutionalization (Rothman, 1971), jails grew in number. Although their functions were more diverse than simply pretrial detention, the place of the bail process as the gatekeeping mechanism for the use of pretrial detention became assured. In spite of diversification in the functions that jails were ultimately called upon to perform, a major use of jails was, and continues to be, incarceration of people who have been accused but not convicted of crimes.[2]

Concern for issues that surround pretrial confinement and the use of bail as a means for securing pretrial release has a history dating back to the Magna Carta. By 1689, when the English Bill of Rights was drawn up, safeguards against excessive bail became a fundamental legal concept, and the language used closely presaged the wording of the eighth amendment of the Constitution of the United States (Foote, 1965a:967–969). Studies documenting extreme abuse in the administration of bail and the use of pretrial detention were undertaken during the 1920s and 1930s, approximately a quarter century before key studies by Caleb Foote in the 1950s, and by the Vera Institute during the early 1960s.[3]

It was the work of Foote that inspired more than a decade of movement toward reform of bail and detention practices in the United States. Occurring in an era of social action against poverty and of judicial definition of defendant rights, the bail movement of the 1960s sought to reform abuses that plagued both the use of pretrial confinement (*e.g.*, unnecessary detention, overcrowding, poor hygiene, and few medical or other services) and the administration of bail (*e.g.*, misuse of cash bail to secure detention, corruption, and bias against poor defendants). Major attention was focused on these problems during 1964 when the National Bail Conference took place in Washington, D.C. (Freed and Wald, 1964). The increasing momentum toward bail reform was highlighted by the passage of the Federal Bail Reform Act of 1966 (18 U.S.C. §§ 1346–1352) and by the inception of many release on recognizance (ROR) programs around the country. In the 1970s, innovations designed to lessen the economic hardship inherent in cash bail and to reduce the use of detention further were added in the form of Ten Percent bail and conditional release programs.[4]

Of initial concern in the vigorous efforts undertaken by proponents of bail reform were two objectives: (1) to decrease what was seen as inordinate use of pretrial detention; and (2) to make bail practices more equitable so that poor defendants would not be disadvantaged simply because they could not afford cash bail. To accomplish this, reformers emphasized an alternative to cash bail, release on recognizance,[5] that was based on consideration of defendants' backgrounds and ties to the community. Although many ROR reform projects modeled after the original Vera Institute innovation in New York (Ares, Rankin, and Sturz, 1963) sprang up around the United States in the 1960s, the overall impact of bail reform efforts on the American way of bail and detention—and other aspects of the criminal justice system—is not entirely certain (Thomas, 1976). Patricia Wald has written a gloomy assessment of the effect of bail reform in the United States.

> In retrospect, bail reform efforts in the sixties have probably had their greatest impact in releasing good risk defendants who might otherwise have had to pay a bondsman or go to jail. They did not, however, do very

much to solve the problem of the defendant who needs supportive help in the community to succeed on release. Nor have they reduced the staggering costs society and the individual still pay for detaining persons not yet convicted of any crime. Finally, the abhorrent conditions under which presumptively innocent men are detained, have, on the whole, gotten worse, not better, due to overcrowding, physical deterioration of facilities, and a steadfast refusal to allocate adequate funds to this part of our criminal justice system (Wald, 1972:188).

Another observer has similarly characterized the ultimate effects of bail reform as falling short of achieving far-reaching change in the bail process and of eliminating the inequities experienced by poor defendants.

There is reason to doubt that ROR techniques introduced by Vera have spread throughout the country and become institutionalized . . . in the various court systems in an effective manner. There is reason to doubt that the problem of the indigent defendant who could be released has been resolved (Friedman, 1976:307).

Thomas (1976) has reported generally that proportionally fewer defendants were detained in the early 1970s than were detained in the early 1960s in many of the jurisdictions he studied. He noted that this decrease occurred during the height of bail reform, but he wondered if bail reform efforts alone could explain the phenomenon. A major implication of the study presented in the following chapters is that bail reform may not have successfully engaged judicial decisionmakers responsible for current bail and detention practices.

The basic study of bail decisionmaking and pretrial detention pursued in this book is prompted by the knowledge that vast amounts of energy and resources have been invested in bail reform efforts without having resolved a number of fundamental questions.

BAIL DECISIONMAKING AND THE DETERMINATION OF PRETRIAL CUSTODY

A certain amount of confusion commonly exists over what is meant by the terms "bail" and "bail decision." Bail typically connotes the fixing of a dollar amount that must be posted by a defendant to secure his or her release before trial. Equating bail and bail decisionmaking with strictly financial pretrial arrangements is, however, misleading. The original meaning of the term bail is much broader.

Black's Law Dictionary (1951:177) defines bail as securing the "release of a person from legal custody, *by undertaking that he shall appear at the time and place designated and submit himself to the jurisdiction and the judgment of the court*" (emphasis added). Bail decision therefore implies more than deciding dollar amounts. Several decision options are available: the defendant may be detained outright with no hope of release (as in murder cases in many jurisdictions); cash bail may be set in any specified amount (high or low); release may be granted contingent on a promise to appear as required (ROR); or nonfinancial release may be granted, conditioned by supervision or participation in specified programs.

It is difficult to look at one aspect of criminal justice processing without becoming aware of its close relationship to other aspects. For the bail decision and the determination of pretrial release or detention, the implications of this are critical. Bailsetting and pretrial custody outcomes are greatly affected by a number of prior "processing" factors, ranging from local crime patterns and arrest practices to the policies and interests of various bail decision participants. At the same time, these pretrial outcomes themselves may have a great deal of impact on subsequent processing realities. For example, if the jails are filled with detainees awaiting trial, court scheduling is affected and resources destined for other uses are absorbed. Both the extent to which detention is used and the length of pretrial confinement have an effect on the degree to which plea bargaining is used and jury trials are held in a given jurisdiction, and in the long run the quality of justice is affected. Serious questions, in fact, have been raised in a number of studies about the impact of detention on the outcome of defendants' cases at subsequent decision stages.

At the core of the process that screens defendants before trial is the administration of bail. The bail decision may appear relatively simple—but it may be complex, because a number of potential decision participants can influence its outcome. (See Figure 1-1.) Potentially, the police, the district attorney, and the local ROR project staff, in addition to the presiding judge or magistrate, may contribute in some fashion to the outcome of bail and pretrial release or detention decisions. In many cases, whether a defendant has representation when bail is considered mitigates the decision prospects. But, even after bail has been set, in many jurisdictions pretrial release further depends on the availability and willingness of the bondsman.

Complicating the bail decision and the prospects for release is the fact that each potential decision participant brings into play his or her own particular interests and decisionmaking criteria. For example, the police may release defendants charged with crimes of lesser seriousness at the station house (or before) by issuing citations

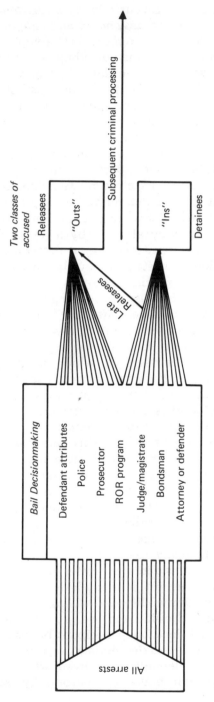

Figure 1-1. Bail Decisionmaking and the Determination of Pretrial Custody: Overview

(Feeney, 1972; Thomas, 1976). Charging decisions, made by police and prosecutors, may prove influential in bail considerations.[6] In some jurisdictions the prosecutor's recommendation is heavily relied upon by the judge or magistrate, and his or her intersts may reflect prosecutorial strategy or be based on the use of an "in-house" bail schedule. Pretrial release programs—where they exist—wield varying degrees of influence in bail decisionmaking, depending upon the nature of the relationships they enjoy with their respective courts. In exercising his or her discretion, the judge or magistrate may depend on one, none, or all of the other potential pretrial decision participants—or may be guided by personal concerns or policy. Finally, when money-bail has been set, the prospects for pretrial release may be further influenced by a bondsman's selection criteria, which may be based purely on business sense or profit motive (Freed and Wald, 1964; Dill, 1972). What is at issue in this study, however, are not the intricacies of possible interactions among prospective pretrial participants, but the final merged effect of their interactions, that is, whether or not defendants are released or detained.

Analysis of this pretrial screening "mechanism" may not be as simple as might at first appear. When either bail is denied or some form of nonfinancial release is granted at the first appearance before a magistrate, bailsetting and determination of pretrial status are the same event. That is, in these two instances, a defendant's pretrial custody status (release or detention) is determined directly by what is decreed at bailsetting. When money-bail is set, however, release or detention is not directly predictable as a result of the bail decision. Other factors, such as the defendant's ability to afford or to raise bail and the availability and willingness of a bondsman or a third-party surety, may mitigate his or her prospects for release before adjudication. In contrast to the bail decision, determination of pretrial custody simply refers to a defendant's custody situation after all of the options have been played out.

THE FORMAT OF THE INQUIRY

The questions asked in this investigation are fundamental: (1) What are the legal purposes for bail and pretrial detention? and (2) How should bail decisionmakers accomplish these purposes? Theoretical analysis begins in Chapters 2, 3, and 4 by reviewing diverse sources of legal policy that include the U.S. Constitution, case law, the Bail Reform Act, advisory standards, and bail guidelines in the fifty states and the District of Columbia. In legal analysis, the aim is not only to discover an "official" definition of the legal purpose of bail and detention but also to learn through instructions to bail judges in these sources the kinds of criteria that "ought" to guide bail decisions.

Chapter 5 anchors the inquiry within the context of the empirical research that has already been conducted in the area of bail and detention. The critical review of research presented there helps to bring the reader up-to-date with what has been learned in earlier studies and with the issues that have been raised in the area of bail. For example, serious questions have been raised concerning the appropriateness (predictive validity) of decision criteria that have been espoused in legal guidelines instructing bail decisionmakers. Methodological considerations in previous empirical studies are stressed and the research needs that shaped the approach taken in later chapters are discussed.

Empirical analysis of the bail decision process—including comparative analysis of detained versus released defendants, the two groups of accused that are the focus of this book—begins in Chapter 6. Of major interest in this next stage of inquiry are the results of a case study of bail decisionmaking and the determination of pretrial custody in Philadelphia, reported in Chapters 6, 7, and 8. Selection of Philadelphia as the site for such a study was undertaken to shift the focus of the investigation from the generalities of the legal framework, and descriptive studies presented in earlier chapters, to the specifics of a large urban jurisdiction that processes daily upwards of one hundred defendants at first appearance.

In order to fix subsequent empirical analyses squarely within the context of the decisionmaking environment of the Philadelphia courts, Chapter 6 begins by describing the characteristics of the study site. Special attention is given to the structural features of the justice system in Philadelphia and the sample design that was employed to accommodate them. Chapters 7 and 8 analyze the bail decisions and pretrial statuses of Philadelphia defendants to derive the factors that appear to have been most influential. Based on knowledge of the determinants of bail and custody, inferences are drawn concerning the nature of the role of pretrial detention when viewed in the context of the decision process that governs its use.

Finally, using the same Philadelphia data, Chapter 9 examines a special issue, the often-cited relationship between pretrial custody and the later outcomes of defendants' cases. A number of studies of the bail system in America have reported that defendants who are detained before trial fare less well then released defendants at adjudication and sentencing. The implications of this possibility are discussed and its applicability to the processing of Philadelphia defendants is assessed empirically.

The book concludes in Chapter 10, where the principal findings are reviewed and their implications considered. Compared to how bail decisionmaking ought or is thought to operate (according to sources of legal policy), how does it *actually* operate (in the case of the major jurisdiction studied)? Generalizing the findings, what appears to be the actual role of pretrial detention—the function served by the creation of two classes of accused—as compared to its "officially" envisaged purpose? Does pretrial custody have an impact on defendants' cases at later decision stages (adjudication and sentencing)?

EQUAL PROTECTION AND THE PREADJUDICATORY CLASSIFICATION OF DEFENDANTS

One useful way to consider the pretrial detention/presumption of innocence contradiction that is at the heart of this inquiry is in terms of competing interests: the interest of the defendant versus the interest of the state. The interest of a defendant not to be detained before adjudication is not difficult to comprehend. At liberty, a defendant does not suffer disruption in social ties, family life, and employment. Nor is a released defendant hampered in his or her efforts to prepare a defense due to lack of access to counsel. The released defendant does not need to cope with the stigma and the numerous emotional, psychological, and physical hardships that accompany confinement. And, finally, the released defendant may fare substantially better than a detained counterpart in terms of final disposition of the case. It may be understating the issue to characterize a defendant's preference for release before trial as a mere interest; one federal district court, in fact, has defined this preference as a "right," in writing that "the right to release under reasonable conditions is a *fundamental right.*"[7] (Emphasis added.)

But, what are the interests of the state in incarcerating defendants (presumably innocent) before trial? More specifically, because all defendants are not routinely held in detention, what interest does the state have in creating two classes of accused—one that suffers the hardships enumerated above and one that does not?

One of the major theoretical tasks of this work is to define precisely the state interest(s) responsible for bail and detention—the raison d'etre for the mechanism that classifies defendants into custody statuses before trial. This task may appear unnecessary to some, because traditionally the state interest behind the bail mechanism and pretrial detention was considered self-evident. The pat answer links bail to a need to secure a defendant's appearance in court. Yet, those familiar with bail are aware of a powerful hidden agenda, the preventive detention of persons deemed dangerous. To address this theoretical task—to provide an important foundation for other parts of the investigation—available legal guidelines are scrutinized in search of definitions of the state interest(s) in bail.

Beyond definition of the state interest motivating the pretrial classification mechanism, a second major thrust of this investigation has to do with the *nature of the classification itself*. In *Baxstrom v. Herold*, the Supreme Court instructed that "equal protection does not require that all persons be dealt with identically, but does require that a *distinction made have some relevance to the purpose for which the classification is made.*"[8] (Emphasis added.)

What are the distinctions on the basis of which defendants may ultimately find themselves in jail or at liberty? How are these distinctions, or decision criteria, defined in legal guidelines? How are they invoked in practice?

Once distinctions are discerned on both a theoretical and an empirical level, the next question is whether these distinctions bear some "relevance to the purpose for which the classification is made." Do the factors most instrumental in differentiating classes of defendants (released and detained) in any way promote the state interest in having such institutions as bail and pretrial detention?

The task of describing a state interest or purpose for the bail decision process begins in Chapter 2, in which legal guidelines are analyzed. Discussion of distinctions to be made between defendants is begun in the same chapter, based on review of a variety of legal guidelines. Investigation of distinctions, or key screening criteria, is pursued within an empirical framework in subsequent chapters—through comparative analysis of released and detained defendants in Philadelphia (Chapters 6 through 9). The equal protection/classification model may provide an especially useful evaluative framework for this investigation, because the results of the present inquiry may raise questions pertaining to the constitutionality of the bail decision process in general and of pretrial detention in particular.

From the scope of these and other issues concerning the nature, existence, and ramifications of the two classes of pretrial accused that are addressed in the pages ahead, it is clear that the project set forth in this book is ambitious. It is hoped that the final result will contribute knowledge to an area of criminal justice where a great deal has been (and is) taken for granted. Sykes has said of prison that it is "an instrument of the state, an organization designed to accomplish the *desires of society* with respect to the convicted criminal" (Sykes, 1958:13). (Emphasis added.) If this description of the role of the prison is apt, then the bail decision process and pretrial detention are also "instruments of the State . . . designed to accomplish the desires of society," but "with respect to" persons accused of crime. Thus, if what society *does* reflects what society wants to do, then the research discussed in this book will contribute knowledge of the "desires of society with respect" to accused persons. If what society *does* does not reflect what society wants, the study will have at least added to the knowledge of what society does.

NOTES

1. The history of bail and detention are adequately treated in existing literature (Foote, 1965a; 1965b; Thomas, 1976). Only a cursory historical review is undertaken here.

2. Analysis of data from the 1972 Survey of Inmates of Local Jails (Goldkamp, 1977; 1978) demonstrates that a greater proportion of inmates were serving sentences in jails than were awaiting trial in detention.

3. Foote's pioneering study of the bail system in Philadelphia appeared in 1954. An offshoot of that effort, actually conducted by his students (Alexander et al.), appeared in 1958. The efforts of the Vera Institute began in 1961 and continued for more than a decade.

4. The Ten Percent plan was first conceived of in Illinois in 1964 but did not become a major innovation until the early 1970s. In its most effective implementation, the Ten Percent plan eliminates the role of the bondsman (*e.g.*, in Philadelphia). Under such a plan, the defendant deposits 10 percent of the amount of his or her cash bail with the court, to be refunded once attendance at court proceedings has been achieved. Thus, the defendant no longer has to pay the bondsman's fee, which was never refundable (whether appearance in court was obtained or not). Under conditional release programs, defendants who are not released on their own recognizance are considered for release under supervision or under probationlike conditions (such as participation in certain programs). Conditional release was designed to provide a more highly supervised form of pretrial release than simple ROR for higher risk defendants, without resorting to a cash bail arrangement. (See Bowman, 1965; National Advisory Commission on Criminal Justice Standards and Goals, 1973; Thomas, 1976.)

5. ROR was available as an option of bail long before bail reform; however, it was rarely used (Beeley, 1927; Foote, 1954).

6. The fact that bail decisionmaking is often dependent on the nature or seriousness of the criminal charge is a theme that will be encountered frequently in the chapters that follow.

7. *Ackies v. Purdy* 322 F. Supp. 38, 41 (S.D. Fla., 1970). See also, *Stack v. Boyle* 342 U.S. 1,5 (1951).

8. 383 U.S. 107,111 (1966).

Chapter 2

Making Sense of Bail Decisionmaking:
A Search for Legal Policy

There exists a variety of sources of legal policy in the area of bail and detention. As will be demonstrated in the analytic tasks commenced in this chapter and continued in the two subsequent chapters, inexplicit goals and diverse means for achieving them are central features of these sources of legal policy. Discussion of certain of these sources in this chapter seeks to examine the theoretical underpinnings of the American way of bail and detention and to portray a legal-theoretical state of affairs against which subsequent empirical findings may be contrasted.

Chapter 2 focuses on four important sources of legal policy: the eighth amendment of the Constitution of the United States, decisions of the Supreme Court of the United States, the Federal Bail Reform Act of 1966, and key Federal cases dealing with bail and detention. Analysis of these sources is guided by two basic questions: (1) What is the purpose or state interest served by the bail decision and promoted by pretrial detention? and (2) On the basis of what distinctions are defendants to be sorted into two classes relevant to serving this purpose? Other kinds of bail and detention guidelines are investigated in the two succeeding chapters.

THE EIGHTH AMENDMENT OF THE
CONSTITUTION OF THE UNITED
STATES AND THE RIGHT TO BAIL

The Constitution of the United States has little to say on the subjects of bail and detention. The eighth amendment merely directs that "excessive bail shall not be required." No definitions of "bail" or "excessive" are provided, nor are instructions of when bail is appropriate or how bail and detention are to be administered made explicit. There is considerable room for interpretation. Without knowing precisely what purposes ought to be served by the bail decision and pretrial detention, it is difficult to define factors to guide the choice between detaining or releasing defendants.

According to Foote (1965a), bail under English law was construed as a device by which a defendant could secure preadjudicatory release while providing assurance of his or her appearance at future court proceedings. Denial of bail, where permitted, served the purpose of confining those defendants who were extremely likely to flee because they were facing the death penalty. Others have contended, however, that denial of bail to protect the community from potentially dangerous defendants always has been a legitimate bail function also (Mitchell, 1969:1225; Hess, 1971:308).

Foote has argued that the eighth amendment of the Constitution of the United States represents an incomplete rendering of the principles of English law that gave birth to the institution of bail and the use of pretrial detention. He contends that the issues surrounding pretrial detention and bail received fuller treatment under English law. Not only did English statutes carefully enumerate offenses under which a right to bail could be expected (it was restricted in capital cases), but the habeas corpus procedure was also viewed as a remedy for unlawful or unreasonable detention. In addition, the English Bill of Rights of 1689 contained an excessive bail clause that proscribed use of high bail as a means of securing the detention of defendants before trial. Foote notes that when these three concepts (*i.e.*, a specified right to bail, habeas corpus, and the excessive bail clause) were borrowed by the Americans, the habeas corpus remedy was incorporated into article 1, section 9 of the Constitution; the excessive bail clause appeared in the eighth amendment; and a specific definition of a right to bail appeared nowhere. He concluded that "thus removed from its English historical context and standing, as it is, incomplete and alone, the excessive bail clause of the eighth amendment represents some of the most ambiguous language in the Bill of Rights" (Foote, 1965a:969).

At a minimum, three interpretations pertaining to the existence of a right to bail have been assigned to the six meager words in the eighth amendment that address bail. A first interpretation, finding no explicit reference to a right to bail in that amendment, conceives of none. Instead, this interpretation defers to statutory provisions to learn when bail would be set as a right and when bail would be discretionary.[1] The excessive bail clause is read only as requiring reasonable bail in cases where it has been decreed by statute that bail is appropriate.[2]

The second interpretation differs subtly from the first. In the absence of constitutional or statutory direction as to the applicability of a right to bail, judicial discretion determines its appropriateness. In this context, the excessive bail clause merely decrees that, in those cases in which judicial discretion has determined that bail will be set, it should not be excessive.[3]

The first two interpretations rely on literal readings of the eighth amendment; that is, since no mention of a right to bail can be found, no right to bail can be said to exist. Consequently, there can be no presumption that defendants should not be detained before trial. Moreover, if either of these two interpretations were to be accepted, it would be extremely difficult to predict on what general bases defendants would be detained or released before trial. For, in the first case, it would depend on the statutory definitions in force in each jurisdiction, while in the second case, it would depend on the discretion exercised by the many judges and magistrates who set bail.

A third interpretation does find a right to bail implicit in the eighth amendment and relies on a reading of the historical evolution of bail under English law to bolster its assertion.[4] This position contends that the eighth amendment concern for excessive bail can stem only from a presumption favoring the release of defendants before trial (Foote, 1965a:979–981); that is, "there is not simply a federally guaranteed right to have bail fixed but a federally guaranteed right to pretrial freedom which may be abridged only under extreme high risk circumstances" (Fabricant, 1969:312).[5]

The concept of a right to bail is important to the present undertaking only if linked to the concept of the "right to release" before trial—or, as a right, it is meaningless. Without placing the right to bail in the context of a right to release, the concept of a right to bail is meaningless since nothing is safeguarded when the bail that is granted as a right may be set unaffordably high. The question of whether or not such a right exists under American law is crucial when looking for the officially envisaged basis for detention and bail. If one determines, for example, that there is a presumed right to release in certain cases, while not in others, one can then begin to examine the basis for the selective granting of that right. Yet, in treatises on the right to bail, a right to release is seldom discussed.

The principal interest in considering the eighth amendment of the

U.S. Constitution lies in seeking possible guidelines for the manner in which the pretrial screening of defendants operates. While much has been written in the debate concerning the right to bail (*i.e.*, whether it may be absolute, statutory, or discretionary), the fact remains that each of the positions represents one *interpretation* of the excessive bail clause of the eighth amendment.

Depending on the interpretation favored, different understandings of how and why the bail decision operates and detention is invoked result. In a statutory scheme, it would be necessary only to examine and explain the kinds of criteria specified in federal and state statutes. For a solely discretionary scheme, it would be difficult to obtain an overall picture of the proper use of bail and detention since guidelines would be absent or communicative of minimal restraint. In a scheme where there was a perceived right to release, it would be necessary only to study exceptions to this right to learn about the uses of pretrial detention. Setting the intricacies and possible merits of such a debate aside, however, it must be concluded that, alone, the eighth amendment raises more questions than it answers and offers little in the way of clear guidance relating to the operation of bail decisionmaking and the role of pretrial detention. But, the very fact that it lends itself so easily to more than one interpretation allows for the possibility that the bail decision may be viewed quite differently by various interested parties.

PRETRIAL FLIGHT AND DANGER: THE JUXTAPOSITION OF TWO BAIL DECISION FUNCTIONS IN COURT CASES (1951-1965)

Traditionally, two different views of the proper function of the bail decision process have coexisted in a state of tension. Early critics of the bail system recognized securing the appearance of defendants at required court proceedings as the only "legitimate" function of bail (Beeley, 1927; Morse and Beattie, 1932; Foote, 1954).[6] They voiced strong opposition to the practice of setting money bail at unafford-able levels so as to effect the preventive detention of defendants who—for one reason or another—were deemed dangerous by the presiding judges or magistrates. On the other hand, the perennial practice of setting bail in line with the seriousness of the offense charged and the recent appeal of preventive detention legislation[7] attest to the durability of the alternate view of the bail function. This latter view would not refute the legitimacy of the interest in assuring a defendant's appearance, but it would accord at least an equal role to "protecting the community" from dangerous defendants in bail determinations.

Two landmark cases—containing the seeds of this bail policy dialectic—were first heard by the U.S. Supreme Court in the fall of 1951. Dicta in *Stack v. Boyle*[8] and *Carlson v. Landon*[9] were contradictory. They have been cited in support of opposing positions on such issues as the right to bail and preventive detention.[10] Neither of the cases produced holdings directly applicable to the administration of bail in state courts, since each dealt with questions of federal law. In fact, *Carlson* dealt with detention in a deportation proceeding—a civil matter. Nevertheless, these cases are acknowledged as the first major treatment of bail and detention issues by the Supreme Court.

The roots of many of the key concepts that evolved in later cases, in bail legislation, and bail reform in general, can be found in *Stack v. Boyle*. In *Stack* dicta, the Court enunciated the following principles: (1) there is a presumption that defendants in all noncapital cases will be admitted to bail;[11] (2) this presumption is based on the *"traditional right* of the accused *to freedom* before conviction"; (3) this right, in turn, relies on the *presumption of innocence*, the need for preparation of an adequate defense, and the need to prevent the application of punishment before conviction; (4) release before trial is, however, "conditioned upon the accused's giving assurance that he will stand trial and submit to punishment if found guilty"; and (5) the fixing of bail "must be based on standards relevant to the purpose of assuring the presence of the defendant."[12]

The emphasis on a specified right to bail linked to a right to pretrial release and the use of bail as a means of permitting release conditioned upon the accused's giving assurance of future appearance clearly suggest that, in principle at least, detention would be appropriate only for *exceptional* defendants. The state interest is securing the attendance at court of persons charged with crimes. Release would appear to depend on two threshold criteria: (1) the offense with which a defendant is charged (whether "capital" or not) and (2) some assurance that a defendant will appear in court. While the first criterion is explicit and concrete (relying on statutory definitions of capital offenses), the second—"standards relevant to the purpose of assuring the presence of the defendant"—is rather vague. In *Stack*, they are linked to rule 46(c) of the Federal Rules of Criminal Procedure.[13] The standards outlined there refer to "the nature and circumstances of the offense charged, the weight of the evidence against him, the financial ability of the defendant to give bail, and the character of the defendant." How these standards might be employed to assess the likelihood of a defendant's appearance and/or how this likelihood might be translated into amounts of money-bail, is not spelled out.[14]

Carlson v. Landon[15] decided only four months after *Stack v. Boyle*, involved the detention without bail of aliens, who were members of the Communist party, for deportation proceedings. Although the decision dealt with a special civil proceeding (deportation) and was therefore, like *Stack*, not directly applicable to the administration of bail in state criminal courts, dicta in *Carlson* did deal generally with the issue of bail, espousing a view quite different from that seen in *Stack*.

In *Carlson* the Supreme Court found neither a constitutional right to bail nor a presumption favoring pretrial release (such as that based on a "traditional right . . . to freedom before conviction" discussed in *Stack*).[16] Discretion to grant or to deny bail was accorded by statute in the federal system: "The eighth amendment has not prevented Congress from defining the classes of cases in which bail shall not be allowed in this country."[17] The admonition against excessive bail in the eighth amendment was interpreted only to mean that where money-bail was deemed proper by statute, it should not be excessive.

In *Carlson* dicta, concern for the appearance of defendants at (deportation) proceedings was not the sole rationale for the bail decision. Rather, the court relied on anticipation of some harm—in this case a perceived threat to the government: "There is *reasonable apprehension of hurt* from aliens charged with a philosophy of violence against this Government."[18] (Emphasis added.)

In the concept of "apprehension of hurt," *Carlson* foreshadowed the later use of "danger-to-the-community" language to reflect a central consideration in pretrial release decisionmaking. Just as *Stack* is seen as authority for the appearance-oriented view of the bail decision process, concerns for defendant dangerousness in bail determinations are rooted in *Carlson*. Cases decided since 1951 can be seen as extensions of either of the two views of the function of the bail decision.

The opinion rendered by Justice Douglas in *Herzog v. United States* further emphasized the presumption expressed in Stack that release before trial ought to be strongly favored over detention in noncapital cases. Douglas wrote in that case that "doubts whether bail should be granted or denied should always be resolved in favor of the defendant."[19] Yet, the following year in *Ward v. United States*,[20] Justice Frankfurter indicated that when a reasonably set amount of money-bail would not assure the presence of the defendant, it was permissable to detain the defendant by denying bail. However, in 1959 in *Reynolds v. United States*,[21] Justice Douglas again alluded to the "traditional right to freedom before trial" and reiterated that the "purpose of bail is to insure appearance and submission to the judgment of the court," adding that "it is never denied for the purpose of punishment."[22]

Consideration of a defendant's ability to afford bail was included in the instructions for fixing bail in rule 46(c) of the Federal Rules of Criminal Procedure at the time *Stack* and *Carlson* were decided. However, it was not until a decade later in the two *Bandy v. United States* cases[23] that the defendant's financial status in bail determinations was addressed by a member of the Supreme Court. It was recognized in *Bandy I* that even low bail may be excessive for defendants who are indigent. Merely because of an inability to pay, such defendants may be forced to await trial in detention, while others with greater financial resources may obtain release.[24] Based on a rationale first voiced in *Griffin v. Illinois*[25]—which held in essence that whether a person received a fair trial should not depend on his or her personal wealth—Justice Douglas in *Bandy* considered the fact that pretrial release may depend solely on the defendant's ability to pay as tantamount to a denial of equal protection. Justice Douglas again emphasized in *Bandy I* that "the right to release is heavily favored" and that where indigency is involved, other (nonfinancial) means for assuring the future appearance of a released defendant should be arranged.[26] Dicta in *Bandy II* went even further, stressing the principle that "a man is entitled to be released on personal recognizance where other relevant factors make it reasonable to believe that he will comply with the orders of the court."[27]

On the other hand, three cases heard by individual members of the Supreme Court sitting as circuit justices in the early 1960s can be seen as descendants of the *Carlson* philosophy of bail, under which bail might be denied because of an "apprehension of hurt." In these cases and in later cases and legislation, two kinds of hurt, or perceived defendant dangerousness, are construed.

The first kind deals with a comparatively narrow definition of pretrial dangerousness and was evinced in *Fernandez v. United States*[28] and *Carbo v. United States*.[29] In *Fernandez*, Justice Harlan ruled that the court of original jurisdiction had the power to revoke bail for defendants who might be engaged in a variety of actions designed to thwart prosecution of their cases. Justice Harlan wrote that "District Courts have authority, as an incident of their inherent powers, to manage the conduct of proceedings before them, to revoke bail during the course of a criminal trial, *when such action is appropriate to the orderly progress of the trial and the fair administration of justice.*"[30] (Emphasis added.)

In *Carbo*, Justice Douglas further developed that bail could not only be revoked but could also be denied in the first place when there was "a substantial probability of danger to witnesses should the applicant be granted bail."[31] Mr. Justice Douglas in that case wrote that "keeping a defendant in custody during the trial to render fruitless any attempt to interfere with witnesses or jurors may, in extreme or unusual cases, justify denial of bail."[32]

The first kind of dangerousness rationale, then, stems from the powers of the judiciary to maintain orderly court processes, and it can be used to revoke the bail of a released defendant or to deny bail to a defendant seen as posing a specific threat to witnesses or jurors, for example. This kind of dangerousness concern can be applied to a defendant regardless of whether the case is capital or noncapital or whether the defendant is on appeal.

The second kind of dangerousness rationale is more general and is usually stated in terms of a threat to the public or the community. In *Leigh v. United States*[33] Chief Justice Warren acknowledged in principle that protection of the community might also be a state interest in the bail decision process: "It is to be denied only in cases in which it seems clear that the right to bail will be abused *or the community will be threatened* by the appellant's release."(Emphasis added.)

This concern was subsequently incorporated into the Bail Reform Act (discussed below) and was there restricted to persons charged in capital offenses or on appeal. The Bail Reform Act usage can, therefore, also be seen within the context of the apprehension-of-hurt concept voiced in *Carlson.*

In sum, the important cases heard by the Supreme Court before the Bail Reform Act of 1966 fell into two groups, each representing a different philosophy of bail and detention in terms of portraying a state interest. One line of cases—comprised of progeny of *Stack v. Boyle*—dealt chiefly with a right to bail that was linked to a right to pretrial release and described the purpose of the bail function in terms of assuring appearance. A preference for release under nonfinancial (nonmoney-bail) arrangements was also stated. But the interest described in the second line of cases—stemming from the *Carlson* outlook—was not premised on a presumption for pretrial release, nor solely on a concern for appearance. While this school did not refute the appearance concern, it pointed out that, in addition, consideration of a defendant's potential dangerousness was a legitimate concern. The *Carlson* apprehension-of-hurt concern subdivides in later cases into two kinds of dangerousness concerns: "potential disruption of orderly court processes or threat to witnesses or jurors" and (2) potential threat to the safety of the community.

It may be concluded from examination of these cases, then, that the state interest in bail determinations consisted of assuring the appearance of defendants at court and/or protecting the community or judicial process from dangerous defendants. Although it has been shown that there is precedent for the dangerousness or preventive detention view of bail decisionmaking, it should be noted that the appearance view has (until relatively recently) been staunchly held by reformers of the bail system and has been the more popularly voiced view. Whichever view is maintained—whether the purpose of the bail decision has to do with pretrial flight or dangerousness—these cases are not helpful in providing explicit instructions to decision-makers as to how to distinguish between defendants likely and un-likely to flee and/or likely and unlikely to be threats to the commu-nity—the classes of defendants that would theoretically derive from such interests. In *Stack*, one is told only that excessive bailsetting should be interpreted to mean "higher than is usually set"[34] and that bail should be set based on "standards relevant to the purpose of as-suring the presence of a defendant."

THE FEDERAL BAIL REFORM ACT OF 1966

The early effort toward bail reform culminated in the enactment of the Bail Reform Act of 1966.[35] The Bail Reform Act was predicated in general upon a view of the bail decision that was colored primarily by a concern for securing the appearance of defendants at court. As a federal statute, it reformed bail procedures only in the District of Columbia and in federal jurisdictions, but it was put forth also as a model for possible progressive bail legislation in the states. Both the presumption favoring pretrial release voiced in *Stack* and the suggestion in *Bandy* that other than financial conditions be em-ployed "as deterrents to bail jumping"[36] were reflected in the spirit and letter of the Bail Reform Act.

> Any person charged with an offense, other than an offense punishable by death, *shall*, at his appearance before a judicial officer, *be ordered released pending trial on his personal recognizance or upon the execution of an un-secured appearance bond* in an amount specified by the judicial officer, unless the officer determines, in the exercise of his discretion, that such a release will not reasonably assure the appearance of the person as required (18 U.S.C.A. section 3146(a)). (Emphasis added.)

An important feature of the Bail Reform Act was that it did not limit its preference for pretrial release to defendants charged in noncapital cases. In fact, the Act mandated that the same consideration given persons held in noncapital cases be extended to persons already convicted but awaiting sentencing or appeal—with two important distinctions. First, the presumption favoring pretrial release through a strong preference for ROR is qualified for capital cases and appeals. (Compare sections 3146 and 3148, for example.) For noncapital cases, defendants *"shall . . . be ordered released . . . on personal recognizance . . . unless"*; for capital cases and appeals, defendants *may* be so released. Second, whereas for noncapital cases, release conditions are established in the context of assuring appearance only, for capital cases and appeals, the judicial officer may consider whether or not the accused may be deemed to "pose a *danger* to any other person or to the community" (18 U.S.C.A. 3148.) Thus, the state interest in protecting the community from dangerous defendants—featured in the *Carlson-Leigh* strain of bail policy—appears in the Bail Reform Act as well, though in a very limited form. By implication, then, if such a release policy were in effect, the vast majority of defendants would be released. Theoretically, those in detention would represent those most likely to flee or, in a small number of cases, those most likely to be dangerous.

Although a presumption favoring own-recognizance release or its equivalent (release on an unsecured appearance bond) is clearly articulated in the Bail Reform Act (in the "shall be ordered released" phrasing shown above), the judicial officer is permitted to set other more restrictive conditions of release in order to guarantee a defendant's appearance at court. The Act introduced a priority for establishing terms of release that would be the least restrictive required to assure a defendant's appearance. Thus, ROR (the preferred arrangement) would be least restrictive of all; release in the custody of an organization or certain members of the community would be next; and release with travel or associations restrictions would be next. Use of Ten Percent cash bail, bail bond, or full cash bail were considered most onerous short of "part-time" custody of the defendants. While a *presumption* of release is implicit in the text of the Act, neither a right to pretrial release nor a right to bail is clearly spelled out. Thus, detention may result even in noncapital cases, especially where the traditional money-bail option is selected.

Another important contribution of the Federal Bail Reform Act is its direct treatment of the manner in which defendants are to be evaluated at bail determinations. At its base, of course, the Act follows the traditional scheme of distinguishing between defendants charged in capital cases (and involved in appeals) and defendants charged in noncapital cases in framing its provisions. (A somewhat more liberal release policy is available for the latter category, in line with the historical evolution of bail policy in the United States.[37])

But, beyond that gross distinction, the Bail Reform Act specifies criteria on the basis of which defendants ought to be evaluated at bail. In *Stack v. Boyle*, reference was made to "standards relevant to the purpose of assuring the presence of the defendant." The Bail Reform Act lists ten criteria to be considered in the pretrial release decision:

[1] . . . the nature of the offense charged, [2] the weight of the evidence against the accused, [3] the accused's family ties, [4] employment, [5] financial resources, [6] character and [7] mental health, [8] the length of residence in the community, [9] his record of convictions, and [10] his record of appearance at court proceedings or of flight to avoid prosecution or failure to appear at court appearances. (Numbers added.) (18 U.S.C.A. 3146(b).)

However, as in *Stack*, no indication as to how these criteria might relate to the likelihood of nonappearance or of pretrial dangerousness is given, nor is the decisionmaker instructed in the appropriate weighting of each consideration in relation to the others. In the brief moment during which the bail decision usually takes place, for example, how does a judicial officer determine the defendant's character or mental health? And, which of these ten criteria is most important? The Bail Reform Act represents considerable progress in the respect that through its provisions, a judicial officer has been informed of the factors upon which he or she must base the bail decision; yet, since no instructions relating to their relative usefulness are supplied, a great deal of room for judicial discretion has also been provided. Finally, it is surprising to learn that, absent explicit instructions, the factors recommended for evaluating risk of flight are to be equally useful in assessing the potential for danger for convicted and/or appealing persons.

THE USE OF DECISION CRITERIA IN COURT CASES SINCE THE BAIL REFORM ACT

Inclusion in the Bail Reform Act of community-ties decision criteria (items 3 through 6 of section 3146(b) cited above) reflected the belief of bail reform practitioners that these criteria provided information that—more than merely relying on the offense charged and prior criminal record—could help assess the likelihood that a defendant would appear at court. That is, by consideration of a defendant's roots in the community, length of residence in the community, employment history, and family ties, bail judges would have more appropriate, factual data for bail decisionmaking than previously.

Risk of Flight

The heavy emphasis placed on the use of these community-ties dimensions in federal courts after enactment of the Bail Reform Act[38] is exemplified by three cases heard by the U.S. Court of Appeals in the District of Columbia. In *White v. United States*,[39] Chief Judge Bazelon overturned a lower court's decision to deny release to a defendant charged in the death of a police officer based solely on the grounds of the "nature and circumstances of the offense charged" and the "weight of the evidence against the accused." Bazelon wrote:

> The District Judge apparently rested his finding of a risk of flight upon the severity of the sentence that could be imposed on apellant if she were convicted on the murder charge; if this factor were alone determinative, however, release would never be possible in a capital case, and the statutory scheme that Congress so carefully established for such cases would be nullified completely. In evaluating the likelihood of flight, the potential penalty has relevance, but here we are much more *persuaded by the stability of the appellant's relationship to the community.* She has lived in the District for ten years, and has displayed a record of steady employment, the continuation of which upon release is assured. These community roots strongly dispute any threat of flight.[40] (Emphasis added.)

In *United States v. Alston*,[41] Bazelon again found fault in neglecting proper consideration of community ties in the setting of bail. He admonished that the "nature of the offense"—translated by the bailsetting judge into "length of possible sentence"—should not be the prime consideration in the pretrial release decision. Although it was a relevant fact (because "the prospect of a long imprisonment certainly reduces the probability that a suspect will remain in custody"), Bazelon instructed that it was only one factor that must be "taken into account as part of a balanced judgment."[42]

At the same time, Bazelon criticized overreliance on a defendant's past record at bailsetting: "It is not the purpose of the bail system either to punish an accused again for his past crimes, or to punish him in advance for crimes he has not yet been shown to have committed."[43]

Past crimes would be relevant only when "violations of a bail or release order", were involved or when a defendant had a previous record of failure to appear.[44] Release was ordered on the grounds of the defendant's long residence in the community and his good employment record and prospects.

In *United States v. Bronson*,[45] the same court ordered a robbery defendant released on recognizance, reversing the decision of a lower court. The court asserted that community-ties criteria should be given "significant, even dominant weight" in the bail decision rather than simple consideration on the nature of the offense charged. The *Bronson* court ruled that it was an error not to credit a serviceman stationed in the District of Columbia with strong local ties, since supervision provided by the army would help satisfy the Reform Act's emphasis on nonfinancial conditions of release.

In *United States v. Honeyman*[46] and *United States v. Briggs*,[47] U.S. Courts of Appeals found fault with the setting of high money-bail in cases where good community ties indicated that other, less onerous conditions of release might secure appearance.[48] In *Harris v. United States*,[49] Justice Douglas, in his circuit justice capacity, overturned a lower court's decision to deny bail to a convicted defendant who was seeking release while on appeal. Justice Douglas justified his decision by relying on the good community ties of the defendant and the lack of a showing that he would not be a good risk. However, the Court of Appeals for the Fourth Circuit, in *United States v. Wright*,[50] ruled, to the contrary, that the "nature and circumstances of the offense charged" and the "weight of the evidence against the accused" were properly given greater weight than the defendant's community ties in the original court's bail decision.[51]

Overall, then, it is seen that in a great many cases community-ties criteria were installed as having the greatest weight in setting bail based on likelihood of appearance. Other factors—such as the offense charged or a defendant's prior criminal record—were given less weight.

Assessing Defendant Dangerousness

A second group of post-Bail Reform Act cases dealt with assessments of dangerousness.[52] It will be recalled that under that Act concern for a defendant's potential danger "to other persons or to the community" was restricted to persons held in capital cases or in cases on appeal. Interpretation and application of the dangerousness focus in the bail decision was a theme in a number of cases heard after 1966.[53]

Cases involving assessments of dangerousness may be understood in the context of the two dangerousness categories discerned in discussion of pre-Bail Reform Act cases. (Recall that concern for "apprehension of hurt" alluded to in *Carlson* engendered consideration of two kinds of defendant dangerousness in subsequent cases.)

Several cases heard after 1966 added to the *Fernandez-Carbo* tradition of defining pretrial dangerousness. In 1967, the Supreme Court ruled in *Bitter v. United States*[54] that a lower court did have the power to detain a defendant without bail in a noncapital case to "ensure the orderly and expeditious progress of a trial." The Court noted then that "this power must be exercised with circumspection. It may be invoked only when and to the extent justified by danger which the defendant's conduct presents or by danger of significant interference with the progress or order of a trial."[55]

Two cases heard in U.S. Courts of Appeals have added qualifications to this special power of courts to confine dangerous defendants. In *Gilbert v. United States*,[56] the court ruled that a denial of bail based on this kind of dangerousness ascription was only proper after a hearing showing that "the necessities of judicial administration require resort to such an emergency power." Relying on *Gilbert* and *Carbo*, the U.S. Court of Appeals for the Sixth Circuit found in *United States v. Wind*[57] that "the defendant is entitled to a hearing and to be afforded an opportunity to refute the charges that if he were released he might threaten or cause to be threatened potential witnesses, or might unlawfully interfere with a criminal prosecution."[58] That court further held that an in camera hearing of the contentions against the defendant would not satisfy the hearing requirement set forth in *Gilbert*.[59]

The second group of dangerousness cases heard after 1966 addressed the proper application of the more general, *Leigh*-like kind of dangerousness consideration adopted in section 3148 of the Bail Reform Act. In that section, when a person charged in a capital case or on appeal is deemed "to pose a danger to any other person or to the community," the bail official may dispense with the presumption favoring release under the least restrictive conditions. Beyond the twelve words alluding to this kind of danger in section 3148, however, no further instructions pertaining to the proper assessment of a defendant's dangerous propensities are found in the Act. How, in practice, is a defendant's potential danger to other persons or to the community to be assessed? And, what connection is there between conditions of release and assurance that a defendant will not pose a danger? In essence, this clause is addressing pretrial confinement or preventive detention of persons deemed dangerous without offering a clear basis for such a practice.

In *Sellers v. United States*,[60] Justice Black, as circuit justice, guarded against an interpretation of "posing a danger" that would be too easy to apply and stressed the gravity of such a determination.

> The idea that it would be dangerous in general to allow the applicant to be at large must—if it is ever a justifiable ground for denying bail as distinquished from a separate proceeding for a bond to keep the peace—*relate to some kind of danger that so jeopardizes the public that the only way to protect against it would be to keep the applicant in jail.*[61] (Emphasis added.)

In effect, Justice Black in *Sellers* held that for a person to be denied bail under the Bail Reform Act, he or she must be very dangerous indeed. Yet, he did not elect to specify how this danger might be measured. Justice Black implied, however, that an alleged offense that did not entail some aspect of "physical violence"[62] would not very likely be used to conclude that the defendant was dangerous under section 3148. As it applies to the phrase, "to any other person," the role of physical violence against the person can be easily understood. But, how is the concept of physical violence extended to relate meaningfully to "or to the community," which is not an individual vulnerable to physical violence but, instead, an ill-defined collectivity?

Certainly, inferences of a defendant's dangerousness are often drawn from the "nature and circumstances of the offense charged," when a crime involving violence against the person is alleged. Judges have traditionally responded to the offense-charged criterion in setting high bail for defendants charged with serious crimes involving violence.[63] In fact, proponents of bail reform strongly criticized this practice, which was seen as a sub rosa means of preventively detaining persons deemed dangerous by bail judges.[64] However, a brief examination of the Reform Act shows that the dangerousness alluded to in 18 U.S.C.A. 3148 is a difficult concept to define.

In *Leary v. United States*,[65] one U.S. Court of Appeals established outer limits to the rationales involved in finding a defendant so dangerous as to justify denial of bail. That court drew a distinction between potentially dangerous "conduct" a defendant might engage in and potential "advocacy" or use of the right to free speech.

> . . . if the "danger" referred to in 3148 includes mere "advocacy" of the use of illegal drugs or of other law violations, the section offends the constitutional guarantee of freedom of speech . . . . To avoid holding the

statute unconstitutional, one must construe the term "danger" as *conduct*, not advocacy falling short of actual incitement to imminent unlawful conduct.[66] (Emphasis added.)

One effect of this decision is to stress the likelihood of actual, concrete, prospective conduct that would be in violation of the law.

The nature of the offense charged, the circumstances surrounding the arrest, the past record of the defendant, the presence of physical violence and/or use of a weapon have been used in a number of cases to find dangerousness. In *Russel v. United States*,[67] a federal court of appeals relied on the defendant's prior record, the fact that he had been arrested before for robbery and for carrying a dangerous weapon, and his poor probationary record to find that he did pose a danger to the community. In *United States v. Tropiano*,[68] a federal district court allowed denial of bail on the grounds of the nature of the offense charged, the previous record of convictions, threats of violence, and the alleged "bad reputations" of the defendants. In *United States v. Jackson*,[69] the seriousness of the charge (kidnapping) and the use of a weapon in the crime were sufficient to have bail denied by a district court. A combination of offense charged, nature of the arrest, use of a weapon (the defendant was charged with robbery in which there was a "running gun battle"), and past record contributed to a dangerousness finding by a federal district court in *United States v. Allen*.[70] In *United States v. Long*,[71] the defendant's prior record of arrests, performance on pretrial release and probation, and the judge's assessment of the defendant's maturity contributed to a finding of dangerousness and a denial of bail by a court of appeals: "Although these matters cannot be accepted as speaking directly to the issue of dangerousness, our conclusion from the findings is that appellant has made virtually *no indication that he is ready to conduct himself responsibly.* "[72] (Emphasis added.)

Yet defendants have been found to pose a danger in cases where neither physical violence nor weapons were present. In several cases, drug trafficking offenses were used to infer dangerousness.[73] In *United States v. Erwing*,[74] a federal district court faced the question of whether a finding of dangerousness under the Bail Reform Act must be grounded on "physical violence."

Specifically, was it the intent of Congress, as defendant now claims, to give a more restrictive definition to the words "pose a danger to the community" so as to limit their application to cases where there is only the threat of physical violence? . . . An examination of the legislative history indicates no such purpose.[75]

That court found that it was appropriate within the framework of section 3148 to consider a narcotics peddler a danger to the community:

> . . . there is every reason to believe that if bail were not revoked the defendant would resume his harmful calling. . . . *The community must be protected from violations of the law which prey on the weakness of mankind.* A wholesale drug peddler, such as the defendant, exploits this weakness and, in doing so, certainly poses a danger to the welfare of the community. . . . For these reasons, and in light of *the known character and conduct of the defendant* . . . he should not be entitled to bail.[76] (Emphasis added.)

Conceivably, then, dangerousness can be perceived by the judiciary without reference to physical violence. In fact, another federal district court in California ruled that a defendant's *"propensity to commit crime generally"* could lead to a finding of dangerousness, even where "pecuniary" and not physical harm might result to the community at large.[77]

Section 3148 itself and the cases reviewed above do provide some clues as to how dangerousness ought theoretically to be assessed by persons making the bail decision. The nature of the offense, the past record of the defendant, and evidence or inferences of physical violence or of weapon use appear to be factors commonly considered. But assessment of a defendant's pretrial dangerousness appears to be carried out in a realm where guidelines are inexact and discretion flourishes. For instance, consider the reliance on such concepts as "the known character and conduct of the defendant" (*Erwing*), the ability of a defendant to "conduct himself responsibly" (*Long*), "bad reputations" (*Tropiano*), and a defendant's "propensity to commit crime generally" (*Louie*).

NOTES

1. The right to bail was traditionally limited by statute to those whose alleged crimes were not punishable by death. In England of the seventeenth century and America of the eighteenth and nineteenth centuries, death as a criminal sanction was available for a wide variety of crimes. Bail statutes formulated then, it is argued by some, excluded defendants who were charged in a vast array of offense activity from a right to bail. Bail was deniable to such a potentially large class of defendants not only on the basis of a concern that persons facing death might flee if released but also on the basis of a concern for the safety of the community if such seriously charged defendants were released. Proponents of preventive detention have contended that, as the death penalty

has become applicable to a narrower and narrower class of criminal cases (at present, generally only murder), bail statutes have not been updated and the power to *deny* bail has been accidentally diminished. Defendants charged with crimes for which no right to bail was formerly authorized (since formerly punishable as capital offense), may now—unjustly, they argue—have bail set as a right. See Mitchell (1969) and Hess (1971).

2. Hess (1971:307), for example, writes:

. . . the omission of a right to bail was deliberate. This right, as it developed, was purely statutory. This is the teaching of the development of English bail history, and it should be noted that, in England, pretrial bail has always been discretionary and remains so today, except for misdemeanors.

3. The New York bail statute, for example, embodies a combination of these first two interpretations. (N.Y. [Crim. Pro.] Law §530.20 (McKinney).) For persons charged with misdemeanors, the legislature has defined a right to have bail or recognizance set. But when the charge involves any felony, bail is left to the judge's discretion. Bail is deniable when the charge is a Class A (the most serious category) felony or when the defendant has a record of two previous convictions.

4. Adherents of the first two interpretations of the right-to-bail question also lean heavily on historical arguments in asserting that no constitutional right to bail exists. See Mitchell (1969) and Hess (1971).

5. For a discussion of the extent to which the right to bail might be restricted, see generally, Note, 79 *Harvard Law Review*(1966:1489): "Even the explicit guarantee of the right to free speech contained in the first amendment is subject to restriction when required by public necessity; the undefined right to bail implicit in the eighth amendment might also be subject to such restriction." (79 *Harvard Law Review* 1966:1500.)

6. See Chapter 5 where early bail studies are described in detail.

7. See generally, Note, 79 *Harvard Law Review*(1966:1489).

8. 342 U.S. 1 (1951).

9. 342 U.S. 524 (1952).

10. Of the principal discussions of these questions, Mitchell (1969) and Hess (1971) rely on *Carlson* to bolster their assertion of no constitutional right to bail and their support of preventive detention. Others, who find a right to bail and who argue against the constitutionality of preventive detention, rely on *Stack* (Foote, 1965a; *Harvard Law Review*, 1966; Fabricant, 1969; Tribe, 1970; Borman, 1971).

11. This presumption was derived from the Federal Rules of Criminal Procedure, rule 46(a) (1), in effect at that time that stated simply that "a person arrested for an offense not punishable by death shall be admitted to bail . . . before conviction."

12. 342 U.S. 1, 4-5 (1951).

13. Rule 46 has been revised four times since 1951 (in 1956, 1966, 1972, and 1975). In its present form it reflects the innovations of the Bail Reform Act of 1966 (18 U.S.C.A. 3146-3152) and the Speedy Trial Act of 1975 (18 U.S.C.A. 3153-3156).

14. Mr. Chief Justice Vinson in *Stack* does advise that "excessive" should be taken to mean "higher than usually set" 342 U.S. 1,6 (1951).

15. 342 U.S. 524 (1952). The Court in *Carlson* was sharply divided: Justices Minton, Vinson, Clark, Reed, and Jackson formed the majority opinion while Black, Frankfurter, Douglas, and Burton voiced strong dissents.

16. The view espoused in *Carlson* that there exists no constitutional right to bail leaves the decision to set bail to the exercise of judicial discretion (within a specified statutory framework). This contrasts sharply with the spirit of *Stack* and the rationale voiced in a Federal Court of Appeals decision in 1926: "The provision forbidding excessive bail would be futile if magistrates were left free to deny bail." *United States v. Motlow* 10 F. 2d 657, 659 (7th Cir., 1926). But, on the other hand, the *Carlson* view does align itself with a tradition of lower court rulings. See, for example, *Vanderford v. Brand* 126 Ga. 67,54 S.E. 822 (1906); *People ex rel. Shapiro v. Keeper of City Prison* 290 N.Y. 393,49 N.E. 2d 498 (1943).

17. 342 U.S. 524,545 (1952).

18. *Id.*, at 541,542.

19. 75 S. Ct. at 348,349 (Douglas, J., Circuit Justice, 1955).

20. 76 S. Ct. 1063, 1066 (Frankfurter, J., Circuit Justice, 1956).

21. 80 S. Ct. 30, 32–33 (Douglas, J., Circuit Justice, 1959).

22. *Id.*, at 32. A case heard by the Supreme Court of Nevada in 1927 stressed the same theme: "It was the idea of the framers of the Constitution that punishment should follow conviction, and not both precede and follow it, or be inflicted in spite of possible acquittal." *Ex parte Malley* 50 Nev. 248,256 P. 512, 514 (1927).

23. *Bandy v. United States* 81 S. Ct. 197 (Douglas, J., Circuit Justice, 1961) (*Bandy I*) and *Bandy v. United States* 82 S. Ct. 11 (Douglas, J., Circuit Justice, 1961) (*Bandy II*). In *Bandy I* the defendant petitioned Justice Douglas for release on personal recognizance while awaiting adjudication of his case. In *Bandy II*, Bandy had been convicted and was petitioning for release on personal recognizance while the Supreme Court considered whether to grant certiorari.

24. 81 S. Ct. 197, 198 (Douglas, J., Circuit Justice, 1961).

25. 351 U.S. 12 (1956).

26. This theme was stressed later in *Pannell v. United States* 320 F. 2d 698 (D.C. Cir., 1963) (Wright, J., concurring): "Special emphasis should be placed on the financial ability of the defendant to give bail, because if the defendant cannot make the bail set, he is effectively denied bail."

But other courts have voiced the view that excessiveness in bail setting need not depend on a defendant's ability to raise bail. See, for example, *Malley*, note 22 above, at 514: "It was not the idea of the Constitutional Convention that the person charged with a crime should be the one to say whether or not he can give bail in a certain amount, or to say when the amount fixed is excessive."

See also *White v. United States* 330 F. 2d 811 (8th Cir., 1964), *cert denied*, 379 U.S. 855 (1964), where it is stated:

We simply point out that the governing criterion adopted by this Circuit to test the excessiveness of bail proscribed by Amendment VIII is not as the defendant suggests his impecunious financial status, but whether bail is set at a figure higher than an amount reasonably calculated to insure that the accused will stand trial and submit to sentence if convicted. (330 F.2d at 814.)

27. 82 S. Ct., 11, 13. In *Pelletier v. United States* 343 F. 2d 322 (D.C. Cir., 1967), Chief Judge Bazelon commented on the equal protection issue: "It is an invidious discrimination to deny appellant release because of his poverty, when, for example, his ties to the community or such devices as release subject to supervision of the U.S. Probation Office, would adequately insure his presence." (343 F.2d at 323.)

28. 81 S. Ct. 642 (Harlan, J., Circuit Justice, 1961).

29. 82 S. Ct. 662 (Douglas, J., Circuit Justice, 1962).

30. 81 S. Ct. 642, 644.

31. 81 S. Ct. 662, 669.

32. *Id.*, at 668. This, then, appears to supersede the presumption favoring release before trial discussed in the *Bandy* cases—where dangerousness was not at issue.

33. 82 S. Ct. 994 (Warren, C.J., Circuit Justice, 1962).

34. See Note 14, above.

35. 18 U.S.C.A. 3146–3152. Of the growth in the interest in bail reform between the early 1950s and the mid-1960s, Foote writes that "unlike other areas of ferment in criminal law administration, this changing attitude toward bail is the only major reform of recent decades in which the courts have played a wholly passive role." (Foote, 1965a:959).

For the legislative history of and commentary concerning the Bail Reform Act, see House Report 1541, 1966 *U.S. Code Cong. and Adm. News*, 2293–2310. See also *Federal Bail Procedures, Hearings Before the Subcommittee on Constitutional Rights and the Subcommittee on Improvements in the Judicial Machinery of the Committee on the Judiciary*, U.S. Senate, 89th Congress First Session, on S. 1357, S. 646, and S. 648; and *Amendments to the Bail Reform Act of 1966, Hearings Before the Subcommittee on Constitutional Rights of the Committee on the Judiciary*, U.S. Senate, 91st Congress, First Session. Also, note that the Bail Reform Act (18 U.S.C.A. 3141–3152) is operational through rule 46 of the Federal Rules of Criminal Procedure.

36. 82 S. Ct. 11,12.

37. Although no explanation is offered in the text of the Act or in the legislative history, the classification of cases in terms of "capital" and "noncapital" for bail purposes is a traditional one. In America of the late eighteenth century, many offenses were punishable by death. No right to bail was legislated for capital cases since it was believed that persons faced with a possible death sentence would have a greater likelihood of fleeing the jurisdiction and of not showing up in court. However, where the distinction remains in many bail statutes, more and more offenses have since that time lost their capital punishment status. See Mitchell (1969) and Hess (1971). Since the reformulation of death penalty statutes that was instigated by the historic decision in *Furman v. Georgia* 408 U.S. 238 (1972), the meanings of capital and noncapital have been unclear and may vary considerably from jurisdiction to jurisdiction.

38. This review treats only cases heard in federal courts, including many appeals. Although procedurally bail setting in federal and state jurisdictions may transpire very differently, it is argued here that the rationales that shape the decisions and the factors considered by the decisionmaker in both jurisdictions will be essentially similar. The advantage in examining case law predicated upon the federal model lies in the relatively explicit nature of the guidelines that inform the pretrial release decision and the sharp focus of the court commentaries that were produced in appeals. A review of case law produced by state courts would—in addition to constituting a sizeable study in its own right—reflect the heterogeneity of the statutes that govern bail procedures in the individual states. State bail statutes will, however, be discussed in a subsequent chapter.

39. 412 F. 2d 144 (D.C. Cir., 1968).

40. *Id.*, at 146, 147.

41. 420 F. 2d 176 (D.C. Cir., 1969).

42. *Id.*, at 179.

43. *Id.*, at 179.

44. *Id.*, at 179.

45. 433 F. 2d 537 (D.C. Cir., 1970).

46. 470 F. 2d 473 (9th Cir., 1972).

47. 476 F. 2d 947 (5th Cir., 1973).

48. The *Briggs* court also held that "each defendant is entitled to know the reasons why the particular conditions of release were imposed in his case." (476 F.2d at 949.) See also, *Weaver v. United States* 405 F. 2d 353 (D.C. Cir., 1968); *United States v. Smith* 444 F. 2d (8th Cir., 1971); and *Wallace v. Kern* 520 F.2d 400 (2d Cir., 1975), where different courts held that reasons for imposing restrictive conditions of release must be spelled out in writing.

49. 404 U.S. 1232 (Douglas, J., Circuit Justice, 1971).

50. 483 F. 2d 1068 (4th Cir., 1973).

51. Perhaps the sharpest condemnation of overreliance on "nature of offense charged," comes in *Ackies v. Purdy* 325 F. Supp. 38, 39 (S.D., Fla., 1970), a case heard by a district court in Florida. This court held that setting bail on the basis of a master schedule fixing given amounts for particular offenses was "violative of the due process clause" and "denied poor defendants their right to equal protection." This case stands out from other available bail cases, since it does not deal with application of the Bail Reform Act but rather represents a class action brought against the bail policies of a particular locality (Dade County, Florida).

52. It is important to note that dangerousness of the variety referred to in the Bail Reform Act is applicable only to persons held in capital cases or to persons whose cases are on appeal. For the most part, cases ruling on the proper interpretation of pretrial dangerousness are linked solely to these statuses. But, the interest in the invocation of pretrial dangerousness in the present inquiry is broader. These cases are examined because they represent the application of a concept in explicit terms that is central to bail decisionmaking and detention in a general sense. That is, dangerousness has traditionally played a role in the bail decision free of legal guidelines. Thus, although the capital/noncapital and pretrial/postconviction statuses of defendants are of great technical and procedural

importance, for the purposes of this review they are distinctions of minimal significance when compared to the general value of the insight provided by cases that have wrestled with the concept of dangerousness in explicit terms.

53. It should be noted that, vaguely defined as it was, dangerousness as alluded to in section 3148 of the Bail Reform Act has been cited by a U.S. Court of Appeals as a precedent showing support for the finding that the concept of dangerousness in the 1970 dangerous special offender sentencing statute, 18 U.S.C.A. 3575-3578, was not "unconstitutionally vague." *United States v. Stewart* 531 F. 2d 326 (6th Cir., 1976).

54. 389 U.S. 15 (1967).

55. *Id.*, at 16.

56. 425 F. 2d 490 (D.C. Cir., 1969).

57. 527 F. 2d 672 (6th Cir., 1975).

58. *Id.*, at 5, 6.

59. *Id.*, at 6.

60. 89 S. Ct. 36 (Black, J., Circuit Justice, 1968).

61. *Id.*, at 38.

62. *Id.*, at 38.

63. This is evidenced, for example, in a decision by a U.S. Court of Appeals in *United States ex rel. Estabrook v. Otis* 18 F. 2d 689 (8th Cir., 1927): "Bail should not be granted where the offense for which the defendant has been convicted is an atrocious one, and there is danger that if he is given his freedom he will commit another of like character." (18 F.2d at 690.)

64. Reliance on the offense criterion has been noted in numerous studies influential in the movement to reform the administration of bail. Among these are Beeley (1927); Morse and Beattie (1932); and Foote (1954).

65. 431 F. 2d 85 (5th Cir., 1970).

66. *Id.*, at 89. In *Carbo v. United States* 82 S. Ct. 662, 667 (1967), Mr. Justice Douglas warned against the possibility that a bailsetting judge might be influenced by the political nature of the alleged offense: "Where the crimes charged are of a political nature, special care is needed lest denial of bail create an inequality in the law between those despised and the rest of the community."

In separate strong dissents in *Carlson v. Landon* 342 U.S. 524 (1952), Justices Black, Frankfurter, Douglas, and Burton (at 547-569) suggested that the appellants had been denied bail due only to their membership in the Communist party not because of any conduct or potential danger they might raise to the community, and that they, therefore, had been deprived of due process and equal protection. In *Christoffel v. United States* 196 F. 2d 560 (D.C. Cir., 1951), a U.S. Court of Appeals held that "the decision of a court must be without respect to persons and without respect to the political affiliations or activities of a party except as the same are shown to be relevant and material to an issue before the court." (196 F.2d at 565.)

67. 402 F. 2d 185 (D.C. Cir., 1968).

68. 296 F. Supp. 280 (D.C. Conn., 1968).

69. 297 F. Supp. 601 (D.C. Conn., 1969).

70. 343 F. Supp. 549 (E.D. Pa., 1972).

71. 422 F. Supp. 712 (D.C. Cir., 1970).

72. *Id.*, at 714.

73. See, for example, *United States v. Erwing* 268 F. Supp. 877 (N.D. Cal., 1967); *United States v. Blyther* 407 F. 2d 1279 (D.C. Cir., 1969); *United States v. Nelson* 467 F. 2d 944 (5th Cir., 1972); and *United States v. Quicksey* 371 F. Supp. 561 (S.D. W.Va., 1974).

74. 268 F. Supp. 877 (N.D. Cal., 1967).

75. Id., at 878.

76. *Id.*, at 879.

77. *United States v. Louie* 389 F. Supp. 850 (N.D. Cal., 1968).

 *Chapter 3*

Other Sources of Bail Policy:
A Chronology

Since the landmark federal bail legislation of 1966, conceptual treatment of bail has evolved further in other sources of legal policy. Examined briefly in this chapter are four sets of advisory standards and recommendations pertaining to bail and detention and one controversial proposal that was enacted into law.[1] Treated chronologically to convey an historical sense of the evolution of bail guidelines, these sources of bail policy include:

1. Standards of the American Bar Association (1968);
2. Preventive Detention Code of the District of Columbia (1970);[2]
3. Standards of the National Advisory Commission on Criminal Justice Standards and Goals (1973);
4. Uniform Rules of Criminal Procedure of the National Conference of Commissioners on Uniform State Laws (1974); and
5. Standards of the National Association of Pretrial Services Agencies (1978).

Review of these guidelines continues analysis of the legally envisaged purpose for bail decisionmaking and of the factors used to distinguish among defendants at their first appearances before a judge.

THE STANDARDS OF THE AMERICAN
BAR ASSOCIATION (1968)

Rather than departing from the Bail Reform Act's conceptualization of bail decisionmaking, the American Bar Association's Standards

Relating to Pretrial Release moved toward clarification and refinement of the reform model. The substance of the Standards was focused on themes that were central to the Reform Act. For example, after the fashion of the 1966 act, the Standards stressed several bail reform principles: the main function of the bail decision was to secure the attendance of defendants at court; there was a strong presumption favoring pretrial release under nonfinancial terms; and the principle of release under the least restrictive of alternatives possible was again voiced. In addition, the Standards adopted lists of factors to be considered by bail judges in making their determinations that amount to variations on the list given in the Bail Reform Act. (See the discussion presented in Chapter 2.)

Yet, the Standards innovated in a number of areas. In a proposal that went beyond the Reform Act, the American Bar Association (ABA) recommended that persons charged with offenses having possible penalties of six months or less be issued citations or summonses and that persons charged with offenses with penalties up to one year be released on personal recognizance with no inquiry into their backgrounds.[3] The ABA called special attention to the use of cash bail, characterizing it as a drastic bail option and specifying factors to guide its limited use. The Standards clearly warned that, when used, cash bail was for assuring appearance, not for punishing, frightening, placating public opinion, or preventively detaining persons deemed dangerous. Moreover, the Standards proposed that any use of cash bail be transacted through a Ten Percent program and not through bondsmen.[4] In fact, prohibition of bondsmen or "compensated sureties" was recommended in the ABA Standards.

The Standards were careful to restrict the role of dangerousness in bail determinations,[5] following the lead of the Bail Reform Act that limited the concern for dangerousness to capital cases and appeals. However, the ABA Standards avoided the vague definition of that concern that characterized the Reform Act wording and referred instead directly to serious pretrial crime, intimidation of witnesses, and attempts to otherwise interfere with justice. Moreover, the Standards required a more specific evidentiary requirement—that such dangerousness concerns be supported by a finding of fact, not left to judicial intuition. Although the Standards would permit outright detention in capital cases where a finding supported such an outcome, they applied the principle of release under least restrictive conditions to defendants viewed as possible dangers and suggested conditions of release resembling those found in probation and parole to minimize the chances that the feared activities would occur. In spite of a more explicit treatment of the danger concerns in bail, however, it should be noted that the Standards, like the Bail Reform Act, offered no instructions on how to discern dangerous tendencies among defendants.

The ABA's approach to factors to be weighed by the judge in bail determinations based on risk of flight was quite complicated and the lists of criteria proposed for various bail decision functions seemed likely to produce considerable confusion. As a refinement of the conceptualization of the bail decision in the Bail Reform Act, the bail task was divided by the ABA into three parts: an "exploratory inquiry into the facts relevant to pretrial release," an assessment of the defendant's risk of flight, and a special procedure for setting cash bail in cases where release under less drastic alternatives is deemed inappropriate. For each of these functions, a list of criteria to be considered by the bail official was provided. And, although the principal focus of each of them involved a defendant's risk of flight, the composition of the lists varied from function to function.

THE PREVENTIVE DETENTION CODE
OF THE DISTRICT OF COLUMBIA (1970)

The Preventive Detention Code paid at least token obeisance to the concept of greater use of nonfinancial forms of release to help assure attendance at court,[6] but it also set forth procedures to enable pretrial detention of defendants deemed dangerous. It extended the concern for dangerousness to include potentially all defendants and not just those capitally charged or on appeals. In this regard, it is philosophically and substantively at odds with the provisions espoused in the Bail Reform Act and ABA Standards. Defenders of the District of Columbia law have contended that its value lies in realistic recognition of the preoccupation of bail decisionmakers with defendant danger and in the attempt to bring this kind of decisionmaking out in the open where it can be regulated. These same defenders have pointed with pride to the procedural safeguards that have been erected to guarantee due process to prospective detainees (Mitchell, 1969; Hess, 1971).

The Bail Reform Act and ABA Standards were characterized above as being relatively nonspecific on the means for evaluating defendant dangerousness in the special circumstances where it was a proper concern. The D.C. Code, to the contrary, certainly attempts to specify criteria on the basis of which presumably dangerous defendants may be discerned. Persons may be eligible for "detention prior to trial" if they are (1) charged with a "dangerous crime," (2) charged with a "crime of violence," (3) charged with obstructing justice, (4) charged with a crime of violence and believed to be an addict.[7]

The two broadest of these eligibility-establishing criteria are defined as follows:

dangerous crime

> The term "dangerous crime" means (1) taking or attempting to take property from another by force or threat of force, (2) unlawfully entering or attempting to enter any premises adapted for overnight accommodation of persons or for carrying on business with the intent to commit an offense therein, (3) arson or attempted arson of any premises adaptable for overnight accommodation of persons or for carrying on business (4) forcible rape, or assault with intent to commit forcible rape, or (5) unlawful sale or distribution of a narcotic or depressant or stimulant drug (as defined by any Act of Congress) if the offense is punishable by imprisonment for more than one year.[8]

crime of violence

> The term "crime of violence" means murder, forcible rape, carnal knowledge of a female under the age of 16, taking or attempting to take immoral, improper or indecent liberties with a child under the age of 16 years, mayhem, kidnapping, robbery, burglary, voluntary manslaughter, extortion, or blackmail.[9]

Perhaps ironically, these provisions of the D.C. Code demonstrate how difficult it is to attempt to specify the kinds of defendants who might be considered dangerous. For what, on the surface, looks like an attempt to link determination of defendant dangerousness to carefully specified criteria ends up potentially including most categories of criminally charged defendants whose possible penalties may exceed one year in confinement. Addicts charged with crimes of violence, further, may be considered potentially dangerous on the vague grounds that they might "endanger the public morals, health, safety, or welfare."[10]

Traditionally, judges have relied largely on the seriousness of the criminal charge in deciding bail. Critics have contended that in so doing judges were exercising the power to detain persons they perceived as dangerous through high cash bail. Seen in that context, the Preventive Detention Code of the District of Columbia represents a continuation of the practice of inferring dangerous propensities in defendants on the basis of the charged offense. For persons charged with a dangerous crime, pretrial detention may be sought when the government "certifies" that no condition of release would assure the safety of the community—based on "past and present conduct and other factors."[11] For persons charged with a crime of violence, a pattern is sought and discerned when it is learned that "the person has been convicted of a crime of violence within the ten-year period immediately preceding the alleged crime of violence for which he is presently charged" or that the "crime of violence was allegedly committed while the person was, with respect to another crime of violence, on bail or other release or on probation, parole, or mandatory release pending completion of a sentence."[12] The finding of dangerousness under the D.C. Code is arrived at through special hearings, during which the defendant is entitled to counsel. The finding of dangerousness calling for detention rests on "clear and convincing evidence," but the information to be relied upon "need not conform to the rules pertaining to the admissability of evidence in a court of law."[13]

Although questions concerning the constitutionality of the Preventive Detention Code can still be raised [14] and in spite of the fact that procedures for detention have proved impractical for the District of Columbia to carry out, the Code's impact has been great. From the perspective of this analysis, the D.C. Code is important because it embodies a model of bail decisionmaking in which the concern for defendant dangerousness has been raised to a legitimate status. Critical questions for the moment aside, the D.C. Code has further significance as an attempt to "specify" criteria to help evaluate potential dangerousness in defendants and to define procedures for the operationalization of preventive detention.

THE STANDARDS OF THE NATIONAL ADVISORY COMMISSION ON CRIMINAL JUSTICE STANDARDS AND GOALS (1973)

At first glance, the Standards of the National Advisory Commission on Criminal Justice Standards and Goals (NAC) look, quite simply, like an updated version of the Reform Act and ABA bail models. But, in the particular context of the espousal of antidetention policies by the Bail Reform Act and ABA and of propreventive detention policy by the D.C. Code, the substance of the Standards proposed by the National Advisory Commission (Corrections Standards 4.4-4.6) is intriguing, to say the least. In one sense, the NAC guidelines fit within both traditions; but in another, the NAC guidelines begin a tradition of their own.

First, NAC standards are similar to those proffered in the Reform Act and ABA guidelines in the following ways: (1) The overriding "interest" in bail decisionmaking is in assuring the appearance of defendants. In fact, dangerousness as an initial concern for bail is nowhere mentioned or alluded to in the NAC standards.[15] (2) There is a high priority placed on ROR and on nonfinancial terms of pretrial release and a low priority on money-bail. NAC guidelines do not set different standards for noncapital and capital defendants. (3) Criteria set forth for determining release alternatives are nearly identical to the lists of criteria found in the Reform Act and the ABA Standards. Thus, in these respects, the NAC guidelines resemble the earlier bail reform-inspired pretrial release models.

The manner in which the NAC standards at once conform to the preventive detention tradition of the D.C. Code and initiate a tradition of their own can be discerned from careful examination of the pretrial release and detention "alternatives" listed in Standard 4.4.

> Judicial officers on the basis of information available to them should select from the list of the following alternatives the first one that will reasonably assure the appearance of the accused for trial or, if no single condition gives that assurance, a combination of the following:
>
> a. Release on recognizance without further conditions.
> b. Release on the execution of an unsecured appearance bond in an amount specified.
> c. Release into the care of a qualified person or organization reasonably capable of assisting the accused to appear at trial.
> d. Release to the supervision of a probation officer or some other public official.
> e. Release with imposition of restrictions on activities, associations, movements, and residence reasonably related to securing the appearance of the accused.
> f. Release on the basis of financial security to be provided by the accused.
> g. Imposition of any other restrictions other than detention reasonably related to securing the appearance of the accused.
> h. Detention, with release during certain hours for specified purposes.
> i. *Detention of the accused.* (Emphasis added.)

Alternatives (a) through (h) contain little that is not a reiteration of the release alternatives presented in the provisions of the Bail Reform Act and in the ABA Standards. It is alternative (i) that makes the NAC guidelines so different from earlier bail reform-type pretrial guidelines. By including alternative (i), detention of the accused, the NAC guidelines depart from the tradition of bail reform (*i.e.*, from the philosophy of the Bail Reform Act and ABA guidelines) and join the tradition of the D.C. Code—where outright detention of defendants *is* a pretrial decision option. That is, in spite of ranking pretrial detention as the lowest priority, the NAC standards present it as an option to be considered among others.

The NAC guidelines differ strikingly from both kinds of earlier models. Detention is permitted, but in the name of securing *appearance—not in the name of dangerousness*. The concept of preventive detention is borrowed from concerns with potential defendant dangerousness for use with defendants considered likely to flee. In NAC commentary, it is not clear that the drafters were aware of the implications of their proposed standards, for the only comment pertaining to the use of full detention is the following statement: "The physical custody of a person awaiting trial should be the last resort where no other means is available to obtain reasonable assurance of his presence for trial." (NAC, 1973:122)

It is not the intention of this discussion to imply that the NAC standards would, if ever implemented, result in an unfettered use of preventive detention under the auspices of a concern for appearance.[16] In fact, protections are provided in the NAC guidelines that look a great deal like the "minimum requirements of due process" enumerated by the U.S. Supreme Court in *Morrissey v. Brewer*.[17] They include a right to notice of the intention to detain or to revoke release; a right to a hearing; a right to representation by counsel or appointment of counsel; a right to "present evidence on his own behalf, to subpoena witnesses, and to confront and cross-examine the witnesses against him"; a right to written notice of the reasons for detention or revocation of release and the evidence relied upon.

THE UNIFORM RULES OF
CRIMINAL PROCEDURE (1974)

Compared to the other advisory guidelines, the Uniform Rules of Criminal Procedure (URCP) of the National Conference of Commissioners on State Laws treat pretrial release decisionmaking only in a very general way. They resemble the ABA Standards in their emphasis on using citations and/or summonses rather than police custody for minor offenses. Preferences for release on a promise to appear characterizes the URCP guidelines, as it did the other models reviewed. In a fashion similar to the D.C. Code, the URCP envisage the task of the pretrial release decision as encompassing assessment of both risk of flight and dangerousness when the alleged offense is "punishable by incarceration" and when the ROR "will not reasonably assure the appearance of the defendant as required for the safety of any person or the community." No criteria are offered to guide the decisionmaker in his or her assessment of risk of dangerousness. The URCP state only that, if a determination is made that ROR will not be sufficient, "one or more of the least onerous conditions" might then be imposed. These include supervision by a person or organization and restriction of travel, associations, and activities (*e.g.*, drinking, drugs, and possession of a weapon) (rule 341, a). The conditions are subject to change, as release is subject to revocation. If these conditions are not satisfactory, money-bail may be imposed. Whether a defendant may be detained outright in any case is not clear, because conditions are not discussed in terms of noncapital and capital cases.

Most significant about the brief release guidelines presented in the URCP—especially because of their possible influence on state-level legislation—is the implicit willingness to allow consideration of potential risk of flight and pretrial dangerousness in all cases. As in the D.C. Code, dangerousness in the URCP is not reserved for a narrowly defined class of defendants. But, in spite of a policy statement that favors "eliminating unnecessary detention" before and during trial, no guidelines for assessing either concern are presented. Thus, the roles of risk of flight and of dangerousness are blended and the bail decision is destined to be carried out in a realm of discretion. The lack of specific criteria for assessing risk of flight and potential dangerousness is accompanied by an equally discretionary use of money-bail as a condition of release.

THE STANDARDS OF THE NATIONAL ASSOCIATION OF PRETRIAL SERVICE AGENCIES (1978)

The Performance Standards and Goals for Pretrial Release of the National Association of Pretrial Services Agencies (NAPSA),[18] the last model for bail and detention to be reviewed in this chapter, have special significance. They are especially influential because they embody the thinking of an organization that has its roots in the bail reform movement of the 1960s—one that is comprised largely of personnel from pretrial release projects across the United States. The NAPSA Standards are particularly noteworthy because they constitute the most recent conceptualization of bail decisionmaking put together by professionals and practitioners in the pretrial field, and as such they represent the latest stage in the evolution of guidelines for bail.

Many familiar bail reform themes are sounded in the NAPSA

Standards, including the presumption favoring release on personal recognizance and the principle of release under least restrictive conditions. In some instances, statement of reform themes are the strongest encountered in any of the sources reviewed. For example, in order to overcome the presumption favoring unconditional release before trial, "a determination by a judicial officer" is required "after a due process hearing" (Standard IV). Moreover, the burden for rebutting that presumption is placed squarely on the prosecution—to be met by a showing of "clear and convincing evidence" (described as falling somewhere between a "preponderance of the evidence" and "proof beyond a reasonable doubt"). And, in addition to implying a greater and earlier role for the prosecution in bail proceedings, the NAPSA Standards further insist that judges issue written statements describing conditions of release and reasons for their imposition. Most notable of all, however, is the Standard calling for the elimination of cash bail altogether. Although abolition of cash bail may seem rather radical given current practices in the United States, it is a notion with a long history (Foote, 1954: 1073; ABA, 1968: Appendix C).

In spite of these kinds of provisions, a reader who expects to find a reaffirmation of the appearance view of the bail decision and a denunciation of the drift toward preventive detention will be certainly mistaken. In fact, rather than resembling a Bail Reform Act "revisited," the NAPSA Standards wed together two separate tendencies toward greater use of preventive detention: that based on perceived dangerousness (as exemplified by the D.C. Code) and that based on perceived risk of flight (as implied in the NAC guidelines).

The rationale for acceptance of preventive detention practices in the NAPSA Standards is nearly identical to the one that was employed to secure enactment of the Preventive Detention Code of the District of Columbia (Mitchell, 1969). The reasoning in both instances resembles the following: Preventive detention has occurred traditionally and unavoidably through the setting of high cash bail. In a process characterized by unfettered judicial discretion, it is better to bring it out in the open, where procedural safeguards may be administered and discretion may be structured (NAPSA, 1977: Commentary, 23; NAPSA, 1978:38, 77-78). The due process rights to be accorded defendants at the detention hearing under these Standards included the right to a hearing, to counsel, to disclosure of the evidence, to confront and to cross-examine, to appear in person, and to present evidence (Standard VII). The wish to force sub rosa detention practices "into the open" with due process protections is made credible and enforceable only in conjunction with abrogation of cash bail.

It is further important to note that the extent to which such a scheme might accomplish its goals would depend on two other features of the bail process: (1) clear definitions of the criteria by means of which judges could invoke danger- or flight-related detention and (2) clear definition of the evidentiary basis for a finding that would result in pretrial detention.

Although it does not serve the purpose of the present inquiry to examine procedural matters in much detail, it should be noted that the evidentiary standard for detention proposed in the NAPSA Standards is the same as that adopted in the D.C. Code, "clear and convincing evidence."[19] Presumably, that standard would be demanding enough to prohibit abuse of the detention option, yet, not so demanding as to render it inaccessible to the state in appropriate cases.

Also, crucial—and more pertinent to the present analysis of bail guidelines—is the second requisite: specification of criteria by means of which detention for dangerousness or flight-risk might be considered. In order to be a candidate for detention proceedings on either grounds according to NAPSA, the judge must first find a "substantial probability" that the defendant committed the offense—clearly involving an assessment of guilt. (Such assessments at the bail stage raise due process issues because they conflict with the notion of presumption of innocence.) Beyond the substantial probability threshold requirement, the NAPSA guidelines specify further conditions for preventive detention (Standard VII). Detention to prevent flight, for example, further requires that the defendant be charged with a felony *and* that he or she (1) absconded before, (2) expressed an intent to flee, or (3) committed acts strongly suggesting such an intent. Detention to prevent danger to the community would require that the defendant be charged with a "crime of violence" (to be defined by each jurisdiction), "pose a threat to the safety of the community" *and* that he or she (1) was convicted of a crime of violence in the past ten years, (2) be on probation, parole, or pretrial release for a crime of violence, or (3) exhibit a "pattern of behavior" (past or present) that poses a threat to the safety of the community.

Certainly, proponents of the NAPSA approach can point to relatively explicit definition of classes of defendants for whom preventive detention might be deemed desirable. Yet, critics of these guidelines may still object to the vagueness inherent in such phrases as "threat to the safety of the community," or "pattern of behavior" and allusions to "acts" or "behavior" from which "intent" (to flee or commit dangerous acts) might be "inferred."

CONCLUSION: DETENTION UNDER
THE VARIOUS MODELS

In comparison with the Bail Reform Act, the ABA's Standards offered no reformulation of the state interest behind the pretrial release decision. Concern for appearance at court was still predominant, although dangerousness was an allowable consideration in capital cases. The Preventive Detention Code of the District of Columbia, however, represented a break with tradition in the sense that it enlarged the interest in screening dangerous defendants into detention, so that dangerousness assessment was to be given a role at least coequal with appearance concerns. NAC guidelines were framed in terms of the "pretrial release and detention decision." Pretrial detention—although rated as of lowest priority—was simply one decision option to be considered along with the others, such as ROR, money-bail, or release under supervision. The NAC Standards opened the door to the use of preventive detention in the name of appearance concerns. It was in the NAPSA Standards that procedures for preventive detention on both grounds (danger and flight-risk) were openly advocated for the first time. The URCP represented a passive, nondiscriminating acceptance of both appearance and dangerousness orientations. But the NAPSA guidelines stand as a more thoughtful and direct acceptance of dual-purpose detention practices. Of course, both the Bail Reform Act and the Preventive Detention Code of the District of Columbia are, more than models for bail decisionmaking, legislation that has been enacted and, to varying degrees, implemented.[20] However, the ABA Standards and the URCP guidelines have been influential in the formulation of state bail and pretrial release statutes.[21] The new NAPSA guidelines will certainly become influential in the states.

If each of these models were implemented in full force, what kinds of defendants might be awaiting trial in the nation's jails? From the Bail Reform Act guidelines, it can be predicted that all defendants receiving good community-ties ratings (based on the ten criteria discussed in Chapter 2) will have secured release, probably on their own recognizance. Those remaining in detention will be those considered most likely to flee, that is, those who scored poorly on offense, past record, residence, family ties, employment, financial status, character and mental condition, prior criminal record, and such. It can be assumed that defendants in detention for failing these tests in some regard would have had unaffordable bail set. From the Reform Act, it is not possible to ascertain which of the recommended factors would weigh more heavily. The Reform Act's detainees would presumably be the most transient, those with the longest past records, and/or those of poorest "character" or "mental condition." An additional group of defendants charged in capital cases would be found held—either on unaffordable bail or without bail—because they posed "a danger to any other person or the community." While it would not be clear how they were distinguishable from others (apart from their capital charges), it would be clear only that they were the dangerous defendants.

The ABA Standards would first consider the seriousness of the offense and the possible penalty. If the offenses with which defendants were charged were considered minor or if they called for sentences of less than one year, they would not be found among pretrial detainees (unless law enforcement officials made a special showing that they might flee). These defendants would be released on citation, summons, or ROR. But for defendants charged with offenses having possible penalties of more than one year, those who remained in jail would be comprised again of those deemed most likely to flee. These defendants would have had unaffordable bail set according to ABA criteria. To what extent the necessity of setting bail was influenced by any of the criteria, including "possible penalty," "likelihood of guilt," "character, reputation, or mental condition," "the possibility of violations of the law," or any of the community-ties measures would not be ascertainable. In addition, some of the defendants would have been found to be potentially dangerous under vague ABA guidelines and would have been jailed without bail.

If the guidelines of the D.C. Code were fully implemented, the jails of Washington, D.C., would be filled with an unsortable mix of defendants who were either deemed poor release risks (*i.e.*, likely to flee) or dangerous (*i.e.*, charged with one or more crimes from a list of about twenty offenses or addicts charged with such crimes). These detainees would also be distinguished by their poor ratings on community-ties criteria. If dangerous and held without bail, they might also be characterized by some significant past conduct. Presumably, a certain proportion of the D.C. detainees would have been detained on unaffordable bail, and part will have had bail denied under preventive detention proceedings.

Persons detained under NAC provisions would resemble those confined under Bail Reform Act or ABA guidelines—with some exceptions. Most would have been detained outright because they were considered very poor appearance risks. They would have been ordered detained—not held on unaffordably high bail. In addition, theoretically, no defendants would be detained (with bail denied or with high bail) because he or she was deemed dangerous by a bail official.

Further, no clear distinction would be found between capitally and noncapitally charged defendants.

Consideration of the URCP yields only the following formulation: most defendants charged with minor crimes would not have been detained—because they would have received citations, summonses, or ROR instead. Most of those detained would have been jailed as the result of being considered either a flight-risk or a danger (based on unknown considerations) and having had unaffordable bail set.

Under the NAPSA guidelines persons deemed either dangerous or likely to flee would be held in jail, but only after benefiting from a detention hearing. In that sense, the NAPSA guidelines most resemble those promulgated under the D.C. Code, except that detention on the grounds of likely flight would also be allowed. In spite of detention criteria that are rather narrowly drawn so as to limit its use, the NAPSA guidelines give strong emphasis to preliminary assessment of guilt.

NOTES

1. For a more detailed analysis of these guidelines, see Goldkamp (1977).
2. D.C. Code §§23–1321 to 1331.
3. The Standards do permit law enforcement officials to petition the judge not to grant ROR in exceptional cases.
4. See Note 3, Chapter 1.
5. The ABA considered a draft model preventive detention proposal and then rejected it. Under this proposal, money-bail would have been prohibited altogether. Normally, defendants would be released on OR or with some nonfinancial conditions. Eligibility for pretrial (preventive) detention would be determined by the following criteria (see, ABA, 1968: Appendix C, 1.4):

a. where the defendant is accused of a capital crime;
b. where there is reasonable cause to believe that the defendant has committed a felony while at liberty pending trial of a prior criminal charge or pending appeal;
c. where the defendant is charged with a felony involving the infliction of or a threat to inflict serious bodily harm on another and there is a high degree of probability that, if released, he will inflict serious bodily harm on another;
d. where the defendant is charged with a felony and is known to have been convicted within the last five years of a felony involving the infliction of or threat to inflict serious bodily harm on another and there is a high degree of probability that, if released, he will inflict serious bodily harm on another person;

e. where the defendant is charged with a felony and there is found to be a high degree of probability that, if released, he will threaten or inflict serious bodily harm on another for the purpose of intimidating or incapacitating witnesses;

f. where the defendant is charged with a felony and there is reasonable ground to believe that, if released, he would leave the United States for the purpose of avoiding prosecution or for the purpose of secreting or disposing of the fruits of the alleged crime.

6. The drafters of the D.C. Code (D.C. Code §§23-1321 to 1331) added a new criterion, "past conduct," to those suggested in the Bail Reform Act for consideration by judges during bail determination.

7. D.C. Code §§23-1321,1323,1331.

8. D.C. Code §23-1331(3).

9. D.C. Code §23-1331(4).

10. D.C. Code §23-1323.

11. D.C. Code §23-1322(a)(1).

12. D.C. Code §23-1322(a)(2).

13. D.C. Code §23-1321(f). Standard 1.5 (b) of the rejected ABA preventive detention proposal would have required an "evidentiary, non-jury hearing" where the prosecution "should have the burden of proving the necessity for detention by clear and convincing evidence." The aims of the present study do not require analysis of the procedural innovations of preventive detention legislation. Its significance is noted and the reader is referred to the text of the Act (D.C. Code §§1321-1331) and to discussions by Mitchell (1969); Teague (1970); and Tribe (1972).

14. See the policy statement of the National Council on Crime and Delinquency against preventive detention (NCCD, 1971:1). Former Senator Ervin (1971:297-298) writes that:

> The constitutional arguments against preventive detention are so numerous that their recitation looks like the model answer to an issue-spotting question on a law school examination. The preventive detention law is unconstitutionally defective on at least the following grounds:
>
> It violates the eighth amendment right of reasonable bail in noncapital cases.
>
> It imprisons for unproved, anticipated crime, rather than actual criminal conduct.
>
> The offense of "dangerousness" is unconstitutionally vague.
>
> It violates the presumption of innocence.
>
> It convicts on the basis of "substantial probability" rather than "beyond reasonable doubt."
>
> Preventive detention severely prejudices the defendant in the trial of the actual offense.
>
> The bill does not afford procedural due process in the detention hearing.
>
> Detention prejudices the right to access to counsel.
>
> The detention hearing forces the defendant to waive his privilege against self-incrimination.

The hearing forces the defendant to disclose his defense to the prosecution prior to trial.

It imprisons on the basis of hearsay and other forms of "evidence" not admissible at trial under the rules of evidence.

15. Although dangerousness is not addressed in the proposed NAC Standards, a note is included in the commentary to the effect that once a defendant has abused his release before trial by committing a crime, detention would be permitted (NAC, 1973:125).

16. This was not the case, for instance, with the D.C. Code. In fact, due to the procedures required for pretrial detention of persons deemed dangerous, preventive detention has scarcely been used as an option in the District of Columbia (Bases, 1971).

17. 408 U.S. 471 (1972). *Morrissey*, of course, did not grant a right to counsel.

18. The NAPSA Standards published in 1978 show important differences from the earlier draft provisions drawn up in 1977. For a critical review of the 1977 draft Standards, see Goldkamp (1977).

19. One of the major reasons that preventive detention in Washington, D.C., was invoked very rarely in the first year and one-half following its enactment was a reluctance on the part of prosecutors to reveal evidence at the detention hearing that could have been crucial in winning the prosecutor's case later in court (Beaudin, 1970–1971; Bases, 1972). This resulted from the evidentiary standard, "clear and convincing," articulated in the D.C. Code. It must be assumed that in a system like the one proposed by NAPSA—with no sub rosa cash bail/preventive detention option—the evidentiary standard would become a major issue.

20. See Beaudin (1970–1971) and Bases (1972) for a discussion of the implementation of and compliance with these two acts by federal and District of Columbia courts.

21. As the text of this book was being finalized, the ABA published a draft updating its 1968 Standards on pretrial release (ABA, 1978). Although the recency of the second edition of the ABA Standards precludes analysis in the text, it is worth noting several features. First, the new ABA Standards clearly stress a presumption favoring release—including release before trial on citations, summonses, ROR, or conditional release. The abolition of cash bail is not sought, although the Standards again stress that its use should be "reduced to minimal proportions" (Standard 10-1.3 (c)). Prohibitions of compensated sureties and use of cash bail for detention-for-danger are again articulated in the new Standards. Unlike the recent NAPSA Standards, the new ABA Standards do not permit outright detention "based on a generalized prediction of dangerousness" (ABA, 1978:44) at first appearance. Pretrial detention hearings are held only when (a) a defendant is detained for five days as a result of unaffordable cash bail or (b) a defendant has been on pretrial release and has demonstrated that no conditions of release can suffice to prevent his or her flight, commission of a new crime, or interference with the judicial process.

Chapter 4

State Bail Guidelines

PROVISIONS IN STATE BAIL GUIDELINES

Perhaps the most striking feature of the kinds of provisions included in the guidelines of the different states is their heterogeneity.[1] (See Table 4-1.) Most state guidelines for bail and detention, in fact, share but two common traits. First, all states except Illinois have replicated in their constitutions the excessive bail clause of the eighth amendment of the U.S. Constitution. In no state is there an absolute right to bail.[2]

The second trait shared by most state guidelines is statutory definition of a right to bail. The prototypic statutory definition of the right to bail is illustrated by that found in the New Mexico Constitution: "All persons shall be bailable by sufficient sureties *except for capital offenses when the proof is evident and the presumption is great.*[3] (Emphasis added.)

Although the wording may vary slightly from state to state, this formula of a right to bail is classic in its exclusion of persons charged in capital offenses and in making bail in excluded cases contingent upon a showing that "proof is *not* evident" and that the "presumption is *not* great." The proof and presumption criteria suggest that an early assessment of probable guilt and/or likelihood of conviction would wield considerable influence in the exercise of the discretion to set or deny bail when it is not a right. This proof and presumption clause is evident in the statutes and/or constitutions of forty-one states.[4]

Table 4-1. Provisions Included in State Bail and Release Guidelines, by State: December, 1978[a]

	Excessive Bail Clause	Right to Bail, Except in Capital Cases	Right to Bail, Except in Other Exclusions	Not When Proof is Evident and Presumption is Great (in Capital Cases or Other Exclusions)	Purpose (Stated or Implied): To Assure Appearance	Purpose (Stated or Implied): To Protect the Community from Dangerous Defendants	Policy Against Unnecessary Detention Stated	Preference Expressed for Release on Own Recognizance	Mandates Release on Least Restrictive Conditions	District Attorney Recommendation or Approval Important	Bail Schedule Used	Ten Percent Bail
Alabama	A	AB		AB	B	B	B				B	B
Alaska	A	A		A	B	B						
Arizona[a]	A	AB	B[b]	AB	B	B					B	B
Arkansas	A	AB		A	B	B	B	B	B			
California	A	AB		AB	B			B	B	B		
Colorado	A	AB		AB				B		B		

State									
Connecticut	A	AB			B		B	B	
Delaware	A	AB			B		B	B	
District of Columbia		B			B		B	B	B
Florida	A	A	B^c	AB	B				
Georgia	A		B^d	AB	B				
Hawaii	A		B^e		B				
Idaho	A	AB		AB					
Illinois	A	A	B^f	A	B			B	B
Indiana	A	AB	B^g	AB	B		B	B	B
Iowa	A			A	B		B	B	B
Kansas	A	AB		A	B		B	B	B^h
Kentucky	A	A		A	B				
Louisiana	A	AB	B^h	AB	B	B	B		
Maine	AB	A	B^e	AB	B	B		B	B
Maryland	A	B		AB	B	B	B	B	B
Massachusetts	A	B	AB^i	AB	B	A^i			
Michigan	A	A		A	B	B	B	B	B
Minnesota	A	A		A	B				
Mississippi	A	A		A	B				
Missouri	A	A		AB	B		B		
Montana	A	AB	AB^g	AB					
Nebraska	A	AB		AB	B	B	B	B	B
Nevada	A	B		B					
New Hampshire	A	AB		AB	B	B		B	B
New Jersey	A	A	B^j	A	B		B	B	B
New Mexico	A				B	B	B	B	B
New York	A				B	B^k	B	B	B^j
North Carolina	A	A		A	B	B	B	B	B̄^i
North Dakota	A	A		A	B	B	B	B	B̄^i B
Ohio	A	A		A	B	B	B	B	B
Oklahoma	A	AB	AB^g	AB	B				
Oregon	A	AB			B		B	B	B
Pennsylvania	A	AB	A^c	A	B		B	B	B
Rhode Island	A	B	B^c	A	B		B	B	B
South Carolina	A	AB		A	B		B	B	B
South Dakota	A	A		A	B				

Table 4-1 continued

State							
Tennessee	A	AB	AB	B		B	B
Texas	A	A[m]	A	B		B	B[g]
Utah	A	A[n]	AB				
Vermont	A	A	A	B[o]	B[o]	B	B
Virginia	A		B[o]	B	B	B	
Washington	A	AB	AB	B	B	B	B
West Virginia	A	B	B[c]				
Wisconsin	A	AB	A	B	B	B	B[p]
Wyoming	A	AB	A	B	B	B	B

Key: A = Provisions were included in state constitutions.
B = Provisions were included in state statutes or rules.

a. Guidelines for all states reflect status as of December, 1978, except Arizona. Arizona revisions were not available at the time of review; instead, Arizona provisions reflect status as of October, 1976.

b. In Arkansas, bail is granted as a matter of discretion in murder, manslaughter, or any capital offense.

c. Bail is granted as a matter of discretion in Florida, South Carolina, Rhode Island, and West Virginia in capital cases and for offenses punishable by life imprisonment.

d. In Georgia, there is no right to bail in cases of rape, armed robbery, murder, perjury, aircraft hijacking, treason, or selling, giving, offer for sale, or bartering of narcotics.

e. Bail cannot be set in Hawaii or Maryland in cases where the offense charged is punishable by life imprisonment without parole. Bail is discretionary in Hawaii when the offense is punishable by between twenty years and life imprisonment with parole. In all other cases, bail is a right.

f. In Illinois, bail is discretionary not only in capital cases, generally, but in murder, aggravated kidnapping, and treason cases, specifically.

g. In Indiana, Nebraska, and Oregon, bail is discretionary not only in capital cases, generally, but in murder and treason cases, specifically.

h. Bail is discretionary in Maine for offenses punishable by life imprisonment. Rather than Ten Percent bail, a 50 percent plan is available in Maine.

i. By popular referendum, the Michigan Constitution was amended (November, 1978) to permit denial of bail not only for murder and treason defendants but for other categories of seriously charged defendants as well. These include persons charged with violent felonies having prior convictions for violent felonies, persons charged with criminal sexual conduct of the first degree, robbery, kidnapping with the intent to extort, and other categories of defendants.

[j]In New York, when a defendant is charged with a Class A felony or has two previous felony convictions, bail cannot be set by courts of original jurisdiction and is discretionary in higher courts. In lesser felony cases bail may not be set by any court without hearing from the district attorney and having the official version of the defendant's prior record of convictions and arrests.

[k]In Ohio's Rules of Criminal Procedure the dangerousness concept is mentioned only in relation to misdemeanors.

[l]The Ten Percent option is not available on a statewide basis in Pennsylvania but operates in a number of major jurisdictions.

[m]In Texas, in addition to persons charged with capital offenses, persons charged in any felony having two prior felony convictions may be held without bail after a detention hearing and showing of probable guilt.

[n]In Utah bail is discretionary not only for persons charged in capital cases but also when the defendant has been accused of any felony while on probation or parole, or while on pretrial release pending adjudication of a felony.

[o]In Virginia's statutes it is implied that a defendant need not be admitted to bail (*i.e.*, may be detained) if there is "probable cause to believe that: he will not appear at trial . . . or, his liberty will constitute an unreasonable danger to himself or the public." (Code of Va. Ann. 19.2:120.)

[p]Use of bail schedules are authorized by statute for defendants charged in misdemeanors only.

Although statutory definitions of the right to bail vary little in essence from the formula presented above, some variety in the kinds of cases excluded from a right to bail can be noted. For example, in Hawaii, Maine, Maryland, Rhode Island, South Carolina, and West Virginia,[5] it is not only the prospect of the death penalty but also of life imprisonment or life imprisonment without parole that renders a defendant potentially ineligible for bail. In Hawaii, bail is not allowed for persons charged for offenses punishable by life imprisonment without parole; bail is discretionary in cases where the punishment may range from twenty years to life with parole; bail is granted "as a matter of right" in all other cases.

The right to bail in New York hinges not only on the seriousness of the charged offense (in terms of the possible penalty) but also on the defendant's record of prior convictions and arrests. When charged with a felony of the most serious variety (Class A) or when having been convicted previously of two felonies of any sort, defendants in New York may not have bail set in courts of original jurisdiction and may only have bail set, if at all, at the discretion of higher courts.[6] In Texas, a similar arrangement prevails. Defendants charged in capital cases or having had two previous felony convictions may be held without bail after a detention hearing and a showing of probable guilt.[7]

Rather than relying on the seriousness of the offense and the possible penalty, several states specify particular offenses for which bail may be denied (when the "proof is evident and the presumption great"). The longest list of offenses where bail is discretionary is found in Georgia's guidelines. Persons charged with rape, armed robbery, aircraft hijacking, treason, murder, perjury, or narcotics-related offenses may be detained without bail.[8] In Illinois, bail is not set "as a matter of right" in murder, aggravated kidnapping, and treason cases.[9] Nor is bail set as a right for defendants in murder and treason cases in Indiana, Nebraska, and Oregon.[10]

Overall, the right to bail described in state guidelines appears to be defined principally in terms of seriousness of the offense charged, possible penalty, and record of prior convictions. To the extent that detention facilities hold persons for whom bail has been denied, persons charged with the most serious of offenses—those punishable by death or life imprisonment—and having, perhaps, the most serious records of previous convictions would be found among defendants.

Because the right to bail is a right that is given to certain categories of persons charged with criminal offenses and withheld from certain others, it is logical to examine state guidelines for indications of the purpose of the bail and detention decision. In as many as thirteen states, no statement of the general purpose of the bail decision is provided—nor is it implied.[11] In the guidelines of twenty states, however, the only purpose for bail—either stated or implied—is to assure the appearance of defendants at required proceedings.[12] Yet, guidelines in eighteen states and the District of Columbia suggest, implicitly or explicitly, that the chief business of the bail decision encompasses both evaluation of risk of pretrial flight and assessment of potential pretrial dangerousness for all defendants.[13] In one state, New Hampshire, a presumption favoring release before trial is included without a statement that bail is for assuring appearance; however, a statement relating to defendant dangerousness is present. In Virginia, it is implied that pretrial detention may be invoked as an option for either dangerousness or flight-risk concerns. (See Note O in Table 4-1.) In the November election of 1978, Michigan voters approved a constitutional amendment permitting preventive detention.

Six states pay obeisance to a policy "against the unnecessary detention" of defendants before trial;[14] and more than a decade after the first major bail reform efforts, only twenty-three states (plus the District of Columbia) have adopted guidelines stressing a preference for ROR or release on a promise to appear.[15] Twenty-two jurisdictions have incorporated the principle of release under the least onerous of pretrial conditions.[16] As of December, 1978, Ten Percent provisions, modeled after a program first innovated in Illinois in 1964, were included in the guidelines of seventeen jurisdictions,[17] but greater use of this program—and an emphasis on third-party bail—may be anticipated in the near future. Maine has a Fifty Percent bail provision.

The pretrial release model embodied in the Bail Reform Act of 1966 has been adopted without major modification by seven states.[18] Arkansas and Kentucky, however, have adopted legislation closer to the model delineated by the ABA. Fourteen jurisdictions have adopted release guidelines superficially modeled after the Bail Reform Act but allowing broader consideration of pretrial dangerousness—by not restricting it to just capital cases and appeals as done in the Act.[19]

Other kinds of provisions deal with the role of the prosecuting attorney in the bail decision and the use of bail schedules. Three states define a role for the prosecuting attorney in setting bail and fixing conditions of release. In Arkansas, for example, a defendant charged with an offense punishable by more than one year in confinement may not be granted ROR without the stipulation of the prosecuting attorney.[20] In Colorado, a defendant charged with a crime while on release pending adjudication of another crime (another felony or Class One misdemeanor) having a prior Class One misdemeanor conviction within two years or a felony conviction within five years may not be released on OR without approval of the prosecuting attorney.[21] Felony defendants in New York may not have bail set unless the district attorney has received a copy of the records of prior conviction and arrest.[22]

Provisions for limited forms of bail schedules are evident in three states, California, Alabama, and Tennessee.[23] Tennessee guidelines, for example, outline maximum limits for money bail when set in conjunction with certain broad classifications of offenses. For misdemeanors, the maximum allowable bail is $1,000; for felonies not involving crimes against the person, $10,000; for felonies against the person, $50,000; and for homicides, $100,000.[24] Wisconsin provides that money-bail set in misdemeanors be fixed according to a schedule.[25]

DECISION CRITERIA RECOMMENDED IN STATE BAIL GUIDELINES

In defining a right to bail, every state employs factors or criteria that will be influential in the overall sorting of defendants because defendants falling into categories excluded from bail as a right may be held without bail or, in effect, may be screened into detention. Although such factors as charge seriousness, possible penalty, and prior convictions certainly determine who is likely to be held in detention without bail, an unknown proportion of persons falling into categories where bail is discretionary will secure release. Furthermore, many more persons than those held without bail will be found awaiting trial in jail. Denial of bail is an important, but small, factor in the overall use of pretrial detention. In this section, an important question is whether the same factors specified in right-to-bail provisions (thus determinative of bail denial policies) are equally influential in bail guidelines for less exceptional cases where a right to bail exists.

In this part of the examination of state guidelines, results of an analysis of factors recommended for consideration at bail are presented. Of interest are any criteria endorsed by states—in constitutions, statutes, rules of criminal procedure, or court rules—as the proper basis for bail and pretrial custody decisionmaking. The aim of this undertaking is to learn from sources of legal policy which criteria, if any, *ought* to determine the outcome of the bail decision in various states and the District of Columbia.

The kinds of criteria encountered in reviewing the guidelines ranged from the very concrete, such as "prior criminal record," to the very vague and speculative, such as "past conduct" or "character." As can be seen in Table 4-2, these decision criteria were arranged under three general groupings. The first, legal factors, includes the offense and criminal history data traditionally relied upon in bailsetting. The second group is more representative of the kinds of information relied on by bail reform practitioners in trying to improve the ability of the court to assess risk of nonappearance. This group includes family ties, residence, employment, character, reputation and mental condition, ties to the community, and so forth. The last grouping contains items that reflect the different ways in which defendant dangerousness was alluded to in statutory provisions.

When it is recalled (from the discussion of Table 4-1, above) that no statements describing the purpose of the bail decision can be found in the guidelines of thirteen states, it is not remarkable to learn, further, that six states provide no instructions pertaining to how the decision might be arrived at or to the factors that ought properly to be considered in the bail decision.[26] But, more common than statutory silence are brevity and vagueness in states where instructions are found.

Examples of vagueness in state bail guidelines follow. In these particular instances, the judge or magistrate making the bail decision is instructed on the subject of when ROR as an option ought to be granted. Maryland guidelines, for example, inform the decisionmaker only that "when *from all circumstances the Court is of the opinion* that any accused person in a criminal case will appear as required for trial . . . the person may be released on recognizance."[27] (Emphasis added.) The court is instructed to form an "opinion from all circumstances" concerning a defendant's likelihood of appearance—but is not told how.

In Arizona, similar instructions are evident: "Any person bailable as a matter of right shall be released pending or during trial on his own recognizance, *unless the court determines, in its discretion,* that such a release will not reasonably assure his appearance as required."[28] (Emphasis added.) The Arizona decisionmaker is no more informed than his or her Maryland counterpart as to the differentiation of those likely and unlikely to appear.

In New Hampshire, a final example, all persons charged in noncapital cases "shall, before conviction, be released on recognizance *or* by sufficient sureties, *whichever justice may require.*[29] (Emphasis added.)

Table 4-2. State Bail and Pretrial Release Guidelines: Prescriptive Decision Criteria, by State: December, 1978[a]

State	Legal Factors									Community-ties Factors											Dangerousness Factors					General Considerations		Total
	Nature of Charge	Probability of Conviction	Possible Penalty	Prior Criminal Record	Prior Arrests	Prior Record of Court Appearance (FTAs)	On Probation or Parole when Presently Charged	On Pretrial Release for a Previous Charge	General Community Ties	Age	Residence, Length of Residence	Family Ties	Employment, Employment History	Defendant's Financial Resources	Character	Reputation	Mental Condition	Past Conduct	Persons to Assist Accused in Attending Court	Addiction to Drugs or Alcohol	General Consideration of Dangerousness	Danger to Self	Danger to Others (Other Persons, Witnesses)	Danger to Community (Public)	Likelihood of Violation of Law if Released	Risk of Nonappearance	"Not Oppressive" but "Sufficient" Bail	
Alabama	B	B								B	B	B	B										B	B				8
Alaska	B	B		B		B					B	B	B	B	B								B	B				11
Arizona[a]			B																									1
Arkansas	B	B	B	B		B					B	B	B	B	B	B			B						B			13
California																									B	B	B	3
Colorado	B	B		B		B			B		B	B	B	B	B		B		B						B	B	B	15
Connecticut																												0
Delaware	B	B		B		B					B	B	B	B	B		B						B	B				12
District of Columbia	B	B		B		B					B	B	B	B	B		B	B					B	B				13
Florida											B	B	B	B	B		B	B								B	B	9
Georgia	B																											1
Hawaii			B											B														2
Idaho																												0

Key: A = Provisions were included in state constitutions.
B = Provisions were included in state statutes or rules.

[a]Guidelines for all states reflect status as of December, 1978, except Arizona. Arizona revisions were not available at time of review.

In Maryland, the court must consider "all circumstances," in Arizona the decisionmaker must consult his own "discretion," and New Hampshire guidelines presume that the presiding judge will have an intimate acquaintance with "justice" and will, consequently, be informed of its "requirements." These are but three examples of the vagueness of instructions characteristic of bail and pretrial release guidelines in some states.

Consideration of the number of decision criteria included in bail decision instructions by different states, of course, says little about the relative clarity or completeness of such instructions; yet, examination of the number of criteria specified by states does, at least, offer an indication of the extent to which instructions are found. (See Table 4–3.) In addition to the six states providing no instructions, six states set forth only from one to three factors to be considered by bail judges; eight states list from four to six decision criteria; fourteen states list from seven to ten; and seventeen include eleven or more such considerations. The Colorado, Pennsylvania,

Table 4.3. Bail Decision Criteria: Number of Criteria by State: 1978[a]

Number of Criteria	Number of States Having Criteria	States
0	6	Connecticut (0)[b], Idaho (0), Indiana (0), Mississippi (0), Oklahoma (0), Rhode Island (0)
1–3	6	Arizona (1), Georgia (1), Maryland (1), Hawaii (2), California (3), Nevada (3)
4–6	8	West Virginia (4), Illinois (5), Louisiana (5), New Jersey (5), Utah (5), Montana (6), New Hampshire (6), Texas (6)
7–10	14	Alabama (8), Kentucky (8), Michigan (8), Nebraska (8), Wisconsin (8), Florida (9), Iowa (9), North Dakota (9), South Dakota (9), Kansas (10), Massachusetts (10), Missouri (10), South Carolina (10), Wyoming (10)
11–16	17	Alaska (11), Maine (11), Minnesota (11), Ohio (11), Oregon (11), Tennessee (11), Vermont (11), Delaware (12), Virginia (12), Arkansas (13), New York (13), North Carolina (13), District of Columbia (13), New Mexico (14), Colorado (15), Pennsylvania (15), Washington (16)

[a]This table summarizes information presented in Table 4–2.
[b]Number of decision criteria specified in state guidelines.

and Washington guidelines offer the longest lists, showing fifteen and sixteen factors properly to be considered by bailsetting judges.

No single decision criterion is prescribed by every state. Among the forty-four states listing at least some criteria, thirty-nine specify the nature of the offense charged as a decision consideration. The language used to denote this decision criterion varies from state to state. In some, it is the "seriousness" of the present charge (*e.g.*, in California), in some it is that bail should be "commensurate with the nature of the offense charged" (*e.g.*, in Illinois and Kentucky), while in others it is phrased as the "nature and circumstances" of the offense charged, after the language of the Bail Reform Act. In Alabama, very specific indicators of charge-seriousness are listed, including the violent nature of the offense, weapon use, threats to victims or witnesses, value of property taken or damaged, and sales of drugs.

What is meant by the "nature of," by "seriousness" or "commensurability," or by the "nature and circumstances of" a charged offense is not made clear. There is often an implied connection between offense seriousness and risk of flight—where defendants charged with the more serious offenses will be facing longer prison sentences and will, therefore, be deemed more anxious to flee. Yet, consideration of an explicit "possible penalty" criterion is mandated in only seven states.

There are two additional ways in which offense seriousness may be interpreted by bailsetting officials. In the first, the judge relies on offense seriousness as an indication of a defendant's general and/or potential dangerousness; the more serious the offense, the more dangerous the defendant is deemed, the more likely the judge will want him or her detained, and the higher the cash bail set. In the second, the judge, presuming the defendant's guilt, reacts to offense seriousness as an indicator of the magnitude of punishment that ought to be forthcoming and fixes money-bail punitively in an amount commensurate with the gravity of the offense charged. Thus, in addition to contributing to inferences about risk of flight, the popularity of the offense seriousness criterion—state by state the most common criterion of all—may be due to its use in assessing dangerousness in defendants and in meting out pretrial punishment.

Prior criminal record is specified in the guidelines of thirty-six states. The possible interpretations and uses of this criterion closely parallel those described for offense seriousness. Prior records of conviction (or even of arrests, as in New York) may be used by officials to discern "patterns" of general criminality in defendants. Defendants deemed "generally" criminal may be considered (1) more likely to flee, (2) more "generally" dangerous, and/or (3) more worthy of high punitive cash bail. In addition, it is possible that by reviewing a defendant's criminal record, judges may discover that he or she was on parole or probation at the time of arrest and that the present charge might constitute a violation that could result in the defendant's serving "back-time." This use of prior criminal record suggests a "possible penalty" type of consideration. Yet, probation/parole considerations are mentioned explicitly in the guidelines of only three states, Maine, Michigan, and Utah.

Specified in the guidelines of thirty-five states—thus, the third most prevalent criterion—is consideration of a defendant's financial resources or ability to afford bail. The prevalence of this criterion may be related to criticism by bail reformers that a money-based bail system discriminates against the poor. The guidelines of Illinois and Kentucky, for example, instruct that bail shall be "not oppressive."[30] This concern is also reflected in the statutes of Texas and Hawaii among others. In Hawaii the bailsetting official is advised that bail "should be so determined as not to suffer the wealthy to escape by the payment of pecuniary penalty, nor to render the privilege [of a right to bail] useless to the poor."[31] Texas guidelines warn the official that "the power to require bail is not to be so used as to make it an instrument of oppression."[32]

These three prevalent criteria are among the most concrete and specific of all factors to be taken into account by decisionmakers according to state guidelines. Not so concrete, however, is the criterion that—listed in twenty-five states—constitutes the fourth most prevalent "officially" endorsed consideration, "character." What statutes might mean by a defendant's character is a question very difficult to answer. It is certain only that character, as a deciding factor employed by a bailsetting judge, is likely to be quite subjective. (In sixteen states, this criterion is paired with another equally vague criterion: "mental condition.")

To bail reformers, rating defendants according to community ties was considered a more objective, appropriate, and fair means of assessing risk of flight than the traditional reliance on seriousness of the offense charged. Three community-ties indicators—employment history, family ties, and residence in the community—are in abundance as prescribed criteria in more than half of all states. Consideration of a defendant's prior performance on pretrial release is called for in twenty-five states. Assessment of a defendant's probable guilt or likely conviction is mandated in twenty-three states, where consideration of "weight of the evidence" is specified.

Consideration of a defendant's potential dangerousness if released before trial is evident, in various definitions, in eighteen states and the District of Columbia. "Danger to self" is specified as a relevant decision fact in only five states. More frequently, dangerousness in state guidelines is assessed in terms of a defendant's likely danger to "other persons," to "the community," or to the "public." In North Carolina, the concern is framed in terms of potential "danger of *injury* to any other person";[33] in Minnesota, the question, more generally, is whether a defendant's release would be "inimical to public safety."[34] In Colorado and Oregon, the dangerousness concern is couched in terms of "any facts indicating the possibility of violation of the law if released without restrictions.[35] In Kentucky, the concern is vaguely communicated in "the reasonably anticipated conduct of the defendant if released."[36] Colorado guidelines, further, urge consideration of "any facts indicating a likelihood that there will be any intimidation or harassment of possible witnesses by the defendant."[37]

Finally, a number of other criteria are specified—but rather infrequently— in state bail guidelines. Among these are age, alcohol and drug addiction, whether a defendant was already on pretrial release at the time of arrest, whether a defendant was on active probation or parole status, the district attorney's recommendation as to bail, a defendant's "reputation," a defendant's "past conduct." as well as others.

In summary, several statements can be made concerning these legal data. Bail guidelines are quite diverse in character. Six states provide no bail decision instructions; many more provide few. Beyond criteria used to define the scope of a statutory right to bail (*i.e.*, whether a case is capital or noncapital), no single decision criterion is found to be universally recommended. When criteria are specified, those most commonly found are nature of the charge, prior criminal record, and the defendant's financial resources. After these community-ties criteria, employment, residence, and family ties are most prevalent. Dangerousness is a consideration in nineteen jurisdictions. Procedures for detention of dangerous defendants exist in Michigan, New Mexico and Virginia—not to mention the District of Columbia.

If one were to try to predict which of all possible factors might be most influential in actual bailsetting, it would be logical to turn to the criteria that appear most frequently in the guidelines reviewed. Yet, this sort of prediction would be complicated by two problems.

First, even where decision criteria are specified by guidelines, few instructions as to their relative importance are provided. It follows, then, that bail decisionmakers are left to their own, individual weighting schemes. As a consequence, a great deal of variation in the determination of bail and pretrial custody status might be expected.

But, assuming for a moment that such hypothetical weighting instructions were present in the guidelines, a second problem would be faced: vagueness. Many of the criteria are so vague that their inclusion does not assure that bail decisionmaking will be consistent and based on similar concerns. For example, how should a judge operationalize the following concepts: offense seriousness, probability of conviction, community ties, character, mental condition, or danger to the community?

SUMMARY: BAIL DECISIONMAKING AND PRETRIAL DETENTION ACCORDING TO PRESENT LEGAL GUIDELINES

The theoretical task in the last three chapters has been to examine the legal sources of bail and detention policy in light of (1) definitions of *the purpose* of the bail decision process—or of the state interest behind it—and (2) *the means* whereby classes of defendants (high risk/low risk, dangerous/nondangerous, detained/released) are defined. Since the days of bail reform, the following statement has become almost cliché: "The only constitutionally permissible purpose for bail is to assure appearance." From the present review of existing legal guidelines, it is apparent that this is far from accurate: dangerousness as a state interest in bail decisionmaking is and has been alive and well, *and* permissible. It should be noted that this conclusion is reached from consideration of the legal framework that informs the bail process. Any discussion of principles that might "in real life" guide judicial bail decisionmaking has been assiduously avoided in these chapters.

Although considerable debate rages over its interpretation, the eighth amendment of the U.S. Constitution has little to say about the legitimate purpose of the bail decision process. Historical arguments tracing the early origins of bail and detention have been constructed in support of both appearance and dangerousness functions.

If "constitutionally permissible" means, in addition, what the Supreme Court has said about bail and detention, grounds for both an appearance view and a danger orientation have been uncovered. It is perhaps true that the *Stack* appearance view and the *Carlson* dangerousness view represented the majority and minority positions on bail respectively during the not-too-distant past. (The evolution of these two orientations are summarized in Figure 4–1.) However, it becomes increasingly clear that the concern for a defendant's potential

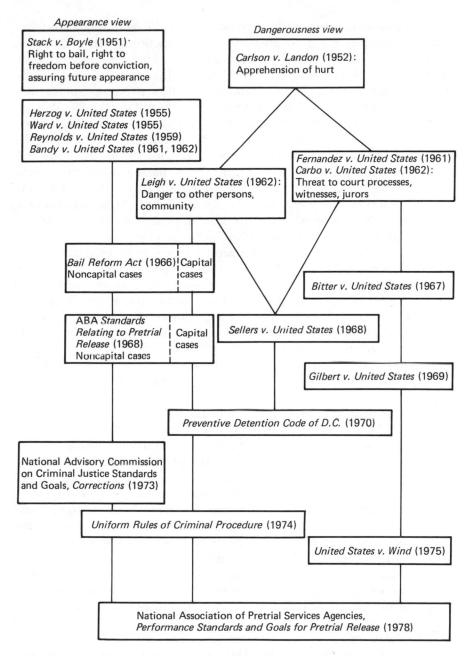

Appearance view

Stack v. Boyle (1951)·
Right to bail, right to
freedom before conviction,
assuring future appearance

Dangerousness view

Carlson v. Landon (1952):
Apprehension of hurt

Herzog v. United States (1955)
Ward v. United States (1955)
Reynolds v. United States (1959)
Bandy v. United States (1961, 1962)

Fernandez v. United States (1961)
Carbo v. United States (1962):
Threat to court processes,
witnesses, jurors

Leigh v. United States (1962):
Danger to other persons,
community

Bail Reform Act (1966) Capital
Noncapital cases | cases

Bitter v. United States (1967)

ABA *Standards
Relating to Pretrial
Release* (1968)
Noncapital cases | Capital
cases

Sellers v. United States (1968)

Gilbert v. United States (1969)

Preventive Detention Code of D.C. (1970)

National Advisory Commission
on Criminal Justice Standards
and Goals, *Corrections* (1973)

Uniform Rules of Criminal Procedure (1974)

United States v. Wind (1975)

National Association of Pretrial Services Agencies,
Performance Standards and Goals for Pretrial Release (1978)

Figure 4-1. The Evolution of the Appearance and Danger Views of Bail Decisionmaking.

dangerousness has not diminished over time. In fact, many contemporary examples point to greater accommodation with or outright acceptance of preventive detention for danger: the Preventive Detention Code of the District of Columbia; the Uniform Rules of Criminal Procedure; the NAPSA Standards; and a pending Senate bill (S.1437). The power of the danger ideology in bail is great; danger is a concern in the guidelines of eighteen states and proposals are before legislatures in many others. The most remarkable example of the viability of the danger view was contributed by the voters of Michigan during the 1978 election. They passed a constitutional amendment[38] mandating preventive detention based on danger concerns for special categories of defendants. The Michigan action demonstrates the unprecedented popular appeal and political assets associated with issues involving pretrial dangerousness.

If the purpose of the bail decision process is to evaluate defendants in terms of flight-risk and dangerous propensities, the role of pretrial detention must be to hold those deemed most flight-prone and/or most dangerous. In summary, after discerning from the various sources of legal policy the purposes of the bail decision process, the next objective was to determine the means by which defendants ought to be classified—either as high risk/low risk, dangerous/nondangerous, or simply detained/released. By source, briefly, the following bail decision criteria were espoused:

1. *U.S. Constitution:* No recommended criteria.
2. *Pre-1966 court cases:* Nature of the offense (including capital or noncapital), weight of the evidence, the financial ability of the accused, and the defendant's character. Criteria for assessing dangerousness were not specified.
3. *The Bail Reform Act of 1966:* Whether a case was capital/noncapital, nature and circumstances of the offense charged, the weight of the evidence, family ties, employment, financial resources, character and mental condition, length of residence in the community, record of prior convictions, and record of appearance at court proceedings. It is not indicated that, in capital cases, evaluation of a defendant's potential dangerousness would be based on criteria any different than those listed for evaluation of risk of flight.
4. *Post-1966 court cases:* Appearance: heavy emphasis on community ties (*i.e.*, residence, family ties, employment history, character), deemphasis of offense seriousness and prior record. Dangerousness: offense seriousness (injury, weapon, drug traffic), prior

record (crimes against person, weapon) and other vague criteria, such as "propensity to commit crime generally" and "reputation."

5. *Other pretrial release models:* The ABA (1968) listed possible penalty (offenses with sentences of less than one year releasable on citation, summons or ROR), whether an offense is capital/non-capital, in addition to the criteria listed by the Bail Reform Act. The ABA Standards also included "any facts indicating the possibility of violation of law if the defendant is released." It is not indicated whether, in capital cases, evaluation of a defendant's potential dangerousness would be based on criteria any different than those listed for evaluation of risk of flight. The National Advisory Commission guidelines relied on criteria similar to those employed in Bail Reform Act and ABA provisions. The Preventive Detention Code of the District of Columbia used Bail Reform Act criteria for evaluation of risk of flight but listed offenses termed as dangerous crimes, or crimes of violence and any person charged with obstructing justice and addicts charged with a crime of violence as criteria determining eligibility for preventive detention proceedings. The Uniform Rules of Criminal Procedure listed no criteria for assessing risk or dangerousness. The NAPSA guidelines called for frank consideration of preventive detention by attempting to define eligibility quite narrowly. Detention was to be permitted on the basis of danger and risk of flight; in conjunction with elimination of the use of cash bail.

6. *State bail guidelines:* A great deal of variety in the number and kinds of criteria prescribed was found. Some states offered no instructions, others a few, and still others emulated the Bail Reform Act, ABA, or D.C. Code models with some additions of their own (such as alcohol and drug abuse in Pennsylvania).

NOTES

1. Bail and detention guidelines may be found under a variety of arrangements in state constitutions and statutes. For example, in one state the constitution and the state statutes may have contained the relevant data, but in another state the key material might have been treated under court rules defined by the supreme court of that state (*e.g.*, Pennsylvania, Alabama). In searching for guidelines, each potential source was consulted and employed when found to be relevant. The analysis of state guidelines presented in this chapter reflects guidelines as of December, 1978—with the exception of Arizona, whose revised code was not available at the time of the review. See Appendix A for a directory of state guidelines.

2. It is especially important in discussions of a "right to bail" to recall that

such a right may have very little connection with a "right to release." In practice, a right to bail may only mean a right to high, unaffordable bail.

3. N.M. Const. Art. II, §13. It is interesting to note that a federal district court in Florida recently found just such a "proof-is-evident" clause violative of a defendant's constitutional rights to due process and equal protection under the law. See *Escander v. Ferguson* 441 F.Supp. 53 (D.C. Fla. 1978).

4. It is absent from guidelines of the District of Columbia, Georgia, Hawaii, Maryland, Massachusetts, Nebraska, New York, North Carolina, Virginia, and West Virginia.

5. Haw. Rev. Stat. §§1-15; Me. Rev. Stat. tit. 15, §942; Md. Ann. Code Art. 27, §638A; R.I. Const. Art. I, §§8,9; S.C. Code, §§17-15-10 to 220; W.Va. Code §62-1c-1.

6. N.Y. [Crim. Pro.] Law, §§530.10-.70 (McKinney).

7. Tex. Const. Art. I, §11(a): "Any person accused of a felony less than capital in this State, who has been theretofore twice convicted of a felony . . . therefore may, after a hearing, and *upon evidence substantially showing the guilt of the accused*, be denied bail pending trial." (Emphasis added.)

8. Ga. Code Ann. §27:901.

9. Ill. Ann. Stat. Ch. 38, §§100:1-15(Smith-Hurd).

10. Ind. Code Ann. §§35-1-22-1 to 7(Burns); Neb. Const. Art. I, §9; Ore. Const. Art. I, §16.

11. No statements describing the purpose of the bail decision or language from which a purpose could be inferred was present in the guidelines of the following states: Hawaii, Idaho, Indiana, Kansas, Massachusetts, Mississippi, Nevada, Oklahoma, Rhode Island, Tennessee, Utah, West Virginia, and Wyoming.

12. These states included Arizona, California, Connecticut, Florida, Georgia, Illinois, Iowa, Louisiana, Maine, Maryland, Missouri, Montana, Nebraska, New Jersey, New York, North Dakota, South Dakota, Tennessee, Texas, and Wisconsin.

13. Jurisdictions with provisions recognizing the dangerousness concern include Alabama, Alaska, Arkansas, Colorado, Delaware, Kentucky, Michigan Minnesota, New Hampshire, New Mexico, North Carolina, Ohio, Oregon, Pennsylvania, South Carolina, Vermont, Virginia, Washington, and the District of Columbia. See Mich. Const. Art. I, §15(1978).

14. These are Alaska, Kansas, Maine, New Jersey, Oregon, and Wisconsin.

15. These include Alaska, Arizona, Arkansas, Connecticut, Delaware, Illinois, Iowa, Kansas, Kentucky, Maine, Massachusetts, Missouri, Nebraska, New Mexico, North Dakota, Oregon, South Carolina, South Dakota, Vermont, Virginia, Washington, Wisconsin, Wyoming, and the District of Columbia.

16. These include Arizona, Arkansas, Iowa, Kansas, Kentucky, Massachusetts, Missouri, Nebraska, New Mexico, North Carolina, North Dakota, Ohio, Oregon, South Carolina, South Dakota, Tennessee, Vermont, Virginia, Washington, Wisconsin, Wyoming, and the District of Columbia.

17. These include Alaska, Arkansas, Illinois, Iowa, Kentucky, Minnesota, Missouri, Nebraska, New Mexico, Ohio, Oregon, Pennsylvania, South Dakota, Vermont, Washington, Wisconsin, and the District of Columbia.

18. These include Iowa, Kansas, Massachusetts, Nebraska, North Dakota, Wisconsin, and Wyoming.

19. These include Alaska, Arkansas, Delaware, Kentucky, Minnesota, North Carolina, Ohio, Oregon, Pennsylvania, South Carolina, Vermont, Virginia, Washington, and the District of Columbia.

20. Ark. Rules Crim. Pro. 8.4,a (i).

21. Colo. Rev. Stat. §16-4-105, m-n.

22. N.Y.[Crim. Pro.] Law, §530.20 (McKinney).

23. The ABA Standards admonished against the use of "predetermined schedules" in the fixing of money-bail. (See ABA, 1968: Standard 5.3,e.) In *Ackies v. Purdy* 382 F. Supp. 38 (S.D., Fla., 1970), Judge Fulton held that use of master bond schedules by Dade County officials violated due process requirements and denied equal protection to poor defendants.

24. Tenn. Code Ann., §§40:1201-1243.

25. Wis. Stat. Ann. §969-01-14 (West).

26. These include Connecticut, Idaho, Indiana, Mississippi, New Mexico, and Rhode Island.

27. Md. Ann. Code Art. 27, §638A.

28. Ariz. Rules Crim. Pro. §§7.1-.6.

29. N.H. Rev. Stat. Ann. §597:1.

30. Ill. Ann. Stat. Ch. 38, §110-5(Smith-Hurd); Ky. Rev. Stat. §431.525.

31. Haw. Rev. Stat §37:709-9.

32. Tex.[Crim. Pro.] Code Ann. tit. 17, §§01-38 (Vernon).

33. N.C. Gen. State. §15a-521 to 547.

34. Minn. Rules Crim. Pro. 6.

35. Colo. Rev. Stat. §16-4-105(j); Ore. Rev. Stat. §135:230-295.

36. Ky. Rev. Stat. §431.525(4).

37. Colo. Rev. Stat. §16-4-105(k).

38. Mich. Const. Art. I, §15.

Chapter 5

Lessons From Previous Research:
Findings and Issues

If the result of the analysis of legal guidelines in the preceding chapters had been to reveal unanimity in (1) description of the purpose of the bail decision and (2) definition of the means for evaluating defendants within the framework of that discerned purpose, the principal task for empirical research would be relatively straightforward: to determine whether or not the specific "means" actually accomplished the desired "ends." Unfortunately, unanimity was not a characteristic either of the definition of means or of the description of ends. Where addressed, the function of the bail decision, in fact, was most often portrayed as (1) securing appearance, (2) preventing the release of dangerous defendants, or (3) both of these. Similarly, agreement on criteria prescribed to guide bail decisionmaking was not widespread. Recommended criteria were either nonexistent, infrequent, or all-comprehensive—thus of questionable practical value.

With these findings in mind, Chapter 5 turns away from analysis of legal guidelines to a critical appraisal of past empirical research relevant to understanding the operation of bail and detention. This review assesses what has been learned through social science research relating to the analytic perspectives noted above.[1] Bail and detention studies are organized in the following fashion: First, general descriptive studies are discussed; second, studies focusing on pretrial flight and its prediction are considered; and, finally, studies concerned with dangerousness or pretrial crime are examined. Methodological themes are addressed in this review to prepare for the empirical study of bail decisionmaking that is presented in subsequent chapters of this book.

DESCRIPTIVE STUDIES

The Chicago Study

A number of descriptive studies have contributed knowledge fundamental to understanding the administration of bail and the use of pretrial detention in the United States in recent decades. The earliest of these, conducted by Arthur Beeley (1927), investigated bail and detention practices in Chicago in reaction to a 1922 survey of the Cook County Jail (Chicago Community Trust, 1922). In that pioneering study, Beeley examined a random sample of defendants detained in the Cook County Jail (n = 170). Background data were collected from official records and defendant interviews. Beeley's staff classified the detained defendants into "dependables" and "undependables" (those likely to appear at future court proceedings and those unlikely to do so) using the following criteria: current charge, "social history" (including family stability, employment, residence,[2] previous criminal record, and personal references), and personal characteristics (including intelligence, education, personality, and habits) (Beeley, 1927:76). As a result of the classification of defendants, Beeley concluded that bail practices were highly ineffective because they acted to detain many times more defendants than was necessary or reasonable. In doing so, Beeley posed a question that would become a central theme of bail reform nearly thirty years later: Can more ("dependable") defendants be released before trial?

In screening defendants, Beeley was clearly influenced by a number of assumptions, including the following: Bail and detention were predicated exclusively on a concern for the appearance of defendants at trial (within statutory restrictions barring bail in capital cases); defendants charged with minor offenses and having no previous records were better risks in terms of appearing at court; social history data comparable in substance to the later reform concept of community ties were helpful in assessing probable risk of flight; and intuitive (staff) assessment of personal character was also a viable basis for measuring dependability.

Although Beeley did not verify the accuracy of his classification (or, really, his prediction) of dependables by release and follow up, his findings were far-reaching. Using his criteria, nearly three-tenths of those detained could have been released before trial and could still have been expected to make their required court appearances. He later discovered that approximately one-third of the detained defendants were eventually acquitted or had charges dropped (Beeley, 1927:159).

Most defendants remained in detention solely because they could not afford bail. Beeley reported:

> The amount of bail in a given case is determined *arbitrarily* and with little or no regard to the personality, the social history, and financial ability of the accused or the integrity and capacity of his sureties. Bail is too often *excessive* and perhaps, equally often, too small. The local policy of standardizing the amount of bail *according to the offense charged* is diametrically opposed to the spirit and purpose of the bail law (1927:155). (Emphasis added.)

Release on recognizance (ROR) and the issuance of summonses—two practices considered very desirable by Beeley—were infrequent. Through findings based on the classification of inmates and a systematic examination of the administration of bail in Chicago, Beeley concluded that the pretrial process was not operating as if ensuring a defendant's appearance was its major concern. Instead, he concluded that the bail system in Chicago was "completely broken down" and that the most desirable remedy was to render "the use of detention unnecessary altogether" (Beeley, 1927:166).

Although Beeley conducted the earliest study of bail and detention practices on record, it is interesting to note that his was not the first voice raised in denunciation of American bail practices. In fact, in 1922 Felix Frankfurter and Roscoe Pound called for the "removal of bail wherever possible, and a relaxation where such a removal cannot be accomplished" to eliminate the abuses they saw plaguing the operation of the bail system in Cleveland (Pound and Frankfurter, 1922:290).

The Oregon Study

Shortly after the appearance of Beeley's study, Morse and Beattie (1932) completed a major study on the flow of felony cases through the system in Multnomah County, (Portland) Oregon. Although their goal was an overall examination of the processing of cases through various stages in a particular setting, a portion of their work examined bailsetting for all felony cases during 1927 and 1928 (n = 1,771) and its relation to later outcomes. Morse and Beattie learned, for example, that in their locale approximately 70 percent of all felony defendants were detained and 20 percent obtained release by posting bail, while only 8 percent were released on their own recognizance (Morse and Beattie, 1932:101–106).

Morse and Beattie also found that whether bail amounts were set high or low depended mainly on the severity of the offense charged.

Greater proportions of felony defendants with low bail were able to secure pretrial release than defendants with high bail. Thus, logically, the amount of bail was the major determinant of whether a defendant was released or detained. Defendants with low bail not only had greater access to pretrial liberty but also tended to have higher dropout rates before reaching the trial stage. Furthermore, felony defendants with low bail tended to show lower conviction rates, and if convicted, sentencing sanctions were less severe than those received by defendants with higher bail (Morse and Beattie, 1932:112).

These early Morse and Beattie findings raised important questions about the function of the bail process and the use of detention. If bailsetting responded mainly to the nature of the offense charged and determined whether or not defendants would be released or detained before trial, and in addition, if high or low bail amounts signaled how well a defendant might fare in later decisions (*i.e.*, dismissal, conviction, sentencing), what purpose was the bail process serving? One implication of the Morse and Beattie findings might have been that the bail decision was cursorily concerned with questions more typically addressed at later dispositional stages. According to this hypothesis, the bail decision facilitated the processing of defendants by assigning bail that reflected the likelihood of guilt and the probable severity of sentence. Consequently, it effected a rough sorting of defendants into two groups, those released and those detained—or, at the same time, those least likely and those most likely to be found guilty and to be subsequently sentenced. In finding that pretrial status was "significantly related to disposition" (Morse and Beattie, 1932:117), Morse and Beattie formulated for the first time an issue that would become one of the central points of inquiry in bail reform criticism and research more than three decades later.[3]

In all, three themes emerge from these very early studies that foreshadow the focuses of later studies associated with the bail reform movement. The first theme is the most comprehensive. It is reflected in the general conclusions that bail had been administered unfairly (*i.e.*, solely according to the offense charged and hinging on defendants' financial resources), in a fashion characterized by abuse, and most importantly, without regard for what was seen as its "legitimate" purpose (*i.e.*, undertaking arrangements that would permit release before trial in exchange for some assurance that a defendant would appear as required at court proceedings). In the same context, it should be noted, the de facto influence exerted by bondsmen in the determination of pretrial status was also sharply attacked (Beeley, 1927).[4]

The second theme revolved around Beeley's hypothesis that, by employing criteria other than the offense charged, it would be possible to screen and release a large portion of defendants ordinarily detained and be reasonably able to expect their appearance at later proceedings. Though the relationship between ratings on his criteria and later appearance at court remained untested, Beeley, nevertheless, pioneered in the development of pretrial classification criteria based on a concern for appearance at court. As a result of their own findings, Morse and Beattie echoed Beeley in declaring: " It is submitted that if provisions were made for investigating and gathering accurate information concerning persons arrested, a much larger proportion could and should be released on recognizance or on lower bails" (Morse and Beattie, 1932:117).

The third theme is, perhaps, the most troublesome because it points to the possible ramifications of the determination of release or detention before trial: the finding that defendants who were detained before trial were more likely to be found guilty and to receive more severe sentences than those who were released.

The Philadelphia Bail Study

More than two decades later, studies supervised by Caleb Foote (Foote, 1954; Alexander et al., 1958) produced findings similar to those generated by the earlier studies. The Philadelphia Bail Study (Foote, 1954) was a wide-ranging undertaking that relied on different sets of data that alternated with the issues examined. Foote's inquiry was guided by several objectives: to survey the methods employed in the bail decision; to determine the extent to which detention was used in the processing of defendants; to contrast the different methods of posting bail in terms of securing appearance; and to gain insight into the situations of the defendants who ultimately remained in detention. To accomplish these objectives, he observed numerous bail hearings and studied samples of cases from court records in Philadelphia and from files obtained from the district attorney's office.

Like his predecessors, Foote found that a defendant's detention did not depend on deliberation about the likelihood of eventual appearance if released before trial. For the cases on which data were collected, the principal determinants of release or detention were the amount of bail and whether or not a defendant could afford to post it. Bailsetting was, once again, linked primarily to the nature of the offense charged. From court observations it was learned that little individual consideration of the defendant's circumstances, character, or ability to afford bail was evident at bail hearings. In fact, in over 70 percent of the hearings observed, no questions relevant to bail were asked (Foote, 1954:1038, Note 32). Foote explained:

> Custom has established a standard related to the nature of the crime charged, a standard which is sufficiently flexible to permit in any crime an amount sufficient to have the practical effect of holding most defendants in prison. The individual is subordinated to the class into which he is placed according to the type of crime with which he is charged, although what relationship to the risk of non-appearance this may have is unknown (Foote, 1954:1043).

In addition to the overwhelming reliance on offense type in setting bail, Foote observed numerous other informal uses of the bail decision. These included use of money-bail as a means of keeping a defendant incarcerated before trial on the belief that he or she was "dangerous," as a tool for "breaking crime waves," as a means of inflicting punishment, and as a vehicle for expressing personal prejudice or whim toward certain defendants (Foote, 1954:1038-39).

About 25 percent of the defendants in the state sample and about 50 percent in the federal sample ultimately awaited trial in detention. Nearly 20 percent of jailed defendants were either eventually acquitted or had charges dropped (Foote, 1954:1050). And, like Morse and Beattie before him, Foote also encountered striking differences overall between the dispositions (conviction/nonconviction and prison/nonprison sentences) of bailed and jailed defendants (Foote, 1954:1052-53).[5]

After examining the rates of forfeiture (involving instances in which defendants failed to appear and thereby forfeited bail) in Philadelphia courts, Foote concluded that bail jumping (failing to appear in court when required) was a negligible problem, occurring in only 2 percent of all cases.[6] Moreover, contrary to traditional logic, bail jumping appeared to be most common for defendants charged with the *least* serious of offenses. Forfeiture rates appeared to be higher for defendants using professional bondsmen as sureties than for those using private sources.

> The use of a financial incentive through bail is the product of long tradition, but under modern conditions the extent to which it deters non-appearance will vary greatly depending upon the type of bail which is posted. If the defendant has to put up his own property or cash or that of a friend or relative whom he does not wish to harm, the resulting restraint upon the accused may be substantial. The amount of deterrence declines, however, when the defendant purchases a bond from a bondsman

or a surety company, especially if there is no procedure for cross-indemnification or if such provision proves to be ineffective (Foote, 1954:1060).

When the defendant pays a 10 percent premium that he forfeits regardless of his or her eventual appearance in court, Foote contended, the effect of deterrence is considerably lessened. In arguing against the utility of financial incentives in preventing nonappearance, Foote concluded that penalties for bail jumping, that is, the "deterrent effect of not wanting to be a fugitive," may serve more effectively to guarantee appearance, because "the likelihood that a defendant will get caught and possibly receive a more severe sentence if convicted may have a much greater impact on a defendant's decision than forfeiture of the bond" (Foote, 1954:1060).

The New York Bail Study

In the New York Bail Study (Alexander et al., 1958), samples representing half of all felony prosecutions (n = 3,223) in three New York City counties (New York, Queens, and Bronx) for 1956 were drawn from docket books kept by the various district attorney's offices. Defendants detained in a number of New York City jails were also interviewed (Alexander et al., 1958:694). Findings in the New York study were quite similar to those generated by earlier studies. Nearly half of all defendants in the sample were detained pending adjudication, and almost 25 percent were detained because bail was simply denied. The seriousness of the offense charged and the defendant's previous record were the prime considerations in New York bail determinations. Little thought was given to the defendant's background or his or her ability to afford bail. ROR was evident in only 3 percent of the cases. Almost exclusive reliance on cash bail had the effect of holding many defendants in jail because of their inability to afford even minimal amounts of bail. As many as 30 percent of defendants with bail set at $500, for example, could not raise that amount (Alexander et al., 1958:712). Other than strictly appearance-oriented uses of bail were again in evidence and, once again, sharp differences were reported in the dispositions of the cases of bailed versus jailed defendants (Alexander et al., 1958:705).[7]

In concluding, the authors of the New York Bail Study called for greater consideration of the defendant's background and ability to pay in determining pretrial status: "It appears that the more a judge or magistrate knows about the strength of a defendant's economic and emotional attachments in the community, the better he will be able to predict his likelihood of appearance, and this makes for an appropriate choice of bail amount" (Alexander et al., 1958:706).

The Vera Foundation's New York Study

In preparation for research carried out in conjunction with the Manhattan Bail Project, Ares, Rankin, and Sturz (1963), under the auspices of the Vera Foundation, conducted a second study of the operation of bail in New York in 1960. The data were drawn from the same sources as those used in the New York Bail Study several years earlier. The findings generated in this study nearly replicated those reported in the earlier study. Bail was not set (*i.e.*, it was effectively denied) in a large proportion of cases, ranging from about 25 percent of all burglary cases to about 13 percent of all sex cases. The controlling factor in bailsetting appeared to be the charge on which a defendant was held. There was an inverse relationship between the amount of bail set and the proportion of defendants able to post it—more than 33 percent of defendants with bail set were unable to raise it and were thus detained. Bondsmen played a major role in determining who could be released. Less than 50 percent of the bonds written in New York County were written by one surety company. Release on recognizance (referred to as "parole" in New York) occurred very rarely, in about 1 percent of all cases. Nearly 66 percent of defendants whose cases were eventually dismissed spent time in jail; and differential judicial outcomes were found for released and jailed defendants. Released defendants fared considerably better than jailed defendants in terms of both conviction and sentencing (Ares et al., 1963:77–85).

The Washington D.C. Study

Another "state-of-the-system" study was conducted in Washington, D.C., in preparation for the inception of the District of Columbia Bail Project (McCarthy and Wahl, 1965). That study examined bailsetting, time spent by defendants in pretrial detention and final dispositions of cases. Data were collected on 2,052 felony cases that originated in or were bound over to the grand jury during 1963. The familiar finding, that bail was set mainly according to the offense charged, was again evident. McCarthy and Wahl found that bail was denied in 9 percent of felony cases (mostly homicide) and that ROR was employed in less than 1 percent of the cases. The remaining cases had money-bail set in varying amounts. About half of these persons had bail set at $1,000 or less and half at more than $1,000. Only 42 percent of those with cash bail were able to post it. Overall, including denials and OR releases, only 38 percent of the total sample of felony cases originally secured release before trial. Another 2 percent were eventually able to gain release after petitioning for reductions or ultimately raising the required amounts (McCarthy and Wahl, 1965: 225–228).

The Washington study also showed that about 80 percent of all defendants charged with felonies spent some time in detention. The median time spent in jail before trial was seventy-five days. Nearly 7 percent of defendants who were detained remained in jail for more than six months (McCarthy and Wahl, 1965:229).

Final dispositions of cases were examined by time spent in detention and by whether or not they were able to secure release. A strong relationship was found between final dispositions and time in jail for defendants who did and did not go to trial: the shorter the pretrial stay, the greater the likelihood that defendants would have their cases dropped (dismissed, nolle prossed, or "ignored"). The longer the stay in detention, the greater the proportion of defendants pleading guilty. Nearly 80 percent of defendants with stays of ten days or less, 65 percent of defendants in jail for one month or less, and 64 percent of defendants confined for two months or less had their cases, in effect, dropped. Only 20 percent, 35 percent, and 36 percent of these groups of defendants, respectively, pled guilty. However, for stays longer than two months, increasingly larger proportions of persons pled guilty than had charges dropped (dismissed, nolle prossed, or ignored). Of defendants choosing to go to trial (26 percent of all who spent time in detention), 89 percent were convicted and 11 percent were acquitted. In general, time spent in detention did not change the proportion of tried defendants who were convicted; however, the median time in jail for persons electing to go to trial was ninety-five days—among the longest stays of all defendants. Of all defendants who were eventually acquitted, approximately 16 percent spent four months or more in jail (McCarthy and Wahl, 1965:230–235).

McCarthy and Wahl also contended that detained defendants in their sample fared less well in terms of case outcomes (acquittal/conviction, suspended sentence, or probation/imprisonment) than released defendants (McCarthy and Wahl, 1965:236). Yet, it is highly questionable from their data whether this has been adequately demonstrated, since the differences they report between classes of defendants are minute.

The National Bail Study

In an effort to characterize the operation of bail and detention over time, the National Bail Study (Thomas, 1976) contrasted samples of both misdemeanor and felony defendants drawn in each of twenty major urban jurisdictions for the years 1962 and 1971.[8] Samples of approximately two hundred felony and two hundred misdemeanor defendants who appeared at initial appearance in those years were selected from the court records of the lower courts in each jurisdiction. Care was taken to include defendants processed throughout the year,[9] so that the small samples would not be biased by any unusual monthly variations in the kinds of defendants who were processed.

Rates of detention and method of release were derived for each of the twenty jurisdictions for both "before" and "after" years. In his reporting of the study, Thomas (1976:38, 65) found generally that between 1962 and 1971 the percentage of felony defendants detained dropped by one-third and the percentage of misdemeanor detainees fell about one-quarter.[10] The reduction in rates of detention in the twenty cities was accompanied by an apparent increase over the decade of the use of own-recognizance releases (ROR): from about 5 percent to 23 percent of all felony defendants and from 10 to 30 percent of all misdemeanor defendants.

Thomas inferred from these data that the growth of ROR projects in these diverse jurisdictions during the bail reform era may have greatly influenced bail practices to rely more on ROR and less on money-bail, with the overall result that detention rates were generally lowered. Thomas noted at the same time, however, that judges were releasing more defendants on OR than just those who had earned positive recommendations for such release from the ROR project staffs in several jurisdictions. In addition, increased use of ROR was evident in jurisdictions having no ROR projects at all during the period studied. The idea of bail reform, Thomas suggested, had an impact more widespread than effects traceable to local reform projects.

The Survey of Inmates of Local Jails

One final analysis by Goldkamp (1977; 1978; 1979(a)) sought to examine the characteristics of defendants who were detained in the nation's jails. The Goldkamp study utilized data obtained by the Law Enforcement Assistance Administration through the U.S. Bureau of the Census for the Survey of Inmates of Local Jails of 1972. In spite of the massive resources required to conduct the survey interviews of jailed inmates, surprisingly little use had been made of the unique data by the government before the Goldkamp analysis.[11]

In focusing specially on defendants detained in local jails during

1972, the Goldkamp study produced a number of basic findings that add to knowledge concerning pretrial detention in the United States. For example, rather than comprising most of the population of American jails, the estimated 43,000 detainees accounted for only three-tenths of jail inmates. Detained defendants were found to be disproportionately young, male, low income or unemployed, and black, when compared to the total noninstitutional population of the United States. Detainees were charged with a wide variety of offenses, ranging from very minor to very serious.; (More than four-tenths, however, were held for murder/kidnapping, rape, robbery, or burglary.) Nearly four-tenths of the detained defendants had been in jail under different circumstances during the previous year. Only about 25 percent reported that they had never been convicted or sentenced for any offense in the past. More than one-quarter were detained without bail, either because of procedural delays or through outright denial of bail. For those detained with cash bail set, the median amount was approximately $2,500. The median length of confinement for the defendants surveyed was about one month (Goldkamp, 1977:191-290).

Summary: Descriptive Studies in
Bail and Detention

These descriptive studies have seriously questioned the uses to which bail and detention apparently were being put and the criteria relied upon by those whose responsibility it was to decide bail.[12] In addition, they call into question exclusive reliance on cash bail and its discriminatory effects. In these studies as well a striking difference between the case outcomes at adjudication and sentencing of released and detained defendants surfaces as a major equity theme. It is striking that issues confronted during the 1960s, when the interest in bail reform was at its height, had, to a large extent, been raised decades earlier. The best example of this, perhaps, can be found in Beeley's attempt to screen dependable defendants based on information not exclusively offense-oriented and the close resemblance of his criteria to those later used by the Vera Institute. The Thomas study is the only one to examine the operation of bail and detention in numerous jurisdictions after the effects of a decade of bail reform. In addition to noting an apparent increase in the use of ROR and pretrial release in general, his study indirectly raises the question of disparity in bail decisions by documenting the variety of procedures affecting the pretrial release of defendants in different American jurisdictions. Similar defendants could conceivably receive different bail outcomes depending only on the idiosyncrasies of the practices in different jurisdictions. The Goldkamp analysis of government data suggests that the persons originally seen as most disadvantaged by the American system of bail and detention—minorities and low-income defendants—may still be the principal "clients" of pretrial detention.

COMMUNITY TIES, ROR, AND FLIGHT

As the bail reform movement unfolded, the 1960s saw the introduction of fact-finding mechanisms (of the sort conceived by Beeley, Morse and Beattie, and Foote) designed to provide the court with information about defendants deemed relevant to bail decisionmaking but not exclusively offense-oriented. These new procedures sought to foster pretrial release of greater numbers of defendants before trial under nonfinancial conditions (principally ROR), by using criteria that would help assess each defendant's likelihood of flight.[13]

In 1961, the Manhattan Bail Project pioneered in the preliminary testing and operationalization of such a concept under the auspices of the Vera Foundation (Ares, Rankin, and Sturz, 1963; Freed and Wald, 1964). To that end, an instrument was developed that rated defendants according to certain "objective criteria," pertaining to such background information as residential stability, employment history, family contacts, and prior criminal record.[14] Defendants were scored on these dimensions and recommendations for ROR were forwarded if required scores were obtained. In accordance with the appearance orientation of Vera's innovative release-on-recognizance program, an improved system for notifying defendants of their upcoming court dates was an important innovation as well.

In the Manhattan Bail Project experiment, a sample of defendants was interviewed before initial appearance at criminal court.[15] Defendants who scored sufficiently high on the Vera scale to warrant recommendations for release on recognizance (on the grounds that they would be quite likely to make their scheduled court appearances) were randomly divided into experimentals and controls. The recommendations concerning the defendants in the experimental group were forwarded to the court for its consideration at the bail decision. Recommendations for the control group defendants were not forwarded and their cases were allowed to proceed through pretrial processing in the customary manner. Only 14 percent of the controls were released on ROR by the court (without benefit of project recommendations), but 60 percent of the experimentals (with recommendations considered by the court) were so released. By use of the Vera recommendation procedure, the study concluded, approximately four times the proportion of defendants usually released through ROR could be freed.[16] Furthermore, failure-to-appear (FTA) rates and rearrest rates for defendants released on the basis of project recommendations were reported to be acceptably low (Ares, Rankin, and Sturz, 1963:86).

Given the appearance orientation of this reform, it is not surprising that, in addition to a more favorable release rate, the rate of bail jumping (failure-to-appear) was adopted as a measure of success. Within this context, it is assumed that a certain proportion of released defendants ultimately will not appear at court as required. Although there are no acknowledged guidelines that delimit an acceptable percentage of nonappearing defendants, it can be assumed that the proportion of released defendants who abscond ought to be kept at a minimum.

The Extent of Bail Jumping

A number of studies have presented data that describe what might be considered customary jump rates of released defendants. At the same time, failure-to-appear rates for ROR releasees are offered in contrast—to reflect the ability of the community-ties criteria used by ROR projects to distinguish "good" appearance risks from "bad." This approach appears to represent a genre of bail study; several selected examples are discussed.

In an investigation of FTA rates for a sample of defendants appearing in Manhattan Criminal Court during the first three months of 1967,[17] Schaffer reported that 10 percent of all released felony defendants failed to appear at court, while 11 percent of defendants charged with misdemeanors and 24 percent of defendants charged with violations absconded (Schaffer, 1970: Table 7-a). When examined by method of pretrial release, defendants released on cash bail were the most likely not to appear (19 percent), defendants released on ROR but not after a project recommendation were next highest (15 percent), while only 9 percent of those recommended for ROR and released and 4 percent of those released on bond failed to appear in court (Schaffer, 1970:Table 8-a).

Schaffer also found that jump rates for defendants did not increase with the severity of the offense charged, as conventional judicial wisdom might postulate. On the contrary, some of the highest jump rates were recorded for defendants charged with offenses of lesser seriousness (*e.g.*, prostitution and petty larceny), and high bail was not associated with lower rates of nonappearance (Schaffer, 1970:Table 9-a). In addition to showing the degree of nonappearance associated with both traditional and ROR release, Schaffer's findings further fuel the criticism that reliance on offense charged does *not* offer a useful assessment of propensity toward flight, nor does imposition of excessive money-bail necessarily offer an effective deterrent against nonappearance.

Using a survey questionnaire, Wice (1970, 1974) assembled data bearing on estimated jump rates in eight large American cities.[18] These estimates by officials based on forfeitures of bail or bond ranged from a low of 4 percent in Washington, D.C., to a high of 24 percent in Detroit. Only Detroit's estimate exceeded 10 percent of all released defendants. From his survey of seventy-two cities, Wice obtained similar FTA estimates for defendants released on money-bail and those released on recognizance. Eighty-seven percent of the cities showed ROR jump rates of 9 percent or less, 80 percent showed the same range for money-bail releases (Wice, 1974:68).

In a separate report on the same study, Wice (1970:63) contrasted cities using traditional bail practices with cities that had incorporated ROR reforms into their systems. In the traditional cities, about 7 percent of all defendants were released on ROR, with an overall FTA rate of 12 percent. Cities using "reform" procedures released 27 percent of all defendants on ROR with a 10 percent FTA rate. Wice's findings support the notion that the proportion of defendants likely not to appear (based on standard release policies where substantial proportions are detained) is small and that ROR enables the release of greater proportions of defendants before trial without noticeably increasing the jump rate. It should be stressed that many other studies have reported essentially similar findings (based perhaps on more reliable data) pertaining to the feasibility of using ROR.[19]

In the National Bail Study, FTA rates for each of the cities were computed for felony and misdemeanor defendants for 1962 and 1971 (Thomas, 1976:89, 90). The FTA rates for felony defendants in 1962 ranged from a low of 1 percent in Hartford to a high of 15 percent in Wilmington. In 1971 the felony rates ranged from a low of 3 percent in Des Moines and Peoria to a high of 17 percent in Boston and Chicago. (The median felony jump rate was about 6 percent for the twenty cities in 1962 and about 11 percent in 1971.) The FTA rates for misdemeanor defendants in 1962 ranged from a reported low of zero percent in Detroit and Washington, D.C., to a high of 16 percent in Wilmington. The misdemeanor FTA rates in 1971 ranged from 3 percent in Hartford and Sacramento to 29 percent in Los Angeles. (This represents a shift in the median rates for the cities from about 6 percent in 1962 to about 10 percent in 1971.)[20] Overall, the FTA rates do not appear to have been substantially high. Yet Thomas's findings demonstrate also that FTA rates fluctuate widely from jurisdiction to jurisdiction.

In sum, available data appear to confirm the claim by reform activists that Vera-like community-ties criteria may be used to release greater numbers of defendants before trial without adversely affecting the appearance problem. However, two notes of caution deserve mention. First, further study is clearly needed before one can feel confident about the ability of community-ties criteria to distinguish potential absconders from good risks. Important questions must be raised about the quality of the data used and the definition of the criterion variables. Obviously, the most informative experiment would entail release of all defendants before trial and subsequent examination of the characteristics of those who do not appear. The impracticality of such an undertaking necessitates other kinds of experimentation employing the proper controls.

It is conceivable that community-ties criteria *do* help differentiate the two groups, but it is also known that notification procedures greatly affect whether or not defendants show for trial.[21] *More specifically, the question that remains unanswered is whether good court attendance by ROR releasees is produced by the selection criteria (community-ties ratings) or the supervision imposed through telephone notification and other procedures.*

The second caveat concerns the potentially biasing effect of criteria used in pretrial release decisions. Early studies and reform efforts both cite unfairness inherent in pretrial detention practices, when the likelihood of securing release depends on the defendant's ability to afford bail. As ROR projects have spread throughout the country, implementation of Vera-like criteria have made some inroads into the widely criticized practice of framing release solely in financial terms. Yet, it is conceivable that the community-ties criteria may generate unfair effects of a different sort. For instance, are certain defendants (whom Beeley might classify as dependables) discriminated against because they do not meet residential/family stability measures? If so, is this form of discrimination reasonably related to the task of determining who the good appearance risks might be? Thomas (1976: 148), among others, has questioned whether the use of community ties—reflecting as it does "middle-class" (his wording) employment, residential, and social standards—might be operating to the disadvantage of minority and low-income defendants. This is a crucial point, when it is realized that the criteria used have questionable validity in the minds of a number of researchers.

Efforts have been made in many jurisdictions to liberalize release procedures by reducing the number of points that would be required for a positive ROR recommendation. Lazarsfeld (1974) has attempted to refine the Vera instrument to permit broader release policies with no increase in FTA rates. Among numerous other jurisdictions, Philadelphia engaged in a reanalysis of the criteria it employed in its pretrial release program (Ozanne et al., 1976; Wilson, 1975:32-34).

THE PREDICTIVE VALIDITY OF CRITERIA EMPLOYED IN THE BAIL DECISION

Except when bailsetting is used in a purely punitive fashion, the aims of the bail decision are largely *predictive*. In order for bail decision-making to be rational, the criteria relied upon must be reasonably helpful in distinguishing defendants who are likely to flee or commit crimes before trial from those who are not. The longstanding complaint by critics of bail that charge seriousness was inappropriate for assessing risk of flight, for example, was in part a question concerning the *predictive* validity of that criterion. In this section, studies that have examined the relationship of decision criteria—such as criminal charge and community ties—to the outcomes of interest are briefly reviewed.

It has been argued that consideration of offense seriousness has validity, since a defendant's propensity to flee might well be heightened as the possible penalty becomes more severe. Yet, findings reported by Welsh (1977), Feeley and McNaughton (1974), Landes (1974), and Schaffer (1970), to mention but a few, shed some doubt on this assumption.

Schaffer reports that among the defendants released before trial in his Manhattan sample, the rate of FTA did not increase with offense severity. As noted previously, absconding was most characteristic of those charged with the least serious offenses (violations), and those charged with misdemeanors showed generally lower FTA rates than those charged with felonies (Schaffer, 1970:Table 7-a). Feeley and McNaughton (1974:33),[22] studying the processing of defendants through the Sixth Circuit Court in New Haven, found that defendants charged with serious offenses were no more likely to abscond than those charged with minor offenses. Landes reported that "the more severe the charge, the greater the number of prior felonies and the more likely that a defendant is on parole, the lower the estimated probability of disappearance, other things constant" (Landes, 1974: 324). Based on these related findings, the ability to predict nonappearance on the basis of severity of offense charged would appear to be rather doubtful.

In substantial part, bail reform involved selling the use of alternative decision criteria that were considered more equitable and more appropriate for predicting appearance/nonappearance. With growing acceptance of the Vera community-ties criteria in many jurisdictions with ROR programs, the question of their predictive validity becomes more and more urgent: Can ratings of defendants based on the Vera criteria effectively distinguish between those who will appear and those who will not appear? If so, how effectively?

Because favorably rated defendants recommended for ROR typically show acceptably low FTA rates, it does not necessarily follow that these criteria can effectively screen bad from good risks. There is no proof that those defendants who remain in detention (*i.e.*, having scored poorly on the Vera items) would not also show acceptably low FTA rates. Gottfredson explains:

> The Vera Institute instrument has been found to work only in a restricted sense. That is, research reported to date indicates that defendants released as a result of recommendations based on the criteria developed rarely fail to appear for trial and have low arrest rates during the period of pretrial release. However, in order to be valid as predictors, it must be shown that they can discriminate between the groups of individuals who subsequently appear for trial and those who do not. It is necessary that such a demonstration be based *on a total sample of defendants* for release on recognizance, not simply those traditionally released as good risks (Gottfredson, 1974:289). (Emphasis added.)

Relatively few studies have dealt with the questions of predictive validity that surround the use of these criteria. In their study, Feeley and McNaughton (1974:34) attempted to distinguish between defendants who absconded and those who appeared in court by using variables describing their backgrounds and community ties, as well as offense-related variables, with no statistically significant results. Landes (1974:324) was unsuccessful in predicting nonappearance using the variables he found to be most influential in determining the amount of a defendant's bail (*i.e.*, severity of offense charged and previous record). Lazarsfeld (1974) demonstrated that an alternative screening instrument may be employed with as much success as the original Vera scale. Clarke et al., (1976) studied 763 defendants released on bail in Charlotte, North Carolina, during 1973. Court disposition time, criminal record, and method of release (cash or promise-to-appear) were reported as most important in distinguishing between defendants who appeared and who did not. However, the Gottfredson study (1974), focusing on defendants arrested in Los Angeles between November, 1969, and July, 1970, is the only study to date to have aimed specifically at validation of the predictive criteria employed in the Vera scale by drawing on a sample approximating the "total sample" ideal.[23]

Gottfredson describes his sample and design as follows:

> Each defendant was unable to obtain bail release and applied for OR consideration by the Los Angeles Superior Court OR Project. All of the defendants were evaluated in the normal manner by the OR project and those favorably recommended by the project and approved by a judge were later released on OR in the normal manner . . . . Of the 619 defendants released by the court in this manner during the period of study, 201 were randomly selected to represent the OR releases. Three hundred twenty-eight defendants deemed not eligible for OR release by the project were also released under special arrangement with the court. These defendants constituted the Experimental Release Group (ER) (1974:289-290).

Although the FTA rate for the ER group (27 percent) was noticeably higher than that for the ROR group (15 percent), Gottfredson found that "the vast majority of defendants were successes while on pretrial release." An alarming implication is that while the Vera-type criteria correctly recommended the release of (and predicted the appearance of) 85 percent of the ROR sample, they erred in leaving for detention 73 percent of the ER sample.

Thus, using the community-ties criteria, the following results were achieved. For every eighty-five defendants correctly released, fifteen were released who should not have been (since they failed to appear). For every twenty-seven correctly detained (since they would later have failed to appear), seventy-three would have been erroneously kept in jail to await trial (Gottfredson, 1974:293-294). Gottfredson further found that scores on the Vera scale were minimally correlated with FTA. In addition, none of the individual scale items was substantially related to nonappearance. In fact, resident points—a key theoretical link to the community-ties rationale—was shown to be the weakest item (Gottfredson, 1974:296).

In a second part of his study, Gottfredson tried to move beyond the Vera scale to utilize any additional information that would have been available to decisionmakers at the bail stage to achieve a better prediction of nonappearance. Using his best predictors in a regression equation, he was unable to fare any better than when Vera items were used.[24]

The importance of studies that attempt to validate the predictive ability of criteria used in screening defendants at the bail stage is obvious. The Gottfredson study suggests that criteria commonly used in many of the ROR projects around the country may have little predictive power. If this is so, a large number of defendants may be sorted "in" and "out" of detention on the basis of a classification scheme that bears little relevance to predicting future appearance. Conceivably, defendants may be detained merely because they fail the Vera community-ties test.[25]

CRIME ON PRETRIAL RELEASE
AND PREVENTIVE DETENTION

As with the concern for appearance, pretrial decisionmaking based on concern for a defendant's potential dangerousness involves prediction. Certain assumptions relating to the defendant's past and present dangerousness are made, and subjective forecasts of his or her future dangerousness on pretrial release are formulated, usually based on the criminal charge.[26] The measure of whether a released defendant turns out to be dangerous (in existing research) is typically whether or not he or she has been rearrested while on pretrial release. If predicting dangerousness is to be considered an acceptable bail decision task, then what the decisionmaker must predict successfully is the amount (and kind) of crime committed by released defendants.

The Extent of Bail Crime

The amount of crime committed by released defendants is very difficult to estimate chiefly because (1) all those committing crime are not arrested and (2) all those arrested may not have committed crimes. In spite of their questionable validity, rearrest rates are usually employed as estimates of the criminal activity of defendants who have been released before trial. (Reconviction rates are considered more appropriate measures by some (Angel et al., 1971:308-309)).

Estimates of the extent of pretrial "recidivism"[27] vary considerably. In the *Report of the President's Commission on Crime in the District of Columbia* (1966), rearrest rates were examined for felony defendants (n = 2,776) who had originally been released on bail between January, 1963, and October, 1975. Of chief interest to the commission were rearrests for felonies alleged to have been committed while on pretrial release.[28] Of all releasees, the commission reported, only 8 percent were rearrested for felonies. Releasees originating exclusively with the D.C. Bail Project showed a somewhat lower rate, only 5 percent (1966:515).

In 1970, a pilot study exploring the ability to predict bail crime (or, in effect, dangerousness) was carried out by the National Bureau of Standards (Locke et al., 1970). The NBS study showed that for a sample of misdemeanor and felony defendants, the overall rearrest rate was about 11 percent. Of defendants originally charged with offenses termed by the D.C. Preventive Detention Code as "crimes of violence," 17 percent were rearrested for crimes committed on pretrial release, and of those charged with crimes defined as "dangerous," 25 percent were rearrested. However, overall only 7 percent of those originally charged with a felony were rearrested for a felony, and only 5 percent of those originally arrested for violent offenses were rearrested for violent offenses (Locke et al., 1970:2).

Based on a retrospective examination of the sample used in his study, Landes (1974:309) reported a rearrest rate of about 7 percent. In their study of defendants in New Haven, Feeley and Mc-Naughton (1974:40)[29] reported a rearrest rate of about 4 percent. Data from the Charlotte study showed a rearrest rate of about 10 percent (Clarke et al., 1976). The Gottfredson study, however, showed high overall rearrest rates, but low rates for serious crimes. In his sample of defendants in Los Angeles who ordinarily would not have been released on OR, 47 percent were rearrested—mostly for property crimes and seldom for crimes against the person. About 26 percent of those meriting OR release recommendations and released on OR were rearrested. Although this might at first glance suggest that that ROR decision was operating rather well in terms of discriminating between defendants likely and not so likely to commit pretrial crime, Gottfredson (1974:292) reported that only about 5 percent overall (both samples) were rearrested for dangerous crimes.[30]

These estimates appear to indicate that rearrest of defendants on pretrial release may not be that infrequent, but that rearrests for serious or dangerous crimes might be quite rare indeed. It is difficult to feel very confident about such a conclusion, however. The principal reason for lack of confidence in present knowledge of this phenomenon is that all estimates rely on arrest or conviction rates. Obviously, the difficulty with arrest rates is that arrested defendants may not have committed any dangerous or seriously criminal acts, just as some of those not arrested may have. It is important to stress another caveat concerning the measuring of pretrial crime in terms of rearrests: If the interest in pretrial arrests stems from a concern with potential defendant *dangerousness*, then the measure should clearly be arrests for serious crimes—however defined—not arrests per se.

Gottfredson (1974:293) and Clarke et al. (1976:34) found that rearrest rates may depend to a great extent on the duration of pretrial release. In fact, Gottfredson reported a correlation of .53 (p < .001) between rearrests and length of time on release before trial. Clarke found court disposition time to be the single most influential factor in explaining rates of rearrest (and failure-to-appear). Thus, the longer a defendant waits while at liberty, the greater his or her chances on being arrested for a crime while on release. (An important implication of this finding might be that, rather than using the bail decision to predict pretrial dangerousness in a necessarily inefficient manner, bail crime could be more effectively curbed by shortening the length of time between arrest and adjudication—a major goal of proponents of "speedy trial" legislation.)

Predicting Pretrial Dangerousness

From available data, indications are that serious or dangerous pretrial crime may not be a frequent occurrence and that rearrest of released defendants for serious crimes may be quite rare indeed. The extent to which detention practices effectively confine dangerous defendants is presently unclear, and it is a question that may not be resolved definitively—short of the unlikely event that a study is conducted in which all defendants are released before adjudication and their subsequent arrests are charted.[31] The difficulty encountered in predicting statistically rare events is well known and it is a difficulty that has hampered research in other areas of criminal justice where dangerousness is an issue.[32]

In the pretrial area, Feeley and McNaughton, for example, reported difficulty in isolating characteristics that might distinguish defendants who were rearrested from those who were not. They concluded "there is simply no likelihood of establishing anything approaching predictive capacity" (Feeley and McNaughton, 1974:42) and "reliable predictors of those likely to be rearrested while free on pretrial release are not likely to be forthcoming on the basis of any of the currently gathered types of information" (Feeley and McNaughton, 1974:vi).

Upon validating the best prediction equation by using the random split-half technique on his sample, Gottfredson (1974:300) realized little more success in predicting rearrest than would have been possible by relying on chance alone. Similarly, the NBS study (Locke et al., 1971) reported little predictive success.

Unlike other researchers in this field, Landes (1974) believes his findings show that by using traditional bailsetting procedures, judges actually achieve a respectable amount of success in detaining defendants who would have been dangerous if released.

The variables that are statistically significant determinants of the defendant's bond (e.g., severity of the charge and criminal record) also provide information on the likelihood that a defendant will be charged with committing an offense during the period of pretrial liberty, and that variables that are not significant determinants of bond (*e.g.*, age, residence, other income, previous employment) do not provide such information (Landes, 1974:312).[33]

Kirby (1974) and Welsh (1977) also purport to show a relationship between the nature of the initial criminal charge and subsequent rearrest.

On the whole, however, it appears that the intuitive prediction of dangerousness practiced by pretrial decisionmakers is an undertaking with little promise of success, given that studies employing statistical techniques have encountered such difficulty. Because in terms of *magnitude*, bail crime does not appear to be a great problem and because predicting pretrial crime is in fact so difficult, inevitable questions are raised concerning the appropriateness of present bail practices that may be directly or indirectly guided by concern for dangerousness. (It would be naive, certainly, to suppose that empirical findings would have much of an impact on preventive detention policy, while pretrial crime remains such a source of public and judicial concern.)

The Harvard Preventive Detention Study

One study in particular stands out as an effort to evaluate the feasibility of applying dangerousness (in this case as defined in the District of Columbia statute) as a criterion by which defendants might be screened. Angel, Green, Kaufman, and Van Loon (1971) studied a sample of 427 defendants, who were arrested in Boston in 1968 for crimes that would have qualified for preventive detention procedures had the D.C. law been in effect in Boston at the time and who were released before trial. To obtain their sample of released defendants who would have qualified for preventive detention under the D.C. Code, Angel et al., obtained a list of all persons arrested for violent crimes in Boston during the months of January, March, May, August, September, and November, 1968. Of all such arrestees, it was determined that 427 released persons would have fallen under the provisions of the D.C. Code. (Juveniles and persons arrested for violent crimes not covered by the preventive detention provisions of the Code were excluded.) The sample included defendants who had been arrested for all possible D.C. detention crimes, but more than half were charged with robbery and burglary, and about one-fifth were charged with crimes of personal violence.

By searching through court and probation files on state and local levels, it was learned that 14 percent of these defendants on pretrial release were rearrested before trial (but only two-thirds of this number were *convicted* of these pretrial crimes). Only 5 percent of the sample were convicted for crimes termed "dangerous" or "violent" by the D.C. Preventive Detention Code (Angel et al., 1971: 308-309). In terms of actual outcome, only the defendants included in this small group (5 percent) would have earned the label dangerous, and would have had their dangerous crimes prevented, had they been detained.

The Angel study further sought to determine whether or not it would be possible to distinguish between dangerous and nondangerous releasees by employing variables designed to reflect criteria recommended for pretrial screening purposes in the Act (see 23 D.C. Code 1321, b). Because the D.C. Code gives no instructions as to the relative importance of each of the factors it lists for consideration, two approaches were employed to create dangerousness indexes for the sample defendants. A first dangerousness scale (DS-1) was constructed by assigning weights to twenty-six variables on the basis of subjective assessment of their importance in determining a defendant's dangerousness. After having ascertained the statistical relationship between each included variable and pretrial recidivism, a second dangerousness scale (DS-2) was constructed, which weighted each index variable relative to its correlation with recidivism.

The range of possible scores on the intuitive scale (DS-1) extended from a low of 1 to a high of 70. The actual scores of the sample defendants ranged from 1 to 45. In order for the scale to be considered a useful tool for distinguishing the dangerous from the nondangerous, it was necessary to select a cutting point above which, ideally, scores of the actual pretrial recidivists would fall and below which scores of the nonrecidivists would fall. By choosing 30 as the optimal cutoff point on DS-1, the researchers would have designated seventy (or 16 percent of the total sample) as dangerous and therefore, eligible for preventive detention. However, of these only eighteen (or 26 percent) were actual recidivists, while fifty-two (or nearly 75 percent) would have been inappropriately detained. Moreover, the eighteen correctly selected (since they were among the real recidivists) did not represent the most dangerous offenders. That is, defendants committing the most serious crimes while on pretrial release had DS-1 scores that were lower than 30 (Angel et al., 1971:315), and would have been designated as good risks or nondangerous releasees.

Statistical procedures were used to weight variables on DS-2, the nonintuitive dangerousness scale.[34] Scores for defendants on this scale ranged from 13.5 to 52.1 While DS-2 was somewhat more effective in distinguishing between dangerous and nondangerous defendants, no cutting point on the scale could be selected that would result in the detention of more recidivists than nonrecidivists. When the optimal cutting point of 35 was chosen, 14 percent of the entire sample still would have been detained. Of the sixty-three defendants in this group with scores above 35, twenty-six were actual recidivists. About 60 percent of those eligible for preventive detention based on scores from this scale would be detained incorrectly. Somewhat ironically, the five highest scoring defendants (those receiving the highest dangerousness ratings on DS-2) were nonrecidivists (Angel et al., 1971:316).

On the whole, the study concluded, had all defendants been detained under the preventive detention provisions tested, only 10 percent would have been prevented from committing crimes for which they were later convicted. Had this kind of detention policy been in effect, less than 1 percent of all Boston arrestees and 2 percent of all convicted defendants during the six-month period under study would have been incapacitated.

In a final component of the study, 102 defendants who would have been eligible for preventive detention in D.C., based on criminal charge, and who were, in fact, detained in Boston were scored on DS-1 and DS-2. These defendants scored more poorly on each of the variables used on the scales. Their dangerousness scores were significantly higher than those of their released counterparts. Yet, if all of the detained group had been released, a barely perceptible increase in the incidence of bail crime among sample defendants (2 percent) would have been observed (Angel et al., 1971:330-332).

Summary: Predicting Dangerousness

In summary, although it has been shown that pretrial detention—as administered through the bail decision—is greatly concerned with the dangerousness of defendants (as interpreted through the offenses charged and measured in terms of rearrests), available research has demonstrated that predicting a defendant's propensity to commit (dangerous) crime while on pretrial release is at present nearly impossible. Given the state of this sort of predictive art—and the likelihood that bail officials will continue to concern themselves with the volatile issue of defendant dangerousness—it may be worthwhile to confront the question of just what magnitude of error in the prediction should be considered acceptable. That is, the pivotal question regarding detention policy would seem to hinge on how many falsely detained defendants would be legally, morally, or in any other way acceptable in the process of correctly detaining a certain (small) proportion of potentially dangerous defendants.[35]

CONCLUSION: THE PRESENT
STATE OF KNOWLEDGE

Findings produced by early descriptive studies (from 1927 to 1960) served to characterize the operation of pretrial processes (the administration of bail and the use of detention) and to focus on important issues. Several important themes were frequently stressed in these studies: (1) bail was set rather arbitrarily—based more on a mechanical appraisal of the offense charged than on an assessment of a defendant's likelihood of absconding; (2) bail was often fixed at unaffordably high amounts—without regard for the defendant's ability to pay or for the role of the bondsman; (3) a substantial proportion of defendants were unnecessarily detained prior to trial (in terms of *any* apparent rationale); (4) whether a defendant was released or detained before trial seemed to have an important bearing on his or her later outcomes in the judicial process. From these findings it can be inferred that pretrial detention served to hold those defendants who were seriously charged (*i.e.*, considered dangerous), those who were without financial resources, and those who were most likely to be found guilty and sentenced.

Subsequent studies were more specialized, focusing on such issues as how to release more defendants, how to predict failure-to-appear or pretrial crime, and the relationship between pretrial custody and final disposition. Although studies have shown that defendants released on OR as a result of evaluation of their community ties may show favorably low FTA and rearrest rates, none has demonstrated that these criteria can help distinguish good from bad bail risks.

The extent to which both offense and community-ties-related criteria are prevalent in bail and detention guidelines has been described in the earlier chapters. In many guidelines, these criteria were deemed instrumental for classification of defendants into low risk/ high risk, nondangerous/dangerous, and released/detained groups of defendants—according to the apparent purpose(s) of the bail decision. Considering (1) the apparent flexibility of the bail decision function and (2) the kinds of criteria that have been included in legal guidelines, the following findings from the second and third sections of this chapter are especially germane to the present inquiry:

1. Use of ROR as a bail decision option can be increased without affecting the rates of nonappearance or of bail crime (*e.g.*, Ares, Rankin, Sturz, 1963; Schaffer, 1967; Wice, 1970; Thomas, 1976).
2. The rates of nonappearance and pretrial crime appear to be minimal to begin with.

3. Persons released on (high) money-bail generally exhibited greater rates of nonappearance than persons released on OR. This has been interpreted as demonstrating that cash bail does not provide an effective deterrent against absconding—at least not one that is noticeably more effective than release on a promise to appear.
4. The risk of nonappearance or of pretrial crime does not appear to increase with the seriousness of the offense charged; however, it may increase with the length of time between release and disposition of a case.
5. There is no hard evidence that either community-ties or offense-charged criteria can effectively distinguish between persons likely and not likely to be dangerous or to abscond before trial.
6. To the extent that offense or community-ties-related criteria result in the detention of defendants before trial, there is no indication that their detention will in fact or by intention be related to a likelihood that they will flee or be dangerous if released.

Not only are there questions concerning the appropriate use of the bail decision process, but the ability of the decision criteria most commonly relied on to do their job is highly questionable as well. They cannot effectively select out the poor risks, based on either dominant bail ideology, from among defendants processed by the courts.

It is conceivable, certainly, that this state of affairs could be altered by findings produced in future research. Nevertheless, even when viewed tentatively, consideration of these findings raises a number of difficult questions for present policymakers. For example, what policy should be adopted in bail guidelines when it is known that, statistically at least, "nothing works" effectively in bail prediction. Should policymakers then opt for the "least objectionable" or fairest of (ineffective) decision criteria? If it were found that whether a defendant has a telephone or has utilities listed in his or her name or that previous arrests (as opposed to convictions) were very good predictors of flight-proneness or dangerousness (Ozanne et al., 1976; Lazarsfeld, 1974), would these criteria—though effective—be legally acceptable?

Overall, these studies have contributed greatly to a knowledge of bail decision themes (such as the importance of the offense charged, a defendant's ability to afford bail, community-ties ratings, predictions of dangerousness, and differential case outcomes for detained versus released defendants). Moreover, they have raised questions that underscore the importance of learning about the role of pretrial detention. *Clearly absent from this research, however, is a basic empirical examination of the overall filtering process that leaves some defendants in jail while granting others pretrial release—and a sound examination of the "effects" of the process.*

The Importance of Methodological Rigor

A review of the research in the area of bail and detention raises many questions pertaining to the nature of the pretrial screening process. As the aims of research in the pretrial area have shifted from the broad and descriptive to a narrower focus on specific issues, questions of methodological rigor have become more central. The greatest challenge has been encountered in the collection of data, because the issues of interest have implications that are potentially system-wide (affecting arrest, initial appearance, and other preadjudicatory stages; detention, adjudication, and sentencing stages). Previous studies have had to rely on data sets that, for the most part, have differed greatly from one another and have suffered from the exclusion of cases of potential interest.[36]

Beeley, for example, interviewed a sample of defendants detained in the Cook County Jail in Chicago in 1924 but did not consider defendants who were released. Morse and Beattie tracked all felony defendants *forward* through the system in Multnomah County, Oregon, during 1927 and 1928 but had nothing to say about defendants arrested for crimes of lesser seriousness who might have been detained. In the two studies supervised by Foote in Philadelphia and New York (in 1954 and 1958), a more eclectic approach to data gathering was adopted, as different issues were addressed. He obtained data from the records of state and federal courts, from the files of district attorneys' offices, and used other data based on observation of initial appearances and interviews with detainees. Feeley and Mc-Naughton (1974) sampled cases passing through a New Haven court that handled cases mostly of lesser seriousness and traced their courses *backward* through the system from dispositional stages. Most studies addressing relationships between community ties, criminal charge, or other decision criteria and performance on pretrial release suffer from the major bias, noted earlier, that an important group of interest (those detained) was not included in the designs. Relationships discussed pertain only to released persons; thus, little has been shown about the ability of these criteria to distinguish among *all* defendants at bail. As will be seen later in the specialized studies that are treated in Chapter 9, Rankin (1964) compared the dispositions of "bailed" and "jailed" defendants in New York, but excluded jailed defendants who had bail denied outright, and bailed defendants who were released on OR. Single (1972) and Landes (1974) based their analyses on a restricted sample of cases from the files of the Legal

Aid Society in New York, excluding, among other defendants, persons who may have been able to afford their own counsel. Studies were also subjected to exclusions based on offense. Gottfredson's study, to mention but one, did not include defendants charged with homicide, sexual assault, robbery, and other assaults (in his experimental group). Considering the diversity of the data and designs evident in these studies, an obvious and crucial question concerns the extent to which different designs influence the findings that have been produced. As research in this area moves to a narrower treatment of specific issues, studies appear to have become more sophisticated and methodology has become more of an issue in itself. This will be demonstrated more clearly in Chapter 9, where the statistical relationship between pretrial custody and later judicial outcomes will be examined.

NOTES

1. Rather than serving as a broad review of all empirical research undertaken in this area, Chapter 5 represents a more selective approach that emphasizes research with implications for legal guidelines as they presently exist. Two excellent general reviews are National Center for State Courts (1975) and Mullen (1974).

2. Beeley reported that:

> Contrary to expectations, the unsentenced jail prisoners are not transients, taken as a whole. According to several samples taken during 1923 and 1924 about 90 percent of the unsentenced population at any one time are persons who, at the time of arrest, have lived in Chicago over one year (Beeley, 1927:158).

3. For treatment of this question, see Chapter 9.

4. The role of the bondsman, first decried by Pound and Frankfurter (1922), Beeley (1927), and Morse and Beattie (1932), also came sharply under attack in studies and writing during the bail reform years. See, for example Foote, (1954); Freed and Wald (1964); *National Conference on Bail and Criminal Justice: Proceedings and Interim Report* (1965); Goldfarb (1965); and Wice (1974). Beeley referred to the bondsman in the bail context as that "anomalous" and "extra-legal parasite" (Beeley, 1927:156).

5. No tests of significance were included, but percentage differences were generally large between the two groups. This reported relationship is treated specially in Chapter 9.

6. Rates of forfeiture are likely to minimize the extent of failure to appear, although they may represent an accurate accounting of funds acquired by the court. Foote (1954), for example, reports that bondsmen frequently were not required to forfeit funds they had placed with the court.

7. Specifically, 24 percent of the bailed, but only 10 percent of the jailed defendants had their cases dismissed. About 90 percent of the detainees entered guilty pleas, compared with about three-quarters of the defendants who were released on bail. Of those who went to trial, 80 percent of the jailed defendants were convicted compared to about two-thirds of the bailed defendants. Fifty-four percent of the bailed but only 13 percent of the jailed received suspended sentences. Eighty-four percent of the jailed defendants were sentenced to imprisonment in contrast to 45 percent of the bailed defendants (Alexander et al., 1958:726-727).

8. The cities in the study included Boston, Champaign-Urbana, Chicago, Denver, Des Moines, Detroit, Hartford, Houston, Kansas City, Los Angeles, Minneapolis, Oakland, Peoria, Philadelphia, Sacramento, San Diego, San Francisco, San Jose, Washington, D.C., Wilmington. In Champaign-Urbana and Peoria, the base year was 1964, due to unreadable court records for the desired year (1962). In Oakland the base year was 1963. In Philadelphia, only defendants reaching the trial court level were included.

9. See Thomas (1976:65, note 1).

10. A considerable number of methodological problems were encountered—and are in fact honestly pointed out—in the National Bail Study. For example, court records were often incomplete in a number of jurisdictions. The sample sizes were relatively small—and based on definitions ("felony" versus "misdemeanor") that were highly variable from jurisdiction to jurisdiction. Moreover, sampling problems were posed by the varied nature of the structure of the court systems in the various jurisdictions. In some cities, locating a sample representative of all initial appearances during a given year was relatively simple, because the courts were unified in structure. But in other jurisdictions, initial appearances were held by different courts for different kinds of cases, thus making the sampling task very difficult and prone to biases. These problems are discussed in Thomas (1976:34-36; and in various footnotes throughout the text). Thomas writes (1976:34): "the results of the study are not offered as conclusive proof but rather only as indication of what has been the apparent effect of the bail reform movement. The results are also quite obviously limited to the cases studied." The innumerable methodological difficulties pointed out require considerable qualification of the results. It is therefore questionable, for example, whether one may combine noncomparably derived city data to produce general indexes of change, such as those cited here—prior disclaimers notwithstanding.

It may be useful to point out a very important descriptive finding generated in a number of studies not described in detail in this section, which serves to underscore the kinds of difficulties encountered in a multijurisdictional study such as the one reported by Thomas. That finding documents the extent to which bailsetting and detention practices are not uniform across jurisdictions, in part due to the different legislative guidelines provided in the statutes of different states and in part due to the differences in bailsetting traditions in jurisdictions. Teague (1965), for example, documented the variety of decision structures found in Texas. Silverstein (1966) reported the results of American Bar Foundation survey that found a great deal of diversity in bailsetting in 800 sample counties from all fifty states. Wice (1973, 1974) also reported on a wide variety of decision arrangements in various large American cities. This impression should also have been garnered from analysis of the guidelines presented in earlier chapters.

11. The only government publication based on the inmate interview data was a very short "advance" report released by LEAA in 1974. That report of several pages (U.S. Department of Justice/LEAA, 1974) summarized some of the data in a very preliminary fashion. For a comprehensive analysis of the characteristics of defendants detained in the nation's local jails during the summer of 1972, see Goldkamp (1977:Chapter 4).

12. At least two other basically descriptive studies should be noted. In 1963, the Attorney General's Committee on Poverty and the Administration of Federal Criminal Justice released a report (entitled *Poverty and the Administration of Federal Criminal Justice*) that documented problems in the operation of the Federal bail system that paralleled those reported in earlier descriptive studies. In 1966, a portion of the expansive report issued by the President's Commission on Crime in the District of Columbia described bail and pretrial release statistics in the District. As this book was going to press, the General Accounting Office was releasing its report on bail and release in federal jurisdictions as mandated by the Speedy Trial Act of 1975 (18 U.S.C.A. 3152 to 3156).

13. Freed and Wald (1964:58) described some of the variations encountered in fact-finding innovations in the United States during the early 1960s.

14. See the discussion in Freed and Wald (1964:xxviii).

15. The data analyzed included (1) records of cases in the Court of General Sessions kept by the Office of the District Attorney of New York County; (2) case files in Manhattan Court of Special Sessions; and (3) records of cases disposed of in Manhattan Magistrates' Felony Courts. A total of 3,459 cases were examined comprising about 60 percent of the total cases handled by the Court of General Sessions in 1960 (Ares, Rankin, and Sturz, 1963:76).

16. What is not made explicit in the presentation by Ares et al. (1963) is whether the increased number of ROR releases subtracted from the number of defendants who would have been released on money-bail or from defendants who would have been detained. In a later study, Wice (1970) suggests that the ROR releases generally represent defendants who would have been detained. In his book, Thomas (1976:147) contends that this has not been demonstrated.

17. The cases studied by Schaffer were those scheduled for any postarraignment proceeding in Manhattan Criminal Court from January 1, 1967, to March 31, 1967.

18. For a discussion of the great problems associated with these estimated forfeiture rates, see Wice (1974:66-67). In addition, it should be noted that FTA rates may not be comparable across jurisdictions due to the variability in ROR practices. For example, FTA may be affected by the proportion of all defendants who are considered for release and for whom release is granted; when only a few very good risks are released, the FTA will be lower than when a more liberal release policy is in effect. Also, FTA rates may be calculated on the basis of different periods of time; fewer defendants will abscond within a one-month period than within a three-month period.

19. See, for example, McCarthy and Wahl (1965); Lewin (1969); Kennedy (1968); Hawthorne and McCully (1970); Groege (1970); Stochastic Systems

Research Corporation (1972); San Francisco Committee on Crime (1971); O'Rourke and Carter (1970); Obert (1973); Bogomolney and Gau (1972); Kuykendall, and Deming (1967); and Clarke, Freeman, and Koch (1976).

20. Thomas (1976:87–88) acknowledges that these FTA rates are derived in spite of serious difficulties with the data that undermine the reliability of the estimates.

21. See, for example, Wice (1974:34–35, 70). Wice points out that supervision of releasees may contribute greatly to low FTA rates (1970:61). See also, Gottfredson (1974); Clarke (1976); Thomas (1976); and Welsh (1977) for similar observations.

22. In their study, Feeley and McNaughton employed a "100 percent sample" (population) of postarraignment cases (n = 1,642) from June to August, 1973, in the Sixth Circuit Court in New Haven. Intoxication and noncriminal motor vehicle offenses were eliminated from consideration. There is some question concerning the ability of this study to generalize its findings to include the more serious offenses, since this particular court typically handled only misdemeanors and Class D felonies (felonies whose maximum penalty did not exceed five-years imprisonment and/or a fine of $5,000). While guilty pleas for more serious felonies could be accepted there, it is not clear if sentencing followed as well. Perhaps more importantly, the proportion of all serious felonies processed in New Haven represented by Sixth Circuit cases is unknown. Since this study relied on taking cases at their disposition, it is not known to what extent the more serious cases adjudicated in the Sixth Circuit Court could be considered representative of other more serious felonies.

23. Although Gottfredson's design more closely approximated the desired quasi-experimental approach than others, important categories of defendants were nevertheless excluded from his Experimental Release group (homicide, sexual assault, and robbery defendants).

24. After validating his solutions by means of the random split half technique, Gottfredson experienced a considerable loss in predictive efficiency. Formulas that, before validation, were able to explain about 20 percent of the variance in FTA rates, could explain little more than 3 percent after validation (1974:300).

25. Such a danger remains largely theoretical, however, as (a) ROR projects move increasingly away from reliance on community-ties indicators in the ratings (offense and prior record screening variables have begun to take precedence), and (b) judges appear to act in accordance with the ratings only when other (offense and priors) dimensions have been first weighed by them.

26. Another interpretation of reliance on the offense-charged criterion, however, does not involve prediction. It sees this reliance as a means of punishing the accused on the basis of the charge, as a form of kangaroo justice. This model operates along the following lines: (a) offense charged, (b) guilt assumed, (c) punishment (through high bail or denial) exacted in the form of detention.

27. This expression is, of course, technically incorrect. There can be no recidivism where guilt has *not* been established on the first charge.

28. Rearrest for felonies had been adopted as the measure of pretrial "dangerousness" by some because it is serious criminal activity that, logically, is of greatest interest.

29. For a description of the New Haven sample, refer to note 22 above.

30. "Dangerous crimes" in the Gottfredson study refer primarily to crimes against the person.

31. In a related area, Steadman's study of the Baxstrom patients incorporated such a design when the Supreme Court ruled in *Baxstrom v. Herold* (383 U.S. 107) that "criminally insane" patients were being held unconstitutionally and had to be released to "civilian" mental health institutions. Thus, it was possible to observe so-called "dangerous" persons in regular mental health settings and to compare them with other patients. See Steadman and Cocozza (1974).

32. See Morris (1974); Dershowitz (1970); and von Hirsch (1972).

33. However, this conclusion must be interpreted with a great deal of caution. First, it should be remembered that for those defendants unable to gain pretrial release, the propensity to be rearrested remains unknown. Furthermore, Landes bases his accounting of pretrial crime on a retrospective look at his sample—that is, if a defendant, arrested on the charge of *current* interest had at the time of that (the current) arrest already had a charge pending, he or she was counted by Landes as a bail recidivist. In addition, a problem in logic arises because included among his "previous-record" variables are indicators for whether or not the defendants had charges pending and previous arrests. Since these variables are *already used* in setting bail, it does not make a great deal of sense to then turn around and say that the amount of bail set enables one to predict whether or not a defendant had a charge pending at the time of his arrest and then to call bail a predictor of pretrial recidivism..

34. The scores of subjects on the prediction of recidivism variable showed a correlation of only .361 (significance not reported) with the variable recording actual recidivism.

35. See von Hirsch (1972).

36. Three exceptions can be noted: First, the 1960 state-of-the-system study of the New York Bail System carried out by Ares, Rankin, and Sturz (1963) as background for Manhattan Bail Project experiments attempted to rely on data taken from the same sources as the 1958 New York Bail Study. Second, Landes (1974) reworked the data collected by Single (1972) and drew different conclusions. The third exception is the National Bail Study (Thomas, 1976), which took small samples of comparable data from twenty jurisdictions. In spite of the intention to obtain comparable, cross-system data in that study, many difficulties were encountered because systems were not homologous or their methods of collecting data varied considerably.

✳ *Part II*

Bail and Detention in Philadelphia

Chapter 6

Philadelphia as a Case Study: The Site and Method

In the review of studies highlighted in Chapter 5, serious
issues were raised through knowledge of assorted "details"
concerning bail and pretrial detention in the United States.
Questions may be posed about both the purposes served by the bail
process and the criteria that appear to figure prominently in the use
of detention. The findings concerning defendants detained in the
nation's jails, to cite but one example, suggest the possibility that
age, race, income, and/or sex may be factors in the use of detention.
However, it should be emphasized that the studies reviewed suffered
a significant handicap: In describing a limited aspect of the system,
or in examining only certain groups of defendants, they have failed
to portray the dynamics of the process overall. Thus, little has been
learned about the role of pretrial detention in the context of the decision that governs its use. The empirical study of bail decisionmaking in one jurisdiction introduced in this chapter was undertaken in
an effort to overcome this deficit.

Rather than focusing just on defendants who were detained before
trial, or just on those released, or only on those reaching adjudication
or sentencing, for example, the case study of bail in Philadelphia
draws on a representative sample of defendants moving into the
criminal process at first appearance. By collecting the sample at a
point early in criminal processing—before the differentiation of
defendants into bail categories and custody statuses—this case study
seeks to incorporate the "total" sample ideal.[1] Such a design permits
examination of bail decisionmaking for all relevant cases within a

given period of time[2] and facilitates analysis of the sorting process that results in two classes of accused.

To set the stage for statistical analyses presented in Chapters 7, 8, and 9, the task in Chapter 6 is to describe the study site and the important features of its criminal justice system; to discuss the methodology and the data collected; and to characterize briefly the Philadelphia defendants who were the subjects of the study.

OVERVIEW OF CRIMINAL PROCESSING IN PHILADELPHIA

The criminal justice system in Philadelphia serves an urban population of nearly five million inhabitants.[3] Typically, persons arrested in Philadelphia are first brought to local district police stations. Whether or not the arrest was prompted by a "victim" report to police or by discovery of a criminal act by the police themselves, an official *complaint* is filed. For a considerable number of arrestees, processing may stop before it begins; that is, they may be released soon after their arrests with charges dropped. In addition, a small number of others may be channeled out of criminal routing. These cases, referred to as "special" or "private complaints," usually involve domestic disputes of some sort and are handled informally through arbitration. Of those remaining in police custody, a sizeable share are given citations to appear in district summary court. (Refer to Figure 6–1.) Citations are generally issued for "summary offenses" that include offenses of a very minor nature such as petty larceny or shoplifting and violations of various city ordinances. Arrestees who remain in custody probably[4] constitute only a small proportion of the original group of all arrested persons. In most cases, these persons are transported to the centrally located Police Administration Building where further booking procedures and first appearance before a municipal court judge (called "preliminary arraignment" in Philadelphia) occurs. Since 1975, when the defendants studied first entered the criminal process, the use of closed circuit television to eliminate transportation to the central location and to expedite bail processing has gradually increased.

Most arrested persons, however, appear at preliminary arraignment in the Police Administration Building, after being held temporarily in detention quarters in the basement. Shortly before their first appearance, they are interviewed by a member of the Pretrial Services Division (ROR staff). For the others, the interview and bail may be conducted via television. The ROR interview, modeled after the Vera prototype, is designed to elicit reliable information about a defen-

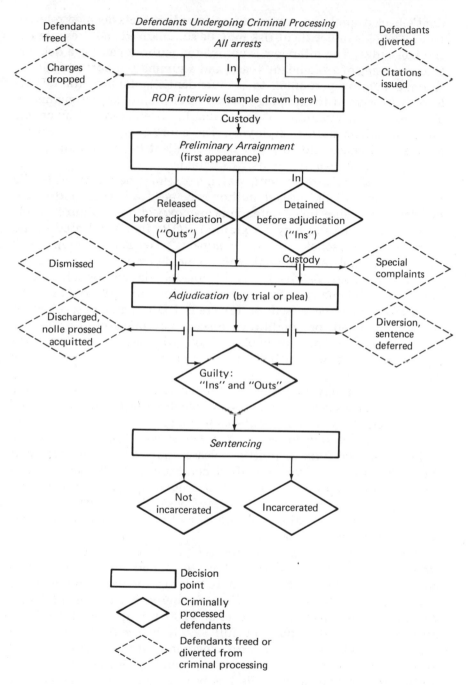

Figure 6-1. Simplified Schematic of Criminal Processing in Philadelphia

dant's background and community ties so that facts deemed relevant to assessing his or her flight-risk may be summarized and presented to the bail judge. The interview is completed without causing a delay in the processing of a defendant's case, and a summary report including a recommendation pertaining to a defendant's suitability for OR release is forwarded to the judge presiding at preliminary arraignment. The interviewer attempts to verify what has been obtained by calling family members and/or employers. The court computer is consulted for a record check and to see if the defendant has outstanding warrants, probation "wanted cards," or detainers.

At *preliminary arraignment,* defendants may be informed of the charge against them,[5] asked if they will need a lawyer, and bail is decided.[6] At bailsetting a defendant may expect one of four possible outcomes: He or she may be granted ROR, that is released on no more than a personal promise to appear;[7] Ten Percent money-bail may be set; bail may be denied in homicide cases;[8] or, the charges may be dismissed. Bail decisions in Philadelphia may be adjusted at any stage subsequent to first appearance (preliminary arraignment). Money-bail may be raised or lowered; ROR may be revoked or belatedly granted; or conditional release may be allowed or discontinued. However, in Philadelphia during the period studied, such modifications of original bail orders appear to have been relatively rare.[9]

Part of the interview preceding the bail decision focuses on defendants who have special problems (*e.g.,* alcohol or drug abuse), so that in the event they do not secure ROR or immediate release on bail, they may be considered for *conditional release.* Conditional release is a nonfinancial form of pretrial release under which the defendant must conform to certain specified conditions, much like a probationer. These conditions may involve frequent contact with the supervisory staff at the Pretrial Services Division, maintenance of regular employment, vocational training, and/or participation in drug or alcohol treatment programs.

Only a few years ago, the release prospects of defendants for whom money-bail was set would have depended greatly on the willingness of a local bail bondsman to put up the cash amount for a nonrefundable 10 percent fee. Thus, formerly, if bail was $2,000, a defendant could pay the bondsman $200 for his release, and the bondsman would then post the full $2,000 bail with the court. The defendant would lose the $200 fee whether or not he or she appeared as required in court. However, the bondsman no longer plays an important role in Philadelphia. He has been replaced by a Ten Percent program that allows defendants to deposit 10 percent of the cash amount of their bail with the court, most of which is refundable upon their attendance at the required proceedings.[10]

After preliminary arraignment, cases move forward into a two-tiered court system, composed of the municipal court and the court of common pleas.[11] In cases where the maximum possible penalty does not exceed five years in prison (*i.e.*, misdemeanors), adjudication and sentencing may occur entirely within the lower or municipal court. Defendants facing more than five years of imprisonment (*i.e.*, felonies) have their cases decided in the higher court, the court of common pleas. Before felony cases advance to the court of common pleas, they are tested at *preliminary hearing* in municipal court, where the task is for the state (the Commonwealth of Pennsylvania) to show that a crime has been committed and that there is "probable cause" to believe that the accused committed it. Misdemeanor cases do not go to a preliminary hearing; instead, they are scheduled for an early trial in municipal court. In felony cases when informations are returned at the preliminary hearing,[12] further processing is scheduled in the court of common pleas. Misdemeanor cases that have been adjudicated guilty in municipal court have the right to appeal to the court of common pleas for another trial.

GUIDELINES GOVERNING BAIL IN PHILADELPHIA

State Guidelines

Bail decisionmaking in the Philadelphia Municipal Court is constrained both by state-level guidelines and policies adopted by the local judiciary. On the state level, provisions relevant to bail are found in the Constitution of Pennsylvania, the state statutes, and rules adopted by the State Supreme Court.[13] The Pennsylvania Constitution resembles those of many other states that employ the traditional formula regarding the matter of bail. In short, it simply announces that bail ought not be excessive and that there is a right to bail, except in capital cases "where the proof is evident and the presumption great." The guidelines most relevant to the purposes of this inquiry—that is, to defining both the "compelling state interest" for bail procedures and the "distinctions" to be drawn—are contained in the Rules of Criminal Procedure drafted by the highest state court.

Provisions regarding bail, more specifically, are found under rules 4003 and 4004 of the Pennsylvania Rules of Criminal Procedure ("Pennsylvania Rules of Court, 1976"). (See Appendix B.) Rule 4003 emphasizes the use of ROR and defines its applicability. Similarly, rule 4004 discusses cash bail and lists criteria to be considered in fixing the amount. However, it must be frankly stated that the content of these two rules fails to address the purpose, use, and method of bail decisionmaking and detention in a comprehensive or coordinated fashion.

Rule 4003 at first appears to present the use of ROR in a singularly positive light, both by alluding to the ROR program in Philadelphia as exemplary (in commentary) and by expressing a presumption favoring personal recognizance release. Provision (a) of this rule reads: "The issuing authority or the court *shall release* a defendant on his own recognizance (ROR) or on nominal bail when . . . ." (Emphasis added.)

But expression of that presumption is followed by conditions that carefully limit its scope. Principally, the presumption only applies to offenses with possible penalties of three years or less (rule 4003(a),1). Moreover, when examining the rule for statements concerning the purposes for bail, it is striking that both danger and appearance themes are voiced in relation to the ROR option. Thus, in addition to limiting the presumption favoring ROR to the most minor cases (in terms of possible penalty), the judge is instructed to ascertain that "the defendant poses no threat of immediate physical harm to himself or to others," while at the same time being required to have "reasonable grounds to believe that a defendant will appear as required" (rule 4003(a),3,4). The reader will recall that, under the Bail Reform Act and subsequent models, consideration of danger had been carefully restricted to special cases (*e.g.*, involving capital or violent crimes). The Pennsylvania use of danger as a concern in determining eligibility for ROR is, therefore, noteworthy.

Without discussion of the bail decision as involving several possible options, the Rules of Criminal Procedure simply moves from provisions for ROR to provisions dealing with cash bail. An implication of this approach is that a judge first screens defendants for suitability for ROR—based on charge seriousness (possible maximum penalty), danger, and risk of flight—and then turns to cash bail for the less promising cases. Surprisingly, however, the rule discussing cash bail (rule 4004) mentions that the purpose for employing that option is to "insure the presence of defendants." No allusion to potential danger is included. Several interpretations of this omission may be suggested: First, danger is a concern in minor cases (with penalties of three years in prison or less) but not in more serious cases; second, cash bail should not be used in responding to assessments of dangerousness (perhaps other procedures would be more appropriate but the Rules are silent); and third, the matter is not addressed and judges are left to draw their own conclusions.

When examining the two rules for instructions pertaining to appropriate decision criteria, a judge might be further perplexed. In considering candidates for ROR (as noted above) judges are told only to consider penalty, danger, and risk of flight. When the cash bail option is treated under rule 4004, a long list of criteria to be weighed by the decisionmaker is provided:

(i)   The nature of the offense charged and any mitigating or aggravating factor that may bear upon the likelihood of conviction and possible penalty;
(ii) The defendant's employment status and history, and *financial condition;*
(iii) The *nature* of his family relationships;
(iv) His past and present residences;
(v)   His *age, character, reputation, mental condition,* record of relevant convictions and *whether addicted* to alcohol or drugs;
(vi) If he has previously been released on bail, whether he appeared as required; and
(vii) Any other facts relevant to whether the defendant has strong ties to the community or is likely to flee the jurisdiction. (Emphasis added.)

Like some of the guidelines reviewed in Chapter 4, these provisions suggest that the judge take into account both the "traditional" factors (*e.g.,* charge, prior record, possible penalty, likelihood of conviction) and the community-ties factors (*e.g.,* employment, residence, family ties)—and more. In fact, in setting bail (but not in considering ROR), bail judges are asked to consider at least as much as judges who are engaging in sentencing determinations. In addition, several slightly unusual variations of standard community-ties criteria stand out, such as, financial condition, the nature of his family relationships, age, character, reputation, and whether addicted to alcohol or drugs. In short, the difficulties pointed out in Chapter 4 pertaining to most state bail guidelines may be reiterated for those used in Pennsylvania: Most of the criteria listed are abstract notions and suffer from lack of definition; the bail judge is not given any indication concerning their relative importance.

Local Guidelines

It is the job of the Pretrial Services Division of the Philadelphia courts to interview all defendants before they appear at preliminary arraignment. How defendants are rated for ROR depends to a great extent on the guidelines promulgated by the Philadelphia courts.

The Pretrial Services Division—in carrying out this evaluation function—serves principally as an advisory resource for the bail judges of the municipal court. It presents defendant information deemed pertinent to assessing risk of flight and submits ROR recommendations; but neither are binding on the judge in reaching his or her decision. To the degree that judges do make use of the Pretrial Services resource, the manner in which defendants are rated for ROR suitability may figure importantly in the bail decision and the use of pretrial detention in Philadelphia. For this reason, a brief description of the guidelines that govern the Pretrial Services tasks will be undertaken here.

Suitability for ROR is determined by the Pretrial Services Division through two kinds of evaluations:

Rating the Defendant. The defendant is interviewed and the information obtained is, if possible, rapidly verified. The defendant is scored on the basis of a number of interview dimensions thought to be indicators of risk of flight (*e.g.*, family and community ties). If the required number of points is obtained, a positive recommendation may be forwarded to the bail judge. If the required number of points is not accumulated by the defendant as a result of the interview, no recommendation is made, although a summary report is still forwarded.

Automatic Disqualification from Positive Recommendations. The defendant is checked against a number of automatically disqualifying factors, legislated by the local judiciary. Regardless of how well a defendant might score based on the interview points, if he or she falls into certain exclusionary categories, no recommendation will be made.

No recommendation for OR release can be made by the Pretrial Services Division, if any of the following are found to be true:

1. if a defendant is charged with the following serious felonies: murder, rape, robbery, burglary of a private residence, arson, aggravated assault, assault with intent to kill; or for certain serious charges where the defendant has prior convictions for the same charges, for example, carrying a concealed deadly weapon and possession of a controlled substance;
2. there are two open cases, or one open case where the charge is a crime against a person (*e.g.*, robbery, rape, etc.);
3. there was a willful failure-to-appear (FTA) within the last three years;

4. the defendant has "wanted cards" that indicate he is to be detained for a probation or parole violation hearing;
5. the defendant is listed as a "fugitive"—for a prior failure to appear, for "prison breach," or for military AWOL;
6. the defendant is on conditional release (release under special conditions) for a prior arrest;
7. the defendant is not a Philadelphia area resident; or
8. the interviewer was not able to verify the address given by the defendant (Gedney, 1976:33–34).

The major emphasis in the disqualifying criteria listed above is for exclusion of defendants charged with serious crimes; that is, crimes against persons and crimes involving repetition (*i.e.*, showing "patterns" of criminal behavior) or use of weapons. Since danger is usually inferred on the basis of the offense charged, the inclusion of this particular variety of disqualifying criteria translates essentially into a dangerousness screening mechanism. Most of the other criteria, however, seek to exempt defendants with prior records of unreliable dealings with the criminal justice system, that is, those who have failed to appear previously or who have violated parole or probation.

The interview employed by the Pretrial Services Division evolved from an earlier prototype designed by the Vera Institute as a means of measuring defendants' community ties (as indicators of flight risk) for the Manhattan Bail Project. However, in the interview instrument employed by the Philadelphia ROR program in the fall of 1975, it is evident that a defendant's community ties were not all that was being measured. Table 6–1 summarizes the five interview dimensions by which a defendant would have been scored. Three of the five pertain to a defendant's ties to the community. They are (1) residence points, (2) family points, and (3) employment points. The two remaining dimensions on which a defendant is scored are (4) prior record points, and (5) "character" points (a mixed indicator of drug and alcohol use, physical and mental health, and prior FTAs).

To receive a "recommendable" score, a defendant at the time of this study would have had to make a score of six or more. A defendant cannot receive negative points on the residence, family, and employment dimensions. If he or she does not have a local residence or local family ties and has not held a job recently, no negative points are recorded—instead no points are recorded. (This has the same effects as assigning a negative score, since without positive points on these three dimensions it is not possible to make the six required for a positive ROR recommendation.) Conversely, a defendant is not credited with positive points for having no prior record of convic-

Table 6-1. ROR Interview Dimensions and Scoring Criteria[a]

Interview Dimensions	Scoring Criteria	Number of Points Earned
I. *Residence* (in Philadelphia area)	Three years or more in Philadelphia area	1
	Present residence one year *or* present and prior one and one-half years	3
	Present residence six months *or* present and prior one year	2
	Present residence four months *or* present and prior six months	1
II. *Family* (in Philadelphia area)	Lives with family *and* has contact with other family member	4
	Lives with family	3
	Lives with nonfamily friend whom he gives as a reference *and* has contact with family	2
	Lives with nonfamily friend whom he gives as a reference *or* has contact with family	1
III. *Employment*	Present job one year where employer will take back	4
	Present job one year	3
	Present job four months where employer will take back *or* present and prior six months where present employer will take back	2
	Present job four months *or* present and prior six months	1
	Current job where employer will take back	1
	Unemployed three months or less with nine months or more single prior job from which not fired for disciplinary reasons	1
	Receiving unemployment compensation, welfare, and so forth	1
	In poor health (regular visits to doctor)	1
	Fulltime student (not getting credit for employment)	1
IV. *Prior record* (within last fifteen years)	Negative points are assessed on the basis of the total number of offense units achieved. The offense code is as follows:	
	One adult felony conviction = 7 units	
	One adult misdemeanor conviction = 2 units	

Units:

0 1 2	0
3 4 5 6	-1
7 8 9 10 11 12 13	-2
14 15 16 17 18 19 20	-3
21 and over	-4

V. *Character*

Prior failure-to-appear for a court appearance within the last 3 years	-1
Definite knowledge of present drug addiction	-2
Definite knowledge of present alcoholism	-2
Number of points required for positive ROR recommendation	6
Maximum points obtainable	12

[a]Based on information presented in Dewaine L. Gedney, *Readings on the Bail System of the Court of Common Pleas and Municipal Court of Philadelphia* (1976).

tions or no character problems; instead, this state of affairs is treated as the norm and no points are given. Negative points are earned for prior convictions (one misdemeanor is allowed with no penalty), prior failures to appear, and definite knowledge of drug or alcohol problems.

It is unclear how the relative weights for each dimension were decided upon. For instance, why can a defendant earn a maximum of three points under residence, but four under family and four under employment? How is it determined that prior convictions should be scored as they are or that drug or alcohol addiction should play the role that it does? These are, for the most part, unanswered questions. In part, too, the weighting scheme employed in the Philadelphia ROR interview was adapted to reflect local experience, local concerns, and common sense.

THE SAMPLE AND DATA

The sampling strategy employed in the Philadelphia study was determined chiefly by the requirement that the sample appropriately include defendants who would be detained before trial as well as those who would be released after initial appearance. This meant drawing the sample at a point prior to the differentiation of defendants into bail categories and custody statuses that occurs at preliminary arraignment.[14] Another aim was to permit a prospective analytic approach— to be able to trace the cases of Philadelphia defendants forward through the criminal process and, consequently, to be able to evaluate the relationship of pretrial custody to later judicial outcomes. In fact, the sample was drawn at preliminary arraignment from a court log of all defendants arriving for bail determinations before judges of the municipal court between August 1 and November 2, 1975, after having been interviewed by the Pretrial Services' staff.[15] To obtain data descriptive of the defendants and of the progress of their cases through the Philadelphia court system, it was necessary to obtain data from two court sources (the Pretrial Services Division and the Data Processing Unit of the Court of Common Pleas) and to merge the two data sets.[16] (For a list of the variables recorded, see Appendix C.)

Exclusions

From listings of persons appearing at preliminary arraignment during the ninety-four day interval examined, the following kinds of cases could be discerned (see Figure 6-2). Overall 10,633 persons appeared, approximately 113 per day. Of these, 6,952 (65 percent) secured immediate release either by posting the required amount of cash bail or through release on a promise to appear. About one-third as many, 2,300 or 22 percent, were detained after preliminary arraignment, either because bail was denied or money-bail was set unaffordably high. The remaining 13 percent consisted of fugitives[17] (279 or 3 percent), dismissals[18] (730 or 7 percent), and special complaints[19] (354 or 3 percent). Because the objectives of the present study involve explaining bailsetting and the determination of pretrial custody, persons designated as fugitives, persons receiving immediate dismissal, and persons handled as special complaints were excluded.[20]

Sample Design

The sample was stratified according to the postpreliminary arraignment status (release or detention) of the cases listed in the court bail logs. This was carried out so that cases of persons who were detained immediately after preliminary arraignment could be oversampled. (It was noted above that three times as many defendants were released at preliminary arraignment as were detained.) The design called for including all detention cases until an adequate number was obtained. For the analyses envisaged, between 2,000 and 2,500 detainees were considered desirable. The time frame (August 1, 1975, to November 2, 1975) was determined principally by the number of detainees that could be included in the sample. All defendants whose immediate postpreliminary arraignment status within that time interval was detention were designated for inclusion in the sample.[21] But, while 2,300 "ins," fell within that interval, three times as many "outs" were processed at the same time. A sample including 1,500 to 1,800 "outs" was deemed adequate for the purposes of the planned analyses; so persons gaining immediate preadjudicatory release were sampled at a ratio of .25. As can be seen in Figure 6-2 (Step Three), the sample to be drawn then tentatively consisted of 1,737 released defendants and 2,300 detained defendants, or a total of 4,037 cases.

Missing Cases

When relying for data on the files of a public agency in a large American city[22] one might expect to encounter a reasonably large proportion of missing cases. Using the identifiers taken from the court bail listings, cases were sought in the files of the Pretrial Services Division of the court. About 89 percent of the designated sample cases were actually located—91 percent of releases and 88 percent of detainees making a total of 3,592 unweighted cases. (See Figure 6-2, Step Four.) Thus, the proportion of missing cases— about 11 percent overall—was clearly within the satisfactory range.

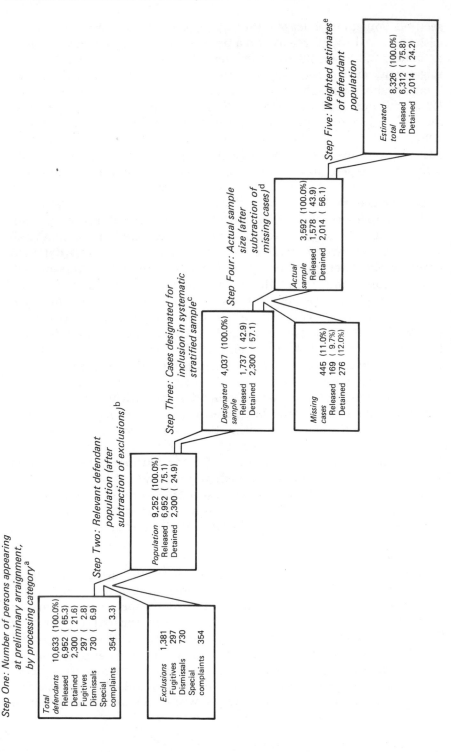

Figure 6-2. Definition of the Philadelphia Sample

Step One: Number of persons appearing at preliminary arraignment, by processing category[a]

Total defendants	10,633	(100.0%)
Released	6,952	(65.3)
Detained	2,300	(21.6)
Fugitives	297	(2.8)
Dismissals	730	(6.9)
Special complaints	354	(3.3)

Exclusions	1,381
Fugitives	297
Dismissals	730
Special complaints	354

Step Two: Relevant defendant population (after subtraction of exclusions)[b]

Population	9,252	(100.0%)
Released	6,952	(75.1)
Detained	2,300	(24.9)

Step Three: Cases designated for inclusion in systematic stratified sample[c]

Designated sample	4,037	(100.0%)
Released	1,737	(42.9)
Detained	2,300	(57.1)

Missing cases	445	(11.0%)
Released	169	(9.7%)
Detained	276	(12.0%)

Step Four: Actual sample size (after subtraction of missing cases)[d]

Actual sample	3,592	(100.0%)
Released	1,578	(43.9)
Detained	2,014	(56.1)

Step Five: Weighted estimates[e] of defendant population

Estimated total	8,326	(100.0%)
Released	6,312	(75.8)
Detained	2,014	(24.2)

[a] Step One shows all persons listed in court bail logs as appearing at preliminary arraignment between August 1, 1975, and November 2, 1975, (a 94-day interval).

[b] Step Two defines the population of all cases of interest to the study.

[c] Step Three shows the stratified sample design that would prospectively include 1 of every 4 "Released" cases (1,737 altogether) and all "Detained" cases (2,300). The "Total" (4,037 cases) represents the total number of cases designated from the court bail logs to be drawn from Pretrial Services Division files.

[d] Step Four shows the number of designated cases actually located in Pretrial Services Division files—with the missing cases for each stratum and the total noted.

[e] Step Five shows the weighted population estimates of the cases actually studied.

When weighted, this sample generated estimates for approximately 8,326 defendants passing through preliminary arraignment between August 1, and November 2, 1975. The analyses presented in subsequent chapters will, therefore, treat *weighted estimates* of characteristics of defendants in Philadelphia.[23]

CHARACTERISTICS OF PHILADELPHIA DEFENDANTS

Before proceeding with an analysis of the bail decision and the determination of release or detention before trial, it will be helpful to describe the Philadelphia defendants (weighted n = 8,326) who reached preliminary arraignment during the interval studied. This descriptive profile of "typical" defendants in Philadelphia will serve as a useful frame of reference in which an understanding of the subsequent classification of defendants—in terms of bail decisions and pretrial custody statuses—can be rooted.

Demographic and Legal Descriptors

1. Philadelphia defendants were quite young when compared with the local population as a whole. For example, persons twenty to twenty-four years old were found proportionately two and one-half times as often among defendants as among the general populace. Nearly half of all defendants were twenty-five years old or younger.
2. In racial/ethnic composition, the local population in 1975 was approximately one-third (33 percent) black, nearly two-thirds white (65 percent), and about 2 percent Hispanic or other minority. *Yet 68 percent of all defendants* appearing for the bail decision *were black, 27 percent were white, and about 5 percent were Hispanic/other.*
3. About 55 percent of the local Philadelphia population were female and 45 percent were male, *but 89 percent of all defendants were male* and 11 percent were female.
4. *About half* (5 percent) *of all defendants were single* (never married), 41 percent were married, and 7 percent were widowed/divorced/separated. Compared with the local population, defendants were disproportionately single (82 versus 34 percent of the local population), almost as frequently married (41 versus 48 percent), and noticeably less often widowed/divorced/separated.
5. *More than half* (55 percent) *of all defendants were unemployed* at the time of their prebail interviews.

6. When incomes of defendants are projected from weekly earnings reported by them to interviewers, it is learned that nearly *six-tenths* (59 percent) *of all defendants earned incomes of less than $3,000.* That is, persons earning projected annual incomes this low appeared *six* times more frequently than would have been expected from knowledge of the income characteristics of the local population.

7. *Defendants were charged with a rather even mixture of offenses* ranked by seriousness.[24] Specifically, 5 percent were charged with violent personal crimes, 8 percent with robbery, 9 percent with aggravated assault, 10 percent with combined drugs, 8 percent with burglary, 11 percent with theft/larceny, 11 percent with simple assault/weapons charges, 5 percent with lesser property offenses, 11 percent with public nuisance/public order offenses, 5 percent with drunk/disorderly offenses, and 15 percent with driving while intoxicated (DWI) or other serious traffic offenses.

8. Less than half (47 percent) of the Philadelphia defendants had no prior records of arrests, 22 percent had one or two previous arrests, and *as many as 30 percent had three or more.*[25]

9. *Nearly eight-tenths of all defendants had no prior convictions,* but 17 percent had one or two, and 4 percent had three or more previous convictions. (See Table 6-2.)

10. Approximately two-tenths (22 percent) of all defendants were charged with offenses processed criminally as felonies, compared with about eight-tenths (78 percent) that were processed as misdemeanors.

Community Ties and Other ROR Evaluation Variables

Although the expression, community ties, refers generally to a defendant's residence in the community, local family ties, employment status, and income, prebail evaluation of community ties has grown to include consideration of a defendant's prior record, prior failures-to-appear (FTAs), and mental health, drug, or alcohol problems. The ROR ratings of Philadelphia defendants are outlined briefly in the sections that follow.[26] (For definitions of the indexes used in scoring defendants, see Table 6-1. For the distribution of the computer-calculated defendant scores on these interview indexes, see Table 6-3).

Residence. The stability of a defendant's residence in Philadelphia is rated on two criteria: first, his or her residence in the general

Table 6–2. Estimated Number of Defendants Appearing for Preliminary Arraignment, by Number of Prior Arrests, Number of Prior Convictions, and Most Serious Prior Conviction, Philadelphia: August to November, 1975

Measure of Prior Record	Number	Percent[a]
All defendants	8,316	100.0
Number of prior arrests		
None	3,937	47.3
1 to 2	1,863	22.4
3 or more	2,516	30.3
Most serious prior arrest		
Violent personal	578	7.0
Robbery	755	9.1
Aggravated assault	351	4.2
Drugs—combined	772	9.3
Burglary	476	5.7
Theft/larceny	355	4.3
Simple assault/weapons	309	3.7
Lesser property	118	1.4
Public nuisance/order	316	3.8
Drunk/disorderly	68	.8
DWI/traffic	269	3.2
Miscellaneous/other	12	.1
None	3,937	47.3
Number of prior convictions		
None	6,552	78.8
1 to 2	1,395	16.8
3 or more	369	4.4
Most serious prior conviction		
Violent personal	84	1.0
Robbery	214	2.6
Aggravated assault	69	.8
Drugs—combined	228	2.7
Burglary	353	4.2
Theft/larceny	190	2.3
Simple assault/weapons	200	2.4
Lesser property	228	2.7
Public nuisance/order	44	.5
Drunk/disorderly	52	.6
DWI/traffic	92	1.1
Miscellaneous/other	10	.1
None	6,552	78.8

Missing cases = 10

[a]Subcategories may not sum to 100 percent due to rounding.

Table 6-3. Estimated Number of Defendants Appearing for Preliminary Arraignment, by ROR Points Scored, Philadelphia: August to November, 1975[a]

Interview Dimensions						Mean	Median
I. Residence							
General: three years or more in area						.9	1.0
Points	0	1					
Percent	6.5	93.5					
Number	(543)	(7,783)					
Specific: past/present						2.2	2.8
Points	0	1	2	3			
Percent	19.9	5.2	7.0	67.9			
Number	(1,658)	(433)	(579)	(5,656)			
II. Family						1.5	1.2
Points	0	1	2	3			
Percent	6.6	63.8	7.4	22.3			
Number	(548)	(5,309)	(614)	(1,855)			
III. Employment						1.5	1.0
Points	0	1	2	3	4		
Percent	28.6	41.5	5.0	4.8	20.0		
Number	(2,384)	(3,455)	(415)	(403)	(1,669)		
IV. Prior Record						-.8	-.2
Points	-4	-3	-2	-1	0		
Percent	8.6	6.7	12.1	3.8	68.9		
Number	(718)	(559)	(1,004)	(310)	(5,735)		
V. Drug addiction or alcoholism							
Alcoholism						-.1	0.0
Points	-2	0					
Percent	2.8	97.2					
Number	(229)	(8,097)					
Drug addiction						-.2	-.1
Points	-2	0					
Percent	7.7	92.3					
Number	(639)	(7,687)					
Point allowed for physically disadvantaged						0.0	0.0
Points	0	1					
Percent	96.1	3.9					
Number	(8,004)	(322)					
Prior failures-to-appear						-.1	-.1
Points	-1	0					
Percent	14.4	85.6					
Number	(1,199)	(7,127)					
Total for points earned						4.8	5.1
Points	0 or less	1 to 5	6 or more[b]				
Percent	10.3	44.5	45.2				
Number	(860)	(3,699)	(4,627)				

Total cases = 8,326

[a]Points were assigned defendants by the author based on the weighting scheme used by the Pretrial Services Division as defined in Table 6-1. See Note 26, Chapter 6 of text.

[b]Six or more total points were required for defendants to earn a favorable ROR recommendation.

Philadelphia area for over three years, and second, the length of specific residence in Philadelphia, past and present. More than nine-tenths of Philadelphia defendants earned the single point achievable on the first (general) residence criterion. From zero to three points could be earned on the second residence criterion as defined in Table 6-1. Approximately 75 percent of the defendants received the highest ratings (two or three points), thus representing the most residence-stable among Philadelphia defendants. However, as many as 25 percent received the lowest achievable residence ratings (zero or one point), thus reflecting the most transient among defendants.

Local Family Ties. The extent of a defendant's family ties in the Philadelphia area was indexed on a scale ranging from zero to three points.[27] Defendants who lived with immediate family and those who had other family relations in the area were considered to have strong family ties; defendants living alone and having no family or relatives in the area scored lowest on the scale. A very large proportion of defendants (70 percent) received the lowest ratings on this scale (zero or one points). A minority (22 percent) received the highest family-ties ratings (two or three points).

Employment History. Employment history[28] was rated on a scale ranging from zero to four points. The highest employment scores were given defendants who held jobs for more than one year—jobs to which it was assured they could return. The long-term unemployed were given the lowest ratings. On this scale as well, the vast majority of defendants scored very poorly: approximately 70 percent received zero or one point. And again, only a small proportion (about 25 percent) received the highest scores.

Prior Record. Table 6-1 depicts the manner in which prior felony or misdemeanor convictions were differentially weighted and translated into (negative) ROR points. Persons with no prior records, of course, received no negative record points. One prior misdemeanor conviction was allowed with no penalty. As Table 6-3 shows, the vast majority of defendants (69 percent) were assigned no negative record points. About 15 percent, however, received the lowest possible scores (three or four negative points), and another 15 percent were penalized one or two negative record points.

Prior Failures-to-Appear. Approximately 14 percent of the defendants were found to have failed to appear at a court during the three previous years, thus earning a negative point.[29]

Mental Health, Drug, or Alcohol Problems. Two negative points were assessable when "definite knowledge" of either alcoholism or drug addiction was obtained during the ROR interview. A very small proportion of defendants (about 3 percent) reported in their interviews that they were either frequent users of alcohol or had undergone treatment in the past for alcoholism. (Defendants who did admit to either use or treatment were assigned two negative points.) Approximately 14 percent indicated heavy drug usage in the present or recent past, but definite (interviewer) knowledge of present drug addiction earned approximately 8 percent of all defendants two negative points. Defendants were not penalized for definite knowledge of hospitalization for mental health problems, but about 4 percent indicated such hospitalization.

Eligibility Based on Points. To be eligible for a positive ROR recommendation forwarded by the Pretrial Services Division to the bail judge, a defendant would have needed to accumulate six or more points across the various community-ties dimensions. When collectively tallied, the scores of defendants ranged from a low of seven negative points to a high of eleven points. Approximately 45 percent of the Philadelphia defendants scored six or more points, and were thus within the positive range. Of the 55 percent not within the recommendable range, 10 percent scored zero or fewer points; 45 percent scored between one and five points. As many as 14 percent scored five positive points, that is, earned only one less than required for a positive recommendation.

Table 6-4 displays the proportions of defendants scoring six or more points (the "good risks") and less than six points (the "poor risks") by selected demographic attributes.[30] It is interesting to note that despite the fact that more than half of all defendants are rated as poor risks, there is little or no variation when eligibility (based on points) is compared by race and sex. Some variation in final community-ties rating, however, can be noted when age is examined: proportionately more twenty-six to thirty year olds were rated as "poor risks" than any other age group; and proportionately fewer of the oldest age group (forty-one and over) than any other were so rated. Considerable variation, on the other hand, *is* found when employment status and income are examined: Only about three-tenths of unemployed defendants (32 percent) were rated eligible for positive recommendations, compared with more than six-tenths of employed defendants (65 percent). Similarly, only 33 percent and 41 percent of defendants with no weekly incomes or with incomes in the lowest category (one dollar to fifty-eight dollars weekly, which

Table 6-4. Estimated Number of Defendants Appearing at Preliminary Arraignment, by Final Community-Ties Rating (Good Risk/Poor Risk), by Age, Race, Sex, Employment, and Income, Philadelphia: August to November, 1975

	Final Community-ties Ratings					
	Total		*Poor Risk (Ineligible)*		*Good Risk (Eligible)*	
Independent Variables	*Number*	*Percent*	*Number*	*Percent*	*Number*	*Percent*
Age (Total = 8,326)	8,326	100.0	4,559	54.8	3,767	45.2
18 and under	546	100.0	279	51.0	267	48.9
19 to 20	1,282	100.0	720	56.2	562	43.8
21 to 25	2,274	100.0	1,311	57.7	963	42.3
26 to 30	1,334	100.0	912	68.4	422	31.6
31 to 40	1,336	100.0	705	52.8	631	46.2
41 and over	1,524	100.0	602	39.5	922	60.5
Race (Total = 8,326)						
Hispanic/other	413	100.0	144	62.0	157	38.0
Black	5,647	100.0	3,094	54.8	2,553	45.2
White	2,266	100.0	1,209	53.4	1,057	46.6
Sex (Total = 8,326)						
Male	7,382	100.0	4,073	55.2	3,309	44.8
Female	944	100.0	486	51.5	458	48.5
Employment status (Total = 7,930)						
Unemployed	4,388	100.0	2,965	67.6	1,423	32.4
Employed	3,542	100.0	1,240	35.0	2,302	65.0
Weekly income (Total = 7,663)						
$0	4,358	100.0	2,938	67.4	1,420	32.6
$1 to $58	182	100.0	108	59.3	74	40.7
$59 to $144	1,854	100.0	717	38.7	1,137	61.3
$145 to $192	632	100.0	163	25.8	469	74.2
$193 and over	637	100.0	309	48.8	328	51.2

corresponds to less than three thousand dollars on an annual basis) scored six or more points, in comparison with 61 percent of the second lowest category, and 74 percent and 51 percent of the highest income categories, respectively.

Summary: Philadelphia Defendants
Before First Appearance

The reader may have been struck by the surprising similarity between the profile of a typical cohort of defendants before first appearance in Philadelphia and the characteristics of defendants detained in American jails (Goldkamp, 1977) noted in Chapter 5. That is, like the nation's *detainees*, Philadelphia *defendants* were disproportionately young, male, black or minority, unemployed or low income, and single. Although it remains to be seen in subsequent analyses what role might be played by demographic and socioeconomic variables in bail decisionmaking and in the determination of pretrial custody, it is apparent that such disproportionality[31] already exists among defendants at the prebail stage in criminal processing.[32] Given this finding, it will be difficult, for instance, to find that the bail decisions will have served to free the rich and incarcerate the poor before trial because, it would appear, the vast majority of all defendants reaching the preliminary arraignment stage were either unemployed or had an exceedingly low income to begin with.

NOTES

1. Recall the discussion by Gottfredson (1974) of the idea of a "total" sample (see Chapter 5). Briefly, total sample refers to a sample design that is not plagued with the exclusion of groups of potential interest to the questions being studied.

2. Included in the sample were defendants appearing for preliminary arraignment between August 1 and November 2, 1975.

3. Estimates pertaining to characteristics of the local Philadelphia population were drawn from U.S. Bureau of the Census data prepared for the U.S. Department of Justice/LEAA (1976).

4. Just what proportion of the original arrestees (during a given interval) is represented by defendants who remain in the system as far as preliminary arraignment is not known. Using police data and preliminary arraignment records, this author estimates that nearly six-tenths of those arrested will drop out by the time bail has been determined.

5. Although the practice may be considered standard procedure, bail judges may or may not have actually taken the time to inform the defendant concerning the nature of the charges. Often, it is taken for granted that the defendant is aware of the charges.

6. Often the bail decision is made in a very perfunctory manner, with little or no interaction between judge and defendants, all in a few brief moments.

7. A variation of release on OR is release on "sign your own bail" (on an unsecured appearance bond). Under this option a defendant is released on a promise to appear, but with a specified amount of cash to be collected as a penalty in the event of a failure to appear.

8. Bail is usually not set until preliminary hearing—if at all—in homicide cases.

9. During 1975, a reported 39,398 persons were interviewed by the Pretrial Services Division. Of these only about 2 percent (796 persons) received bail reductions or conditional release, representing modifications of the original bail decisions (Gedney, 1976:18).

10. Actually, a small service charge of about three dollars is not refunded.

11. At the time of the study, the Philadelphia courts were staffed by eighty-one judges—twenty-one of whom sat on the Municipal Court bench and presided over first appearances.

12. Grand jury proceedings are no longer routinely undertaken in felony cases in Philadelphia.

13. See Pa. Const. I:13,14; Pa. Crim. Pro. 19:51-95; Pa. R. Crim. Pro. 4003, 4004.

14. The court records all preliminary arraignments and subsequently prints out complete lists of defendants who have appeared before a judge on a given date. These listings made it possible to define the total population of defendants passing into the system at a very early stage, and it was from these listings for the time period noted above that the sample was drawn. In the present context, "arrestees" become "defendants" at their first appearance before a judge.

15. An important sample requirement—in order to obtain the dispositional data sought—was to select a time frame that preceded the actual data gathering by an interval (seven to ten months) long enough to allow cases to proceed to their resolutions. Thus, for the data collection to be carried out during the summer of 1976, an appropriate sample frame would be the fall of the previous year.

16. When an individual is first arrested in Philadelphia, he or she receives a six-digit identification (Philadelphia Photo) number that will be used also at any subsequent arrests. But, for each new *case* for which the individual appears at preliminary arraignment, a municipal court case number is assigned. By using these two identifiers it was possible to obtain both pre- and postadjudicatory disposition data on each case included in the sample. Names of defendants were not included in the data, and, once, the data sets were merged, alternative case identifiers were utilized to guarantee the anonymity of defendants. (It was not possible to trace cases in the final form back to actual persons in Philadelphia.) It would be accurate to say that the sample employed in this study consisted of *cases* rather than defendants. Thus, a defendant appearing in the sample more than once would be treated—on the basis of his or her new municipal court case number—as a new individual appearing for a new case. For a more detailed discussion of the methodology employed, see Goldkamp, 1977.

17. In Philadelphia "fugitives" are persons who are wanted for crimes in another jurisdiction, or in Philadelphia for a prior failure-to-appear (but no new charge).

18. By "dismissals" is meant persons for whom all charges are dropped at the preliminary arraignment stage.

19. "Special complaints" represent cases that were diverted from the criminal process to be handled through a process more like arbitration.

20. Briefly, this was because: (a) Fugitives were either automatically detained, detained pending extradition proceedings, or were released into the custody of authorities from the jurisdictions issuing fugitive warrants. Because of the special nature of the handling of fugitive cases, they were considered as falling outside of the interest of the present study. (b) Cases resulting in immediate dismissal at preliminary arraignment were excluded, first, because their inclusion would add little to a knowledge of bail and the use of detention versus release before trial and, second, because of the limited resources (in terms of time and expense) available.

21. A sample drawn from among defendants entering the system during the time interval selected might be expected to vary *slightly* from a sample taken at other times during the year. Little data is presently available to help assess the nature and the extent of such variation, if any. Statistics kept by the Pretrial Services Division do show some fluctuation in the volume of defendants processed each month (Gedney, 1976:7).

22. This study relies on so-called official data—that is, data collected and maintained by criminal justice agencies, rather than by social scientists doing "field research." The reliability and validity of official data has often been questioned (*e.g.*, Sellin, 1938; Kituse and Cicourel, 1963; Sellin and Wolfgang, 1964; Turk, 1969). Depending on the uses to which official data are put, the importance of such questioning is not argued here. On the other hand, it *is* strongly argued here that, for particular kinds of inquiries, official data are the only appropriate data—since they will show most clearly the kinds of decisions that are made about individuals (whether based on accurate information or not). Thus, in the present study, questions concerning the reliability of the data are of secondary importance when compared to the knowledge that can be gained of the decisions made, based on the data actually relied on by the agencies.

23. Due to the large size of the sample and the greater precision of estimates made possible through use of a statified sampling strategy (see Kish, 1953:189–200), the estimates generated in subsequent analyses will be characterized by relatively small standard errors. Thus, they should be considered generally quite reliable. For example, in cases where a particular attribute is shared by approximately half of the sample (considering proportions as a kind of mean), the 95 percent confidence interval would span about two percentage points. The population value for that attribute would fall within plus or minus one percentage point of the sample estimate nineteen of twenty times—were many independent samples to be drawn. In the case where an attribute of interest is more rare in the sample—say, shared by only 10 percent of the sample—the 95 percent confidence interval is only slightly larger, spanning approximately three percentage

points. It is apparent then that the reliability of sample estimates will not pose a threat to their interpretation in subsequent analyses.

24. This may result partially from the classification scheme employed to select the single most serious offense associated with each defendant (see Appendix D) that attempted to combine compatible categories having very small *n*'s. However, this does not detract from the general finding that defendants were being held for a rather evenly mixed assortment of offenses.

25. At preliminary arraignment the presiding judge usually has not only a defendant's prior record of convictions before him or her but also the defendants's prior record of arrests. Because of the potential importance of a defendant's prior involvement with criminal processing in Philadelphia, a special arrangement was made with the Data Processing Unit of the Court of Common Pleas to do a computer search of the records for all defendants included in the sample. Precisely the same kind of search would or could have been made for the judge and/or the Pretrial Services Division before bailsetting. The following kinds of information pertaining to prior record were obtained: the number of prior arrests and convictions, the mean seriousness of a defendant's prior arrest and convictions, his or her most serious prior arrest and conviction. An additional indicator of prior convictions (*i.e.*, either felony or misdemeanor) was obtained from the ROR interview form for each defendant because that measure was used by interviewers in their community-ties evaluation and ROR recommendation procedures. Because the ROR interview is conducted under considerable time constraints (so that the most complete background information possible will be available to the judge in time for a defendant's first appearance), it was thought that a separate record check would both supplement the interview data (indicating only felony or misdemeanor convictions) and correct for any possible inaccuracies.

26. It was not possible to employ the points as recorded by the Pretrial Services interviewers in their ratings of defendants because of the large proportion of cases in which the points were not calculated or in which the calculations were not recorded in the files. Rather, based on the formulas outlined in Table 6–1, it was possible to calculate scores for defendants using available demographic information and the computer. The scores employed in this section may vary slightly from those that might have been assigned by the interviewers were they consistently recorded. For example, it was not possible to assign an extra employment point for those employed one year *with employers who would take them back*. Instead, the extra point was assigned when the defendant had been employed at his present *job for over two years*. In addition, it was not possible to assign four points for family ties because it was not recorded in the data whether a defendant had "contact" with another family member. Such deviations were rare, however, and it is felt, the scoring system employed very closely followed the one outlined by the Pretrial Services Division for use at that time.

27. Because of the adaptation discussed in Note 26 that permitted uniform calculation of community-ties scores by computer, family ties in this study was scored as 0, 1, 2, or 3 family points. In actuality, a fourth family point would have been conceivable for a small but unknown proportion of Philadelphia defendants.

28. The difference between "employment history" and "employment status" discussed above under demographics is simply that the community-ties indicator (history) adds more information than whether or not a defendant was employed at the time of the ROR interview (which is the case for employment status). Employment history contributes knowledge of length of employment (if employed) and length of unemployment (if unemployed).

29. Although evidence of a prior willful FTA within the previous three years resulted in a penalty of two negative points, it was also automatically a reason for disqualification from a favorable recommendation.

30. It should be noted that defendants rated as eligible for a positive *recommendation* for ROR might still be disqualified from such a recommendation based on charge and prior criminal record criteria listed by the local judiciary.

31. "Disproportionality" here refers to the fact that defendants are disproportionately young, male, black, unemployed or low income, poorly educated, and single in comparison with the total Philadelphia population at large.

32. This finding suggests that if one major stage of criminal processing is to be designated as being responsible for disproportionate selection of persons with minority and low socioeconomic status attributes, it logically must be the arrest stage.

✳ *Chapter 7*

Bail Decisionmaking in Philadelphia: An Empirical Analysis

Compared to how bail "ought" to be decided (a theoretical perspective) or is thought to be decided (a conjectural perspective), empirical analysis of bail decisions in Philadelphia will illustrate how—in one urban jurisdiction at least—bail *is* decided. Of necessity, the analysis presented in this chapter will be inductive. Inferences will be drawn concerning the nature of the decision process based on study of specific factors (defendant attributes and legal characteristics) that appear to play the most influential roles. In terms of the sorting or classification analogy discussed in Chapter 1, the objective of this analysis is to gain knowledge of the "distinctions made" among defendants entering the criminal process at first appearance. After delineating the factors most determinative of bail decisions, the empirical focus simplifies in Chapter 8 to consider the determination of pretrial custody.

BAIL DECISIONS IN PHILADELPHIA: AN OVERVIEW

Defendants in Philadelphia may anticipate one of three outcomes at preliminary arraignment: release on OR, Ten Percent cash bail, or denial of bail.[1] Table 7-1 lists the relative proportions of Philadelphia defendants receiving each of the three possible outcomes. Slightly more than half of all defendants (52 percent) had cash bail set; just under half (47 percent) were granted release on OR;[2] about 1 percent had bail (and pretrial release) denied at preliminary arraignment.

Table 7-1 further reveals that patterns characterizing bail deci-

Table 7-1. Estimated Number of Defendants Appearing at Preliminary Arraignment, by Bailsetting Outcomes, by Age, Race, Sex, Marital Status, Employment, Income, Prior Criminal Record, and Criminal Charge, Philadelphia: August to November, 1975

Independent Variables	Total[a]		ROR		Cash Bail		Held Without Bail	
	Number	Percent	Number	Percent	Number	Percent	Number	Percent
All Philadelphia defendants	8,301	100.0	3,874	46.7	4,311	51.9	116	1.4
Age (Total = 8,301)								
18 and under	543	100.0	210	38.7	306	56.4	27	5.0
19 to 20	1,274	100.0	511	40.1	744	58.4	19	1.5
21 to 25	2,269	100.0	849	37.4	1,396	61.5	24	1.1
26 to 30	1,333	100.0	560	42.0	750	56.3	23	1.7
31 to 40	1,360	100.0	661	48.6	688	50.6	11	.8
41 and over	1,522	100.0	1,083	71.2	427	28.1	12	.8
Race/ethnicity (Total = 8,301)								
Hispanic/other	412	100.0	196	47.6	212	51.5	4	1.0
Black	5,625	100.0	2,369	42.1	3,148	56.0	108	1.9
White	2,264	100.0	1,309	57.8	951	42.0	4	.2
Sex (Total = 8,301)								
Male	7,360	100.0	3,295	44.8	3,958	53.8	107	1.5
Female	941	100.0	579	61.5	353	37.5	9	1.0
Marital status (Total = 7,911)								
Never married	4,083	100.0	1,563	38.3	2,447	59.9	73	1.8
Widowed/divorced/separated	544	100.0	303	55.7	234	43.0	7	1.3
Married	3,269	100.0	1,714	52.4	1,522	46.6	33	1.0
Employment status (Total = 7,915)								
Unemployed	4,374	100.0	1,709	39.1	2,528	59.1	80	1.8
Employed	3,541	100.0	1,891	53.4	1,620	45.7	30	.8

	N	%	N	%	N	%	N	%
Weekly income (Total = 7,648)								
$0	4,344	100.0	1,689	38.9	2,576	59.3	79	1.8
$1 to 58	182	100.0	80	44.0	100	54.9	2	1.1
$59 to 144	1,854	100.0	898	48.4	940	50.7	16	.9
$145 to 192	632	100.0	404	63.9	222	35.1	6	.9
$193 and over	636	100.0	416	65.4	215	33.8	5	.8
Prior arrests (Total = 8,301)								
None	3,930	100.0	2,418	61.5	1,458	37.0	54	1.4
1 or 2	1,861	100.0	892	47.9	950	51.0	19	1.0
3 or more	2,510	100.0	564	22.5	1,903	75.8	43	1.7
Prior convictions (Total = 8,301)								
None	6,540	100.0	3,563	54.5	2,891	37.1	86	1.3
1 or 2	1,392	100.0	283	20.3	1,085	51.0	24	1.7
3 or more	369	100.0	28	7.6	335	75.8	6	1.6
Criminal charge (Total = 8,295)								
Violent personal	400	100.0	8	2.0	277	69.2	115	28.7
Robbery	648	100.0	8	1.2	640	98.8	0	.0
Aggravated assault	730	100.0	195	26.7	534	73.2	1	.1
Drugs	819	100.0	249	30.4	570	69.6	0	.0
Burglary	628	100.0	93	14.8	535	85.2	0	.0
Theft-larceny	937	100.0	359	38.3	578	61.7	0	.0
Simple assault/weapons	879	100.0	470	53.5	409	46.5	0	.0
Lesser property	435	100.0	181	41.6	254	58.4	0	.0
Public order/nuisance	884	100.0	742	83.9	142	16.1	0	.0
Drunken/disorderly	433	100.0	352	81.3	81	18.7	0	.0
DWI/traffic	1,261	100.0	1,080	85.6	181	14.4	0	.0
Miscellaneous/other	241	100.0	137	56.8	104	43.2	0	.0

aSubcategories may not sum to total due to rounding.

sions will not be difficult to uncover. Of the independent variables initially examined, for instance, bail outcomes appear to vary noticeably by age, race, sex, marital status, employment, income, past record, and criminal charge.

A brief summary of some of the most striking differences in bail outcomes follows:

Age

Older defendants were considerably more likely to receive ROR and less likely to face cash bail than were younger defendants; for example, seven-tenths of those defendants over forty were granted ROR, compared with only four-tenths of those defendants in the younger age groups.

Race/Ethnicity

Minority versus majority (but especially black versus white) defendants showed some striking differences. Fifty-eight percent of the white defendants were granted ROR compared with only 42 percent of the black defendants and 48 percent of the Hispanic/other defendants. Conversely, greater proportions of black (56 percent) and Hispanic/other defendants (52 percent) than whites (42 percent) had Ten Percent cash bail set.

Sex

Sixty-two percent of the female defendants, but only 45 percent of the male defendants, were granted OR release.

Marital Status

Sixty percent of single persons had cash bail set, compared with noticeably smaller proportions of married or widowed/divorced/separated defendants (43 and 47 percent, respectively).

Employment and Income

Substantially greater proportions of low income and unemployed defendants had cash bail set than did defendants who were employed or earning higher incomes.

Prior Criminal History

Substantially greater proportions of defendants with no prior convictions (55 percent) than with one or two (20 percent) and three or more (8 percent) received ROR. Similarly, considerably more defendants with no prior arrests (62 percent) than defendants with one or two (48 percent) and with three or more (23 percent) were granted OR release.

Criminal Charge

Perhaps the strongest tabular variation in bail outcomes is noted when offense categories are contrasted. Table 7-1 shows that very large proportions of defendants charged with the most seriously ranked offenses had cash bail set instead of receiving ROR. Conversely, large proportions of persons charged in the least serious of criminal matters were given ROR. Nearly all persons having bail denied at preliminary arraignment were charged with the most serious of criminal offenses (homicide).

BAILSETTING AS A TRIFURCATED DECISION PROCESS: AN ANALYTIC MODEL

Rather than regarding bailsetting merely as a simple choice of one of three decision alternatives, greater analytic clarity might be gained by adopting a model in which bailsetting is conceptualized as involving three logical, contingent steps or decision components. (See Figure 7-1.) One scenario in which the bail decision might be viewed as trifurcated and contingent is illustrated in the following manner:[3]

- *Step One* A judge's first and most general consideration under this model is whether or not a given defendant should be released on OR. To illustrate, about 47 percent of Philadelphia defendants were regarded favorably and granted release on this decision step.
- *Step Two* For defendants who are not appraised in a favorable light in the context of the ROR decision component (about 53 percent of the original group in Philadelphia), the judge enters a second logical decision stage where he or she determines whether money-bail will be set or denied. Only about 1 percent of all Philadelphia defendants (those held without bail) are disposed of at this point.
- *Step Three* On the third step, the judge is dealing with defendants for whom it was determined (1) that ROR would not be appropriate and (2) that detention without bail was not appropriate. The decision in this component then simply entails setting a specific amount of cash bail.

By employing a model that conceptually divides the bail decision

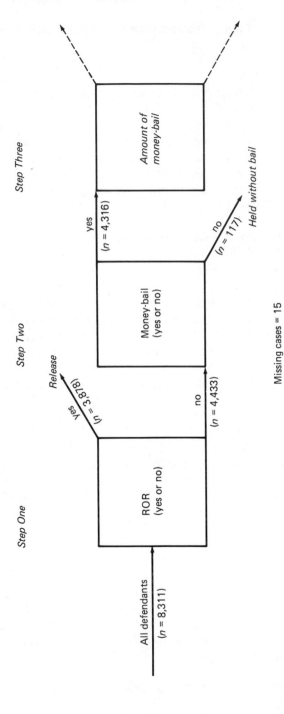

Figure 7-1.   The Bail Decision as a Trifurcated Decision Process

into three logical, contingent components, two principal advantages are obtained. First, analysis of the bail decision may be undertaken with greater specificity than possible through general consideration of the different bail outcomes taken together; second, it will be possible to learn whether the relationships characterizing overall bail outcomes (see Table 7–1) are applicable to each of the decision components, or only to one or two of them, for example. Subsequent analysis will proceed sequentially on the basis of the steps embodied in the trifurcated model shown in Figure 7–1.

GRANTING ROR: STEP ONE

According to the model, all defendants are first evaluated by the bail judge for release on OR. In the Philadelphia sample, 47 percent of all defendants appearing at preliminary arraignment were granted ROR, 53 percent were not.[4] The data presented in Table 7–1 suggest that the decision to grant ROR may be related to a number of independent variables—some, such as age, race/ethnicity, and sex, are highly questionable. To examine more carefully defendant attributes that may have been influential in the ROR decision step, bivariate relationships involving many more independent variables were considered. (For the full list of variables available in the Philadelphia data, see Appendix C.) However, to isolate the factors most determinative of ROR, a multivariate approach was clearly necessitated. Using a multivariate approach, it is possible, for example, to assess the relative importance of particular factors after having exercised appropriate controls. Multiple regression analysis was employed as one useful multivariate technique.[5]

Multiple Regression Analysis
It should be noted at the outset that problems exist when using multiple regression as an analytic technique with this sort of data. Principally, the dependent variable, ROR (no/yes), does not meet the assumption of interval measurement; coding is in the form of a dichotomy. Pearson's correlation, nevertheless, is a robust statistic, and regression results are not substantially affected when an ordinal variable is treated as an interval variable (Hindelang et al., 1978:192; Labovitz, 1967)—or when a dichotomy is represented as an interval measure (Kerlinger and Pedhazur, 1973).[6] In fact, because of the simplicity of the regression technique as a means for explaining variance and exercising controls, there is much to recommend its utility.

Table 7–2 lists most of the nearly fifty independent variables that were examined in both bivariate[7] and multivariate analyses of ROR

Table 7-2. Multiple Regression of ROR Outcomes on Groups of Independent Variables for Defendants Appearing at Preliminary Arraignment, Philadelphia: August to November, 1975

Dependent Variable: ROR Granted by Judge (No/Yes)[a]					
Grouped Independent Variables[b]	*r*	*Beta*	*Multi-ple R*	R^2	R^2 *Change*
I. *Demographic[c]* (Total = 7,631)					
Age	.25	.21	.25	.06	.06
Race/ethnicity	.14	.12	.29	.08	.02
Pays own rent or mortgage	-.10	-.11	.32	.10	.02
Employment history	.19	.06	.34	.12	.02
Sex	.11	.14	.36	.13	.01
Weekly income	.18	.05	.37	.14	.01
II. *Health* (Total = 8,316)					
Narcotics use	-.21	-.20	.21	.04	.04
Hospitalization:					
mental health	-.11	-.09	.23	.05	.01
Frequent alcohol use	-.08	-.07	.24	.06	.01
Physical health	-.03	-.00	.24	.06	<.01
III. *Legal* (Total = 8,316)					
Probable surety:					
immediate family	-.12	.03	.12	.02	.02
Probable surety:					
friends, employer	-.06	.01	.15	.02	<.01
Counsel requested	-.08	-.06	.16	.03	.01
Probable surety: self	.09	.15	.17	.03	<.01
References given	-.07	-.04	.18	.03	<.01
Private counsel	-.02	-.03	.18	.03	<.01
No probable surety	.09	.16	.18	.03	<.01
Probable surety: spouse	.04	.18	.19	.04	<.01
IV. *Prior criminal processing* (Total = 8,316)					
Most serious prior arrest	-.36	-.18	.36	.13	.13
Detainers/warrants	-.21	-.09	.38	.14	.01
Any prior record	-.30	-.03	.39	.16	.02
Open cases	-.21	-.07	.40	.16	.00
Prior FTAs	-.21	-.07	.40	.16	.00
On probation, parole, work release	-.21	-.05	.41	.17	.01
Mean seriousness of prior arrests	-.24	.34	.41	.17	.00
Number of prior arrests	-.30	-.35	.42	.17	.00
Mean seriousness of prior convictions	-.25	-.22	.42	.17	.00
Number of prior convictions	-.26	.20	.42	.18	.01
Most serious prior conviction	-.30	-.05	.42	.18	.00

Table 7-2 continued

Dependent Variable: ROR Granted by Judge (No/Yes)[a]

Grouped Independent Variables[b]	r	Beta	Multiple R	R^2	R^2 Change
V. *Charge-related* (Total = 8,316)					
Charge	−.54	−.47	.54	.29	.29
Number of different offenses charged	−.34	−.12	.55	.30	.01
Number of transcripts	−.10	.03	.55	.30	.00
Weapons charges	−.23	−.02	.55	.30	.00
Prostitution involved	.05	.00	.55	.30	.00

[a]Solutions were significant at the .001 level.

[b]Each group of independent variables (indicated by a roman numeral), represents a separate regression solution. Within each solution, variables were entered in a free, stepwise fashion.

[c]Of the original twenty-two demographic variables entered in the regression solution for this group (I), the contributions of only six are presented here due to limitations of space. None of the remaining demographic variables were able to contribute 1 percent to the overall R^2 and were therefore not considered meaningful.

decisions. Great care was taken in preliminary stages of the analysis to consider several kinds of variables that might have had an impact on ROR. Included were groups of defendant attributes categorized as demographic (including community-ties dimensions), health (including drugs and alcohol use), legal (including surety and counsel indicators), prior processing (arrests, previous FTAs, open cases, convictions), and criminal charge-related. In using the regression approach, the aim is to discover independent variables that account for a large share of the variance (indicated by the R^2 statistic in the table) in ROR (no/yes), the dependent variable.

In order to simplify the task of examining the relationship of fifty-one variables with ROR outcomes, the independent variables were first considered in the generic groups shown in Table 7-2. Each group (for example, first the demographic, then the health) was entered separately in an equation where the dependent variable represented the ROR decision component. Variables within each group were allowed to enter in a free stepwise fashion.[8]

Group I consisting of twenty-two demographic variables, was able to explain 14 percent of the variance in ROR outcomes. The six largest contributions are listed in Table 7-2. Of the six most important demographic variables, age and race/ethnicity were most influential. Missing were any significant contributions by two important community-ties measures, residence and family ties, or other measures closely related to residence and family ties. This regression of ROR outcomes on demographic variables shows that, while a major share of the variance is not explained by the demographic attributes of defendants, it appears in this preliminary sense that *some* variance *may* be explained by demographics.

Variables in the second equation (Group II) include indicators of past or present narcotics use, frequent alcohol use, physical health problems, and past institutionalization for mental health. Together they were unable to account for more than 6 percent of the variance in ROR outcomes, indicating a definite lack of influence.

Group III variables were unable to account for more than 4 percent of the variance in bail outcomes. Thus, whether or not the defendant indicated a probable surety, requested court-appointed counsel, had privately retained counsel, or listed references appears to have made little difference in judges' decisions to grant or deny ROR to Philadelphia defendants.

Prior criminal processing variables (Group IV), on the other hand, were able to account for a more substantial proportion of variance in ROR outcomes (18 percent) than any of the previous groups. Most of this ability (13 percent) was contributed by one variable, knowledge of a defendant's most serious prior arrest.

But, by far the greatest explanatory power was located in the fifth group, consisting of charge-related variables. In fact, one variable alone– seriousness of the present criminal charge—explained 29 percent of the variance in ROR outcomes. Overall, Group V variables taken alone accounted for 30 percent of the variance in the granting of ROR.

Regression Results

From the separate regression solutions presented in Table 7–2, it can be seen that charge variables and prior criminal processing variables are able to explain sizeable, though differing, amounts of variance in the ROR decision. The next step in the attempt to explain the maximum amount of variance possible in ROR outcomes and to compare the relative magnitude of the contributions made by individual variables—regardless of their generic groupings—is to enter them all together in one regression solution. In this manner, one can attempt to learn which among all independent variables appear to exert the greatest influence on the judges' decision to grant or deny ROR. When fifty-one independent variables are entered simultaneously in one equation, a considerable proportion of the variance (43 percent) in ROR outcomes is explained. Table 7–3 does not show the result of regression for all fifty-one variables; rather, the top eight contributors are listed since 40 percent of the variance is already explained by them. (Little insight can be gained from discussion of the remaining forty-three variables that, in minute increments,

Table 7–3. Multiple Regression of ROR Outcomes on All Independent Variables (Eight Variables Entering First in a Free, Stepwise Regression Solution) for Defendants Appearing at Preliminary Arraignment, Philadelphia: August to November, 1975[a]

			Multi-		
Dependent Variable: ROR Granted by Judge (No/Yes) *(Total = 7,631)*					
Independent Variables	*r*	*Beta*	*ple R*	R^2	R^2 *Change*
Criminal charge	−.54	−.38	.54	.29	.29
Most serious prior arrest	−.35	−.09	.59	.35	.06
Mean seriousness of prior convictions	−.24	−.09	.60	.37	.01
Number of different offenses charged	−.34	−.12	.61	.38	.01
Detainers/warrants	−.21	−.05	.62	.38	.00
Telephone	.01	.05	.62	.39	.01
Opencases	−.20	−.06	.63	.40	.01
Hospitalization: mental houlth	−.11	.08	.63	.40	.00
(Abbreviated)			(Abbreviated)		

Semipartial correlations (squared): independent variables entering in the first five steps[b]

Charge	.14
Most serious prior arrest	.02
Mean seriousness of prior convictions	.01
Number of different offenses charged	.01
Detainers/warrants	.01

[a]Fifty-one independent variables in all were entered in the regression equation presented here. Since presentation of more than eight of the first-entering (most influential) variables would be meaningless in terms of explained variance (*i.e.,* the next forty-three variables combined add 3 percent to R^2), the space is saved and the table is abbreviated. The solution was significant at the .001 level.

[b]Figuring semipartial correlations squared is tantamount to calculating the amount of explained variance added to a regression solution by a variable when it is entered last. This was done using only the top five independent variables in the solution. If all fifty-one variables were to be used, additional shrinkage in these correlations might be expected. The solution was significant at the .001 level.

cumulatively add but 3 percent to the total amount of variance explained in ROR outcomes.)

As displayed in that table, the five variables most influential in explaining ROR decision outcomes (accounting for 38 percent of the variance) are representative of neither defendants' community ties or their demographic attributes; instead, they are strictly charge- and prior criminal processing-related. By far, the most influential (entering first) is the charge seriousness variable, alone explaining 29 percent of the variance. The next two variables to enter are indicators of defendants' prior records: their most serious prior arrest and the mean seriousness of their prior convictions.[9] The number of different kinds of offenses with which a defendant was charged and the existence of detainers or bench warrants were the fourth and fifth contributors. It is clear from these findings that the ROR decision (the first step in the trifurcated model), at least, operates primarily according to the seriousness of the criminal charge and the defendant's prior record—not only of convictions but also of *arrests*.

A helpful way of assessing the relative magnitude of the contributions of the top five variables is to compare their squared semipartial correlations.[10] In effect, this amounts to calculating the amount of explained variance contributed by each variable when entered on the last step in the solution. This procedure controls for the effect (*i.e.*, redundancies) of the independent variables entered earlier on the variable entered on the last step. The second part of Table 7-3 lists the squared semipartial correlations for each independent variable. Entered first, charge is able to explain 29 percent of the variance in ROR outcomes; but entered last, its unique contribution is only 14 percent to the explanation of variance. Nevertheless, this still represents a contribution *seven* times the magnitude of the next most influential decision factor, most serious prior arrest, which shows a squared semipartial of only .02. This result may be interpreted as demonstrating the unrivaled dominance of charge seriousness in the judge's decision to grant or deny ROR.

First-Order Interaction Effects

It is conceivable that not only can variance in ROR outcomes be explained by the collective (additive) contributions of the several independent variables described above, but also by some interaction (multiplicative) effect between them that is greater than their mere sums. To check for such an effect in a preliminary way, ten vectors representing all possible first-order interactions between the top five independent variables were created[11] and entered in regression after the five original variables entered as a group. The result was that together the ten vectors added only about 1 percent to the explanation of variance in ROR outcomes. It is concluded from this exercise that no (first-order) interaction effects appear to figure importantly in the explanation of variance in ROR outcomes over and above the main effects of the top five contributing independent variables.[12]

DETENTION WITHOUT BAIL: STEP TWO

Approximately 117 defendants among those not granted OR release are dealt with on the second decision step; that is, 1 percent of all Philadelphia defendants were held without bail. Detention of these defendants is explained by the offenses with which they were charged: murder (116 cases) and aggravated assault (1 case, where presumably it was not yet known if the victim would live). Detention without bail in Philadelphia for homicide defendants is mandated procedurally, at least until preliminary hearing when the charges may be modified and the question of bail reviewed. Although an in-depth analysis of detention-without-bail is not warranted—due both to the small number of cases (n = 117) and to the procedural explanation—the following attributes of these defendants can be gleaned from Table 7-1: Defendants held without bail were predominantly young (70 percent were twenty-five or younger), black (93 percent), male (93 percent), single (63 percent), and unemployed (74 percent).

CASH BAIL: STEP THREE

Defendants who have not been released on OR or detained without bail have cash bail set.[13] For the bail judge, these defendants involve a kind of decisionmaking that differs qualitatively from the ROR or detention-without-bail options. Evidently, they represent cases in which pretrial release issues are less clear. For cash-bail defendants, the presiding judge is not engaged in the selection of *either* release *or* detention but rather in a weighting procedure that results in the fixing of relatively greater or lesser amounts of money. Although a judge may heavily bias a defendant's prospects for release or detention by setting high or low bail, the judge is not assuming the direct responsibility for the defendant's incarceration or liberty that accompanies the granting of ROR or detention-without-bail. In a sense, by deferring to the cash-bail option in the bail decision, the judge in effect passes on the responsibility for the custody decision to the defendant, who assumes it, perhaps questionably, through his or her ability to raise the required amount of cash.

In the analysis of the setting of cash bail that follows, it should be

Table 7-4. Estimated Number of Defendants with Cash Bail Set at Preliminary Arraignment, by Median Amount of Ten Percent Bail, by Selected Attributes, Philadelphia: August to November, 1975[a]

Selected Attributes	Number of Defendants	Median Amount of Bail	Ten Percent Median Bail
All Philadelphia defendants	(4,299)	$ 991	$ 99
Age (Total = 4,299)			
18 and under	(306)	982	98
19 to 20	(740)	968	97
21 to 25	(1,396)	973	97
26 to 30	(746)	816	82
31 to 40	(688)	805	81
41 and over	(423)	579	58
Race/ethnicity (Total = 4,299)			
Hispanic/other	(212)	535	54
Black	(3,144)	996	100
White	(943)	517	52
Sex (Total = 4,299)			
Female	(353)	538	54
Male	(3,946)	993	99
Weekly income (Total = 4,041)			
$0	(2,568)	957	96
$1 to $58	(100)	1,004	100
$59 to $144	(940)	955	96
$145 to $192	(218)	1,000	100
$193 and over	(215)	818	82
Employment status (Total = 4,193)			
Employed	(2,577)	958	96
Not employed	(1,616)	991	99
Marital status (Total = 4,200)			
Never married	(2,443)	966	97
Widowed/divorced/separated	(243)	722	72
Married	(1,514)	991	99
Criminal charge (Total = 4,293)			
Violent personal	(277)	4,931	493
Robbery	(640)	3,458	346
Aggravated assault	(534)	975	98
Drugs–combined	(570)	987	99
Burglary	(535)	1,019	102
Theft/larceny	(578)	503	50
Simple assault/weapons	(405)	489	49
Lesser property	(254)	510	51
Public nuisance/order	(142)	455	46
Drunk/disorderly	(81)	362	36
DWI/traffic	(173)	334	33
Miscellaneous/other	(104)	462	46

[a]The median amounts of cash bail presented in this table are calculated from the actual amounts of bail set by judges. Defendants would be required to post only 10 percent of the actual amounts. Thus, the medians may be divided by ten to obtain comparable medians indicating what defendants were actually required to pay.

recalled that although the dollar amounts may seem large—ranging from $50 to $500,000—defendants were required to post only 10 percent of the amount to gain their release. Table 7-4, for example, reveals that the median amount for all defendants in the sample cohort was $991. When this amount is adjusted to reflect the actual Ten Percent amount, a rather extraordinary finding is derived: *Half of all Philadelphia defendants who had cash bail set*, for all practical purposes, *had it set in amounts less than $100.*

At least from consideration of median bail amounts, Table 7-4 shows substantial differences among defendants when contrasted by race, sex and criminal charge. White and Hispanic/other defendants had median Ten Percent bails of approximately $50, compared with black defendants whose median Ten Percent amount was $100. Female defendants showed a median Ten Percent bail that was about half that of male defendants ($54 compared with $99, respectively). Median bails also fluctuated greatly according to the seriousness of the charge, ranging from Ten Percent medians of nearly $500 for violent, personal offenses to $50 or less for the least serious offenses.

Multiple Regression Analysis

Once again, as was done in the multivariate analysis of ROR outcomes, fifty-one independent variables measuring the attributes of Philadelphia defendants were broken down into five generic groupings and entered into separate regression equations separately. This allows for a preliminary assessment of the relative influence of these kinds of defendant attributes on the judges' decisions to set dollar amounts of bail. Table 7-5 exhibits those results: Twenty-one demographic variables, four health variables, eight legal variables, and ten prior criminal processing variables, grouped separately, were able to account for less than 5 percent of the variance in amount of cash bail in their separate solutions. Only the fifth group, comprised of charge-related variables, was able to explain a sizeable amount of variance in cash bail; knowledge of weapons charges and the number of transcripts or original complaints accounted for approximately 18 percent of the variance in cash bail. Most of this (17 or 18 percent) was due to the weapons-charge variable alone.

Regression Results

Compared with the regression analysis of ROR outcomes, the attempt to explain variance in amounts of cash bail meets only with modest success. (See Table 7-6.) Using the five variables entering first of the original collection of fifty-one, it is possible only to explain 26 percent of the variance. Prime among these independent var-

Table 7-5. Multiple Regression of Amount of Cash Bail on Groups of Independent Variables for Defendants Appearing at Preliminary Arraignment, Philadelphia: August to November, 1975[a]

Dependent Variable: Amount of Cash Bail
(Total = 4,299)

Grouped Independent Variables	*r*	*Beta*	*Multi-ple R*	R^2	R^2 *Change*
I. Demographic —21 independent variables					
II. Health — 4 independent variables					
III. Legal — 8 independent variables					
IV. Prior criminal processing—10 independent variables					
NOTE: Each of the regression solutions for above grouped variables (representing forty-three independent variables collectively) were not able to explain as much as 5 percent of the variance in bail amounts. Presentation of their regression results would be meaningless and are, therefore, omitted.					
V. Charge-related[b]					
Weapons charges	.41	.42	.41	.17	.17
Number of transcripts	.11	.12	.42	.18	.01
Number of different offenses charged	.15	-.07	.42	.18	<.01
Seriousness of criminal charge	.13	.05	.42	.18	<.01
Prostitution involved	-.02	.01	.43	.18	<.01

[a]Each group of independent variables (indicated by a roman numeral), represents a separate regression solution. Within each solution, variables were entered in a free, stepwise fashion.
[b]The solution was significant at the .001 level.

iables are weapons-charges and number of transcripts (or documents filed containing one configuration of charges describing one criminal event). Prior criminal processing variables, number of prior arrests, and mean seriousness of prior arrests rate as secondary contributors; the contribution of the fifth variable is not statistically significant. Noticeable in its absence is the variable so overwhelmingly influential for ROR outcomes, the seriousness of the criminal charge.

In the same table, squared semipartial correlations are presented. It is seen there that, when the effects of the other independent variables are controlled, only three variables appear still to be able to make contributions to the explanation of variance in cash-bail amounts: weapons-charges (by far the most substantial at .16, or 16 percent of the variance), number of transcripts (.02), and number of prior arrests (.01).

Table 7-6. Multiple Regression of Amount of Cash Bail on All Independent Variables (Five Variables Entering First in a Free, Stepwise Solution) for Defendants Appearing at Preliminary Arraignment, Philadelphia: August to November, 1975[a]

Dependent variable: amount of cash bail
(Total = 3,974)

Independent Variables	*r*	*Beta*	*Multiple R*	*R^2*	*R^2 Change*	*Squared Semipartial Correlation*[c]
Weapons charges	.48	.49	.48	.23	.23	.16
Number of transcripts	.13	.13	.49	.24	.01	.02
Number of prior arrests	.07	.25	.50	.25	.01	.01
Mean seriousness of prior arrests	.03	−.17	.50	.25	$<.01$	.00
Probable surety: spouse	.03	.01	.51	.26	$<.01$[b]	.00
(Abbreviated)			(Abbreviated)			

[a]Fifty-one variables in all were entered in the regression equation represented here. Because presentation of more than five of the first-entering (most influential) variables would be meaningless in terms of explained variance (*i.e.*, the next forty-six variables combined add only 2 percent to R^2), the space is saved and the table is abbreviated.

[b]The solution was significant at the .001 level.

[c]Figuring semipartial correlations squared is tantamount to calculating the amount of explained variance added to a regression solution by a variable when it is entered last. This was done using only the top five independent variables in the solution. If all fifty-one variables were to be used, additional shrinkage in these correlations might be expected. The solutions were significant at the .001 level.

First-Order Interaction Effects

When an attempt was made to check for possible interaction effects in the ROR analyses, it will be recalled little that was significant could be reported.[14] But when the same check was made in the present case, a large amount of first-order interaction was detected. In fact, as Table 7-7 demonstrates, first-order interactions were able to increase the amount of variance explained in cash-bail amounts by more than 100 percent. Specifically, using only the top five independent variables, ten multiplicative vectors were created to represent all possible first-order effects. These were then entered as a group after the original independent variables themselves. Table 7-7 shows that, alone, the five independent original variables were able to explain only 20 percent of the variance in cash-bail amounts. But when en-

Table 7-7. Evaluation of First-Order Interaction Effects of the Five First-Entering Independent Variables on the Amount of Cash Bail Using a Group-Stepwise Regression Procedure, for Defendants Appearing at Preliminary Arraignment, Philadelphia: August to November, 1975[a]

Independent Variables	r	Beta	Multiple R	R^2	R^2 Change
Dependent Variable: Amount of Cash Bail *(Total = 4,252)*					
Group I: Summary of five first entering independent variables					
Weapons charges					
Number of transcripts					
Number of prior arrests					
Mean seriousness of prior arrests					
Probable surety: spouse			.45	.20	
Group II: Interaction vectors (first order only)					
Vector 2 (weapons x number of prior arrests)	.52		.55	.31	.11
Vector 3 (weapons x mean seriousness of prior arrests)	.43		.61	.38	.07
Vector 4 (weapons x probable surety: spouse)	.48		.63	.40	.02
Vector 1 (weapons x number of transcripts)	.42		.64	.41	.01
Vector 7 (probable surety: spouse x number of transcripts)	.08		.64	.41	<.01
Vector 5 (number of transcripts x number of prior arrests)	.11		.64	.41	<.01
Vector 6 (number of transcripts x mean seriousness of prior arrests)	.06		.64	.41	<.01
Vector 9 (number of prior arrests x probable surety: spouse)	.06		.64	.41	<.01
Vector 10 (mean seriousness of prior arrests x probable surety: spouse)	.03		.64	.41	<.01
Vector 8 (number of prior arrests x mean seriousness of prior arrests)	.01		.64	.41	<.01

[a]In order to evaluate the possible first-order interaction effects of the five independent variables in question on variance in cash bail, multiplicative vectors were first created for all possible paired combinations of the independent variables. These were then entered as a group (II) after the independent variables themselves (I). The difference between the overall R^2 after both groups are entered and the R^2 for the first group indicates the amount of additional variance in bail amounts that may be explained by first-order interactions. Indications of the relative importance of these interactions is given by the order of entry of vectors within the second group. The solution was significant at the .001 level.

tered in a second step, the interaction vectors contributed an additional 21 percent of explained variance in cash bail.

Because the vectors entered on the second step were allowed to enter in a stepwise fashion, some indication of the kinds of (first-order) interactions that appeared to be influential can be obtained. Apparently, of greatest impact was the multiplicative effect of the weapons-charges/number of prior arrests vector, which added 11 percent to the explanation of variance in cash bail after the effects of the original variables had already been subtracted. A second related vector, weapons-charges/mean seriousness of prior arrests, also made a substantial addition (7 percent). The role of weapons-charges is further underscored in the two remaining vectors that make meaningful contributions, weapons/probable surety: spouse and weapons/number of transcripts.

CONCLUSION

At the commencement of this chapter, it was observed from cursory tabular analysis that overall bail outcomes appeared to be associated with a number of variables, including several demographic measures. Through use of the trifurcated model, it was possible to separate three different aspects of the bail decision process for greater analytic clarity. The principal result was the emergence of qualitative differences in the factors that appeared to influence decisionmaking in each of the decision components conceptualized—especially when the decision to grant or deny ROR and the decision to set a particular amount of cash bail were compared.[15]

Perhaps the most interesting of these results is the finding that bail decisionmaking, in its various facets, seems to operate almost exclusively on the basis of the seriousness of the charge. That is, the ROR decision option appears to screen "out" defendants who are not charged with serious crimes. Bail is denied for defendants charged with murder, the most serious of all charges.[16] And, finally, the setting of cash bail is also affected by charge seriousness but based on a more extreme indicator, the presence of weapons-charges.

In earlier chapters it was pointed out that a great deal of dissatisfaction has been voiced over reliance on charge seriousness as the major criterion in bail decisionmaking. In the Federal Bail Reform Act of 1966, for example, and in the American Bar Association's Standards, consideration of criminal charge in deciding bail was purposely deemphasized in favor of other defendant attributes that were deemed more appropriate, such as community ties. The equity of bail practices that rely on charge criteria may be questioned from a number of perspectives. Among these are (1) charging may be manipulated by police and prosecutors to affect a defendant's chances at bail; (2) bailsetting based on charge seriousness has all the drawbacks of bail set in accordance with an explicit bail schedule; that is, the release prospects of similarly charged defendants may unfairly depend on their differential ability to afford bail; (3) different judges will have different views of seriousness—consequently bailsetting based on charge will vary from judge to judge, creating an inconsistency in bail outcomes among similar defendants.

It is especially surprising that, in a jurisdiction with one of the most progressive pretrial services operations in the nation, *community-ties indicators*, such as family ties and residence in the community, *appear in the face of charge and prior-record concerns to have had almost no impact at all on the granting of ROR or on the setting of cash bail.* This finding may suggest that Philadelphia bail judges do not deem community ties reliable indexes for assessing defendants' propensities toward flight. But, it may also demonstrate a lesser concern for the evaluation of flight-risk, pointing instead to the dominance of other bail decision concerns that may be intuitively linked to charge seriousness and past criminal history criteria—such as a concern for potential defendant dangerousness or a tendency to prejudge or even prepunish defendants at their first appearance.

In fairness, however, these findings may also be viewed more positively. To begin with, it is clear that, in the absence of a statistical ability to predict pretrial flight and/or crime, the bail decision must be transacted by necessity not only in the realm of judicial discretion but also through the exercise of judicial *intuition.* Judicial intuition in bail decisionmaking, in Philadelphia at least, depended heavily on the criminal charge and to some extent on the prior record of defendants. It did *not*, on the other hand, depend on race/ethnicity, sex, employment, or income characteristics of Philadelphia defendants. Had those factors been found to influence bail decision outcomes, equity issues of a more difficult sort would need to be addressed.

NOTES

1. Recall that the scope of the study has been limited to include only these three options. Beyond the scope of the present study were dismissals, fugitives, and special complaints. See Chapter 6.

2. This includes those released on "sign your own bail" (SOB), who were released on a secured promise-to-appear. That is, although no financial guarantees were deposited to obtain release, defendants so released would be liable for given amounts if they subsequently failed to appear in court.

3. It is not implied here that judges might not depart frequently from the three-step procedure posited. For instance, a bail judge might automatically discount ROR and denial of bail and proceed as a first thought to set money-bail. Or a different model, one replacing Step One with Step Two, might be just as useful. The point is that the model assuming the contingent, three-step logic, allows for a meaningful analysis of different aspects of bail decisionmaking.

4. A dummy variable, ROR: no or yes, was created for use in bivariate and multivariate analysis. Recall from Note 23 in Chapter 6 that the percent estimates are generally quite reliable; that is, estimates of attributes shared by about one-half of the sample would have a 95 percent confidence interval of about 2 percentage points, while smaller estimates might have a 95 percent confidence interval spanning three percentage points.

5. It may be worthwhile to introduce briefly the statistics that are employed in the subsequent tables and to explain their meaning before proceeding with a discussion of findings. (a) *Pearson's product moment r*, the coefficient of correlation, is a statistic that summarizes both the strength and direction of the linear relationship between two variables. It may be conceived of as a measure of covariance of scores of two interval level variables when normed to a standardized scale of measurement. (b) *Multiple R*, the multiple correlation coefficient, indicates the relative magnitude of the correlation of one or more independent variables taken simultaneously with a dependent variable. In effect, it represents the correlation of predicted scores falling on a "line of best fit" constructed from knowledge of independent variables with actual scores on a dependent variable. (c) R^2, or the coefficient of determination, is used to show the proportion of variance (between 0 and 1) that may be explained or accounted for by knowledge of given independent variables. On the other hand, $1-R^2$, or the coefficient of alienation, indicates the residual variance or the proportion of variance in a dependent variable not accounted for by given independent variables considered together. It should be noted that R^2 capitalizes on the error variation associated with product moment correlations that contribute to the stepwise multiple regression solution. Thus, R^2 is an upward-biased estimate of explained variance that might be expected to fluctuate if different samples were drawn. Using a formula that takes into account the number of cases compared to the number of variables employed in a solution, a less biased or adjusted estimate of R^2 may be obtained. Due to the large number of unweighted cases in the present sample, when this adjustment is made, less than .02 shrinkage in R^2 was detected. For a comprehensive discussion of these statistics, see Kerlinger and Pedhazur (1973).

6. For a description of multiple regression with a dichotomous dependent variable as equivalent to discriminant function analysis, see Kerlinger and Pedhazur (1973).

7. For measures of bivariate relationships that may not have been presented in Table 7-1, refer to the r statistic in Table 7-2.

8. In stepwise multiple regression, independent variables are entered step by step, according to the amount of explained variance they can add to the regression solution. In other words, the squared semipartial correlations are computed for each prospective independent variable and the dependent variable when the effects of that independent variable's intercorrelation with other independent

variables already entered in the regression equation are controlled. The regression formula (with only four independent variables) can be written as follows:

$$R\overset{2}{y}.1234 = R\overset{2}{y}1 + R\overset{2}{y}(2.1) + R\overset{2}{y}(3.12) + R\overset{2}{y}(4.123)$$

where $R\overset{2}{y}.1234$ (the total amount of variance in y explained by the four independent variables) is conceived of as the sum of the correlations squared of y and variable one and the squared semipartial correlations of independent variables two through four. Note that the squared semipartial correlations will be heavily influenced by the choice of the independent variable entered first. In stepwise multiple regression, the first variable to be entered in the equation is chosen on the basis of the largest simple correlation, since on the first step only the simple, multiple, and semipartial correlation will be equal. On subsequent steps, the squared semipartials of each of the remaining variables are compared. The variable showing the largest semipartial with the dependent variable (controlling for variables previously entered) will enter on the next step. This procedure is repeated until all independent variables are exhausted. See Kerlinger and Pedhazur (1973).

9. The same procedure employed to summarize criminal charges in terms of seriousness (selecting the most serious charge ranked on a scale from 1 to 12) was used to summarize prior arrests and prior convictions. Thus, the single most serious arrest and/or conviction of defendants were recorded in addition, where more than one prior arrest or conviction was involved, the number of each was recorded. Where no priors were recorded, a zero was coded. The mean of the seriousness ratings for each was also calculated.

10. When explanation is the primary objective in regression analysis, it is useful to conceive of the amounts of variance explained by independent variables in terms of their semipartial correlations squared. The most simple method for calculating squared semipartials is by noting the amount of explained variance added by a given variable when all other variables in the equation are entered on earlier steps. This may be done by subtracting the R^2 obtained on the next-to-last step from the R^2 obtained on the very last step. The difference may in interpreted as showing the amount of variance in a dependent variable explained by an independent variable when its redundant properties (properties shared with other independent variables) are subtracted.

11. First-order interaction vectors were created according to procedures described in Kerlinger and Pedhazur (1973). It was beyond the scope of the present inquiry to consider second (or higher) order interaction effects. First-order interaction was examined mainly to raise the possibility of a role for interaction effects inthe explanation variance in a preliminary sense. This does not imply, of course, that where no first-order interactions are located, important higher interaction effects might not still be discovered.

12. These results are not presented here in tabular form.

13. Recall that cash bail in Philadelphia is set under the Ten Percent program.

14. Once again, no claims are made here concerning the possibility of significant higher order interaction effects.

15. The second step was quite different in nature from the first and the third

because it dealt with a small group of homicide defendants who had bail denied as a matter of procedure.

16. That is, the direct detention of defendants on the second step is determined by criminal charge too (homicide), but this step is less influential in terms of volume because proportionately so few defendants fell into that charge category.

Release or Detention Before Trial: An Analysis of the Determination of Pretrial Custody in Philadelphia

Analysis in the preceding chapter has been aimed not only at discerning the principal determinants of bail decisions (and by inference the primary decisionmaking concerns of bail judges) but also at describing the qualitative differences in these criteria as they related to the three aspects of the bail decision process that were posited in the analytic model. For approximately half of all defendants (those granted ROR and those detained without bail), the custody question was determined directly by the bail decision. Yet for half of the Philadelphia defendants in the sample (those with cash bail set), the custody question was not determined directly by what the bail judge decided. Quite conceivably, however, strong clues to the custody preferences of judges in cash-bail cases may have been indirectly communicated through the amount of bail set—whether relatively high or low. In other words, one might assume that a judge who sets high bail in a certain instance is really trying to make it difficult for a defendant (to afford) to be released.[1] Similarly, when the same judge does not opt for ROR in a certain case but still sets very low cash bail, one might assume that the judge is willing for that particular defendant to secure release.

The data presented in Table 8-1 suggest that such an assumption about the setting of cash bail may in fact be warranted. In that table a strong (and logical) relationship between relative amounts of bail and ultimate release or detention can be discerned. Note, first, that approximately four-tenths of all defendants with cash bail set remained in detention after preliminary arraignment. However, the proportion detained varies directly and dramatically with the amount

Table 8-1.   Estimated Number of Defendants with Cash Bail Set, by Amount of Cash Bail and Pretrial Custody Status, Philadelphia: August to November, 1975

Amount of Bail	Total[a]		Detained		Released	
	Number	Percent	Number	Percent	Number	Percent
All cash bail defendants	4,311	100.0	1,867	43.3	2,444	56.7
$1 to $500	1,920	100.0	432	22.5	1,488	77.5
$501 to $1,000	797	100.0	325	40.8	472	59.2
$1,001 to $5,000	1,089	100.0	689	63.3	400	36.7
$5,001 and over	505	100.0	421	83.3	84	16.7

[a]Subcategories may not sum to total due to rounding.

of cash bail set, increasing monotonically from only two-tenths (23 percent) of those with bail set between $1 and $500, to four-tenths (41 percent) of those with bail set between $501 and $1,000, to slightly more than six-tenths (63 percent) of those with bail set between $1,001 and $5,000, to a high of eight-tenths (83 percent) of defendants who had cash bail higher than $5,000.

In this chapter, the apparent complexities of bail decisionmaking are put aside, and, in their place, a simpler analytic framework is adopted. Using this framework, the bail decision is viewed more simply as the gatekeeping mechanism responsible for the "sorting" of defendants into or out of detention. *The aim of the analysis is to learn the bases of the classification of defendants as releasees or detainees* as the result of the brief proceedings that occur at first appearance (or preliminary arraignment) before a judicial officer.

The measure of pretrial custody employed in this analysis dichotomizes pretrial custody into defendants who were released by the time twenty-four hours had elapsed after initial appearance[2] and defendants who remained in detention after that period. This measure of pretrial custody has the advantage of describing the custody statuses of defendants very shortly after the bail decision. As such, it closely reflects the direct or immediate impact of the bail decision on the custody statuses of defendants. What it does not convey, it should be noted, is the extent to which some defendants were detained for periods beyond the twenty-four-hour interval but later released before final disposition of their cases.

CUSTODY STATUS TWENTY-FOUR HOURS AFTER FIRST APPEARANCE

Given Philadelphia's national reputation as a model jurisdiction in the area of pretrial release and other defendant services, it is perhaps not surprising to learn that about three-quarters (76 percent) of all defendants secured immediate preadjudicatory release when this definition of pretrial custody is used. Yet 24 percent had not secured release twenty-four hours after preliminary arraignment, and in spite of the fact that this represents a minority of defendants, enough were being detained that Philadelphia's detention population fluctuated at a level of around one thousand eight hundred detainees at the time.[3] Thus, although it is noteworthy that such a substantial proportion of defendants in Philadelphia were released so quickly after their initial appearances, it is precisely because so many were granted their freedom before trial that one is obliged to inquire why the remaining few were detained. Because pretrial detention is by its nature so selectively apportioned among defendants, it becomes essential to learn what distinguishes defendants who were detained in the sample from those who were released.

Preliminary analysis of independent variables in Table 8-2 shows that differences in the proportions of released versus detained defendants were in abundance. In fact, (judging differences of ten percentage points or more as substantial) the preadjudicatory custody status of Philadelphia defendants appears to have varied substantially by age, race/ethnicity, sex, marital status, criminal charge, prior arrests, and prior convictions. Summarized, these relationships between the principal independent variables and pretrial custody can be characterized in the following fashion.[4]

Age
The proportion of defendants detained declines steadily with age, from 36 percent of the youngest defendants (eighteen and under) to only 4 percent of the oldes defendants (forty-one and over).

Race/Ethnicity
A substantially greater proportion of black defendants (30 percent) than of Hispanic/other (17 percent) and white defendants (11 percent) were detained after twenty-four hours.

Table 8-2. Estimated Number of Defendants Appearing at Preliminary Arraignment, by Custody Status, by Selected Attributes, Philadelphia: August to November, 1975

Independent Variables	Total[a]		Released		Detained	
	Number	Percent	Number	Percent	Number	Percent
All Philadelphia defendants	8,316	100.0	6,308	75.9	2,008	24.1
Age (Total = 8,316)						
18 and under	544	100.0	348	64.0	196	36.0
19 to 20	1,280	100.0	888	69.4	392	30.6
21 to 25	2,273	100.0	1,644	72.3	629	27.7
26 to 30	1,334	100.0	988	74.1	346	25.9
31 to 40	1,362	100.0	1,080	79.3	282	20.7
41 and over	1,523	100.0	1,360	89.3	163	10.7
Race/ethnicity (Total = 8,316)						
Hispanic/other	413	100.0	344	83.3	69	16.7
Black	5,638	100.0	3,948	70.0	1,690	30.0
White	2,265	100.0	2,016	89.0	249	11.0
Sex (Total = 8,316)						
Male	7,372	100.0	5,488	74.4	1,884	25.6
Female	944	100.0	820	86.9	124	13.1
Marital status (Total = 7,911)						
Never married	4,093	100.0	2,836	69.3	1,257	30.7
Widowed/divorced/separated	544	100.0	452	83.1	92	16.9
Married	3,274	100.0	2,668	81.5	606	18.5
Weekly income (Total = 7,663)						
None	4,358	100.0	2,976	68.3	1,382	31.7
$1 to $58	182	100.0	136	74.7	46	25.3
$59 to $144	1,854	100.0	1,512	81.6	342	18.4
$145 to $192	632	100.0	560	88.6	72	11.4
$193 and over	637	100.0	588	92.3	49	7.7

Employment status (Total = 7,930)						
Unemployed	4,388	100.0	3,000	68.4	1,388	31.6
Employed	3,542	100.0	2,980	84.1	562	15.9
Criminal charge (Total = 8,310)						
Violent personal	402	100.0	128	31.8	274	68.2
Robbery	653	100.0	188	28.8	465	71.2
Aggravated assault	730	100.0	548	75.1	182	24.9
Drugs—combined	819	100.0	648	79.1	171	20.9
Burglary	628	100.0	312	50.3	316	49.7
Theft/larceny	942	100.0	708	75.2	234	24.8
Simple assault/weapons	880	100.0	772	87.7	108	12.3
Lesser property	435	100.0	332	76.3	103	23.7
Public nuisance/order	885	100.0	836	94.5	49	5.5
Drunk/disorderly	434	100.0	400	92.2	34	7.8
DWI/traffic	1,261	100.0	1,228	97.4	33	2.6
Miscellaneous/other	241	100.0	208	86.3	33	13.7
Prior arrests (Total = 8,316)						
None	3,937	100.0	3,456	87.8	481	12.2
1 or 2	1,863	100.0	1,488	79.9	375	20.1
3 or more	2,516	100.0	1,364	54.2	1,152	45.8
Prior convictions (Total = 8,316)						
None	6,552	100.0	5,428	82.8	1,124	17.2
1 or 2	1,395	100.0	744	53.3	651	46.7
3 or more	369	100.0	136	36.9	233	63.1

aSubcategories may not sum to 100 percent due to rounding.

Sex

Male defendants (26 percent) were considerably more likely than female defendants (13 percent) to have been detained more than twenty-four hours after first appearance or preliminary arraignment.

Marital Status

A substantially greater proportion of single defendants (31 percent) than of widowed/divorced/separated defendants or of married defendants (17 and 19 percent, respectively) were detained.

Weekly Income

The proportion of defendants detained after the twenty-four hour period was substantially greater for low- or for no-income defendants (32 and 25 percent, respectively) than for defendants in the two upper income categories (about 10 percent).[5]

Employment Status

Proportionately twice as many unemployed defendants (32 percent) as employed defendants (16 percent) were detained.

Criminal Charge

The proportion of defendants detained varied considerably according to the seriousness of the charged offense. Generally, the more serious the charge, the greater the portion detained. For example, 68 percent of those charged with violent personal crimes (murder, rape, and kidnapping) and 71 percent of those charged with robbery were detained, compared with 12 percent of those charged with simple assault or weapons possession offenses and 8 percent of those charged with drunkenness or disorderly conduct.

In spite of the strong general relationship between charge seriousness and the rate of detention, exceptions can be noted. For instance, smaller proportions of persons charged with aggravated assault were detained than might be expected from its ranking as the third most serious offense category.

Prior Arrests

Only 12 percent of those with no prior arrests and 20 percent of those with one or two prior arrests, but as much as 46 percent of those with three or more arrests, were detained beyond twenty-four hours.

Prior Convictions

Only 17 percent of those with no prior convictions were detained, but 47 percent of those with one or two prior convictions and 63 percent of those with three or more were detained.

On the basis of preliminary bivariate analysis, one might be strongly inclined to infer that the occurrence of pretrial detention is associated with a number of defendant characteristics—some of them highly objectionable. For instance, based on these data it would appear that the classification of defendants into custody groups before adjudication operates to the clear disadvantage of defendants who are young, black, male, single, low income, or unemployed as well as to those charged in serious criminal matters and/or having serious prior records. However, before conclusions about the factors associated with the determination of pretrial custody can be made, further analysis will be required to evaluate the power of the relationships encountered when controls are exercised.

MULTIVARIATE ANALYSIS OF PRETRIAL CUSTODY

In a fashion similar to the Chapter 7 analysis of bail, multiple regression is used in this chapter to help isolate characteristics of defendants that appear to be most influential in the classification of Philadelphia defendants into custody statuses.[6] Cautions concerning the use of this technique with these data were mentioned in the previous chapter. It should further be noted that the skewness of the distribution of defendants on the dependent variable (24 percent detained, 76 released) presents an additional issue. Because the variability among cases is minimal in such a distribution, use of *r* or *multiple r* as variance-explaining measures will result in rather small correlations (Hindelang et al., 1978:192). Despite these considerations, it was decided that regression analysis still lent itself well to elucidation of the classification criteria associated with pretrial custody.[7]

To begin the multivariate analysis of the custody statuses of Philadelphia defendants, more than fifty independent variables were organized into five generic groupings (demographic, health, legal, prior criminal processing, and charge-related) as they were in Chapter 7's analyses. Each group was then entered in a separate regression solution where the dependent variable was pretrial custody (detention or release). Results of this procedure are reported in Table 8-3.

The Group I solution based on the twenty-three demographic variables produced less than overwhelming results: Together, all demographic variables were only able to account for 15 percent of the variance in pretrial custody outcomes. The six most influential demographic variables in that equation were employment history,[8]

Table 8-3. Multiple Regression of Pretrial Custody on Groups of Independent Variables for Defendants Appearing at Preliminary Arraignment, Philadelphia: August to November, 1975

Dependent Variable: Pretrial Custody (Detention/Release)[a]

Grouped Independent Variables[a]	r	Beta	Multi-ple R	R^2	R^2 Change
I. *Demographic*[b] (Total = 7,631)					
Employment history	.19	.08	.20	.04	.04
Race/ethnicity (white, nonwhite)	.18	.18	.26	.07	.03
Age	.18	.11	.30	.09	.02
Sex	.09	.15	.32	.10	.01
On public assistance	-.12	-.06	.33	.11	.01
Motor vehicle owned	.15	.10	.35	.12	.01
II. *Health* (Total = 8,316)					
Narcotics use	-.19	-.18	.19	.04	.04
Frequent alcohol use	-.11	-.11	.21	.05	.01
Hospitalization: mental health	-.08	-.05	.22	.05	<.01
Physical health	-.03	-.01	.22	.05	<.01
III. *Legal* (Total = 8,316)					
Counsel requested	-.14	-.13	.14	.02	.02
Probable surety: self	.09	.13	.16	.03	.01
Probable surety: spouse	.08	.12	.18	.03	<.01
No probable surety	.00	.10	.19	.03	<.01
Probable surety: friends, employer	-.01	.04	.19	.04	<.01
Probable surety: immediate family	-.07	.04	.19	.04	<.01
References given	.01	.01	.19	.04	<.01
Private counsel	.03	.00	.19	.04	<.01
IV. *Prior criminal processing* (Total = 8,316)					
Detainers/warrants	-.35	-.23	.35	.12	.12
Most serious prior arrest	-.34	-.10	.44	.19	.07
On probation, parole, work release	-.30	-.12	.46	.21	.02
Open cases	-.25	-.10	.47	.22	.01
Number of prior convictions	-.30	.12	.48	.23	.01
Prior FTAs	-.25	-.08	.48	.23	<.01
Mean seriousness of prior arrests	-.26	.31	.49	.24	<.01
Number of prior arrests	-.33	-.32	.49	.24	<.01
Mean seriousness of prior convictions	-.27	-.15	.49	.24	<.01
Most serious prior conviction	-.31	-.06	.49	.24	<.01

Table 8–3 continued

Dependent Variable: Pretrial Custody (Detention/Release)[a]

Grouped Independent Variables[a]	r	Beta	Multi-ple R	R^2	R^2 Change
V. *Charge-related* (Total = 8,226)					
Charge	–.40	–.34	.40	.16	.16
Number of different kinds of charges	–.28	–.13	.41	.17	.01
Number of transcripts	–.10	.01	.41	.17	<.01
Weapons charges	.02	–.01	.41	.17	<.01
Prostitution involved	–.16	.00	.41	.17	<.01

[a]Each group of independent variables (indicated by a roman numeral), represents a separate regression solution. Within each solution, variables were entered in a free, stepwise fashion.

[b]Of the original twenty-three demographic variables entered in the regression solution for this group, only the top six are presented here in abbreviated form due to limitations of space. Addition of the remaining seventeen variables increases R^2 only .03 and makes little intuitive sense.

race/ethnicity, age, sex, being on public assistance, and owning a motor vehicle. However, variables constituting the health group (II) and the legal group (III) fared even more poorly, accounting for only 5 and 4 percent of the variance in their respective solutions. The prior criminal processing group (IV), consisting of ten independent variables, was able to account for a more substantial amount of variance (24 percent) in the detention versus release custody outcomes in comparison with the first three groups. Most influential among these variables was the variable indicating whether or not detainers or warrants on defendants were outstanding. Detainers/warrants and defendants' prior arrest records (*i.e.*, seriousness) together accounted for 19 percent of the explained variance. Charge-related variables alone (V) explained about the same amount of variance in custody outcomes as demographic variables did; that is, about 17 percent. Most of this (16 percent), however, was due to the influence of one independent variable, the seriousness of the criminal charge, in determining pretrial custody.

From this exercise, where a large number of independent variables have been reduced to five generic groupings, it is learned that only prior criminal processing, charge-related, and, to a lesser extent, demographic variables are likely to prove influential in dividing defendants into classes of releasees and detainees as a result of the bail decision process.

As a next step in the analysis of the determination of pretrial custody, all independent variables were entered in regression simultaneously in a free, stepwise manner. The objective in using this procedure was to be able to assess the collective contributions of all independent variables considered together. The results are presented in Table 8-4.

In terms of the total proportion of variance accounted for, the attempt to explain variance in custody outcomes was rather productive. Using forty-nine independent variables, 37 percent of the variance in pretrial status could be explained. Because inclusion of so many variables does not lend itself well to meaningful interpretation, only the first nine to enter were included in Table 8-4. These nine, however, still explained 35 percent of the variance, a reasonably large amount.

Once again, the seriousness of the criminal charge has entered first, and thus may be interpreted as indicating its preeminence among variables contributing to the explanation of variance in pretrial custody status. In this case, however, it can be seen that the contribution of the second variable, detainers/warrants outstanding, should be considered approximately equal. This may be concluded from the fact that the product moment correlations of these two variables with pretrial status are so similar in magnitude as to be indistinguishable.[9]

Somewhat surprisingly, only one prior-record indicator, the number of prior arrests, entered in the first nine steps shown in Table 8-4. One other charge-related variable (number of different kinds of offenses charged) and two other prior criminal processing variables (whether defendants were on probation, parole, or work release and whether defendants had other open cases pending) figured importantly in the regression solution.

Finally, three demographic variables made marginal but statistically significant contributions to the explanation of variance in pretrial custody: whether or not a motor vehicle was owned, race/ethnicity (nonwhite/white), and whether or not a defendant had a telephone. It is difficult to see how these variables might reasonably relate to the determination of pretrial status. It is possible that defendants without phones have greater difficulty arranging for their release. It is equally possible that defendants with cars have better release prospects because their autos represent assets and can serve, for example, as collateral. But it is much more difficult to explain a possible role for race/ethnicity in the determination of pretrial cus-

Table 8-4. Multiple Regression of Pretrial Custody on All Independent Variables (Nine Variables Entering First in a Free, Stepwise Solution) for Defendants Appearing at Preliminary Arraignment, Philadelphia: August to November, 1975

	Dependent Variable: Pretrial Custody[a] (Total = 7,564)				
Independent Variables	*r*	*Multi-ple R*	R^2	R^2 *Change*	*Squared Semipartial Correlation* [b]
Charge seriousness	-.39	.39	.15	.15	.05
Detainers/warrants	-.34	.50	.25	.10	.05
Number of prior arrests	-.32	.54	.29	.04	.01
On probation, parole, work release	-.30	.55	.30	.01	.01
Motor vehicle owned	.16	.56	.32	.02	.01
Open cases	-.25	.57	.33	.01	.01
Number of different kinds of offenses charged	-.28	.58	.34	.01	.01
Race/ethnicity (nonwhite/white)	.18	.59	.35	.01	.01
Has telephone	.12	.59	.35	$<.01$[a]	.01
(Abbreviated)		(Abbreviated)			

[a]Of forty-nine independent variables originally entered into the regression equation, results are meaningful only for the nine entering first. These are all statistically significant contributors at the .001 level. Addition of the remaining forty variables increased R^2 by only .02.

[b]Figuring squared semipartial correlations is tantamount to calculating the amount of explained variance added to a regression solution by a variable when it is entered last. This was done using only the top nine independent variables in the solution. If all forty-nine variables were to be used, additional shrinkage in these correlations might be expected.

tody—particularly after the effects of other variables have already been controlled.

Examination of the squared semipartial correlations (listed in the same table) supports the contention that clearly dominant defendant descriptors are not in evidence. The variance explaining ability of the two most influential contributors—charge seriousness and outstanding detainers/warrants—shrinks considerably when they are entered last in the regression solution and the redundant effects of the eight other independent variables are held constant. At the same time, more evidence of the coequal status of these two contributors is found: Both show squared semipartial correlations of .05. Although these coefficients appear relatively small, they stand out from the next largest coefficients (.01). Strictly speaking, however, the generally small semipartial correlations indicate a lack of defendant characteristics that are clearly dominant in the determination of pretrial status when controls are exercised.

In the event that interaction among defendant attributes might have been influential in the custody classification of defendants before trial, thirty-six first-order interaction vectors were computed and entered as a group in regression after the nine original principal independent variables. The objective was to learn whether any additional variance—that is, variance not already explained by the original nine variables—might be accounted for by an interaction or multiplicative effect among independent variables. The results indicate that little (first-order) interaction was at work in the determination of pretrial status, for the collective contribution of the thirty-six interaction vectors amounted to only 4 percent additional explained variance.[10]

DEVELOPING A DEFENDANT TYPOLOGY TO PREDICT PRETRIAL DETENTION

So far, the goals of the multivariate analysis presented in this chapter have involved explanation. More precisely, the principal analytic task until now has been to explain as much of the variance in pretrial custody outcomes as possible, using knowledge of various defendant characteristics in multiple regression. The logic and language of this approach, it was felt, lent themselves well to the announced aim of learning which among all defendant descriptors appeared to be "most influential" in determining the custody statuses of Philadelphia defendants. In this section, however, the task of understanding the "sorting mechanism" that determines the use of detention and release before trial is attacked from another perspective, that of *classification* (typology) and *prediction*. The issue of particular interest in this analysis might best be formulated by means of the following question: From knowledge of defendant descriptors, are *types* or *classes* of defendants discernible from which differential rates of detention might be predicted? To address this question, predictive attribute analysis (MacNaughton-Smith, 1963) will be employed.

Predictive Attribute Analysis: A Criterion-Based Classification Method

Predictive Attribute Analysis (PAA) is a divisive hierarchical classification technique (MacNaughton-Smith, 1963; Gottfredson, 1976) that subdivides a sample into attribute-defined classes that are internally homogeneous and externally heterogeneous on a given criterion or dependent variable. PAA lends itself well to predictive uses in that the groups or classes it produces will have differing probabilities of particular outcomes on the dependent variable, and—of great importance—it also has the ability to consider the joint effects of independent variables on the criterion, where they are evident.

In PAA, both the dependent variable (pretrial custody: detained/released) and the independent variables measuring defendant attributes are typically dichotomous.[11] Classes or types are created through the successive partitioning of cases on the independent variable most strongly associated with the criterion at each step. The entire sample is first divided into the two groups that comprise the dichotomous independent variable showing the strongest measure of association (in this case, *Somer's d*) with the dependent variable. Then measures of association are computed again for all remaining independent variables with the dependent variable for each of the two first-level divisions. Once the variables showing the strongest associations in each of the groups are selected, the two groups are partitioned into four groups—defined by subcategories of the variables selected on the second level. After several subdivisions, the final result is an upside-down tree diagram depicting a number of classes of defendants that vary on the dependent variable.

The reader may note a parallel between stepwise multiple regression and predictive attribute analysis. In effect, both methods exercise controls by holding the variables entered on a given step constant while selecting variables that will enter next. Both select newly entering variables on the basis of the strength of their relationships with the criterion after the effects of earlier entering variables are held constant. And, finally, both procedures suffer from the same tendency to capitalize on error associated with the statistics employed at each step.[12] Decisions concerning the inclusion of variables on the early steps in both procedures will greatly affect the selection of variables on the later steps.

To insure that the PAA solution will be as reliable as possible and produce classes that discriminate well between defendants in terms of their rates of pretrial detention, three arbitrary stopping rules were adopted.[13] The first mandates that the number of cases in any subgroup may not—as a result of a split—fall below 200. The second specifies that, for further partitioning to occur, the measure of association (*Somer's d*) between the independent variable and the criterion may not be less than ±.15. The third rule restricts the number of splits to five. Each of these stopping rules helps to promote solutions that are based on sufficient numbers of cases and deal with relationships that are substantial.

The criterion variable, originally dichotomous, was defined in preceding analyses as the custody status of defendants immediately after initial appearance or preliminary arraignment. Of course, the present analysis focuses on the percent detained or the rate of detention. The same independent variables used in regression analyses were employed in predictive attribute analysis. Those not naturally dichotomous were recoded to comply with that requirement.

PAA Results

Figure 8-1 presents the classification diagram resulting from the analysis. Note that each cell representing a subdivision contains a description of the variable of interest or attribute selected for partitioning on each step, the total number of defendants included in a particular subdivision, and the percentage of defendants in the subdivision who were detained.

Cell I at the top of the PAA dendrogram initiates the procedure by indicating that approximately 24 percent of all the Philadelphia defendants were detained twenty-four hours after first appearance when bail had been decided. On the first subdivision or step, the variable most strongly associated with pretrial custody was whether or not the defendant had detainers or warrants outstanding ($d = -.65$). Understandably, the percentage of defendants with warrants and/or detainers outstanding who were detained was very high, about 86 percent. In contrast, only 21 percent of those having no warrants or detainers were detained.

For the other subgroup of defendants derived from the first partitioning—defendants with *no* warrants or detainers (Cell III)—the attribute most highly associated with pretrial status was whether or not a defendant was on probation, parole, or work release at the time of preliminary arraignment ($d = -.38$). When partitioning on this attribute is carried out, it is seen that more than half (55 percent) of defendants who had *no* detainers/warrants but who *were* on probation, parole, or work release were detained (see Cell VII). But, considerably fewer of those who had *no* detainers/warrants and who were *not* on probation, parole, or work release were detained, only 17 percent (Cell VI).

Defendants who had no warrants or detainers outstanding *and* who were not on probation, parole, or work release could be further subdivided by the charge seriousness variable ($d = .27$). Slightly more than one-third (35 percent) of defendants with both of those attributes specified *and* charges of greater seriousness were detained after preliminary arraignment (Cell X), compared to a mere 8 percent of

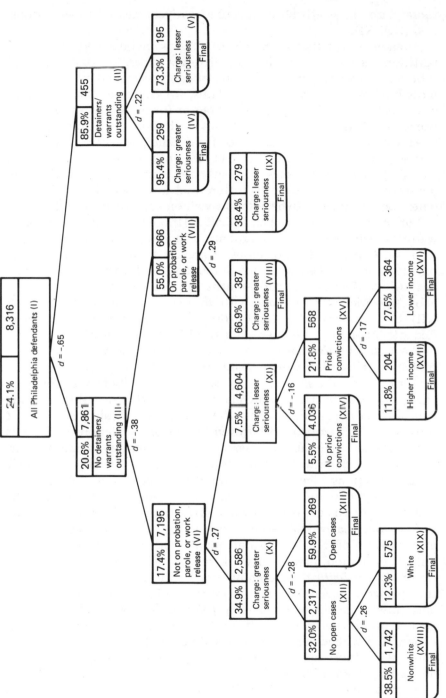

Figure 8-1. Predictive Attribute Analysis of Rate of Detention Among Philadelphia Defendants

those with those attributes specified *and* charges of lesser seriousness (Cell XI).

Already one of the advantages of PAA is encountered: Successive partitionings have shown that for different subgroups of defendants, different attributes may be most strongly associated with—that is, most predictive of—the criterion. Thus, for example, charge seriousness was the important partitioning factor for persons with detainers/warrants (Cells II, IV, and V[14]), but probationary, parole, or work release status was the crucial factor for defendants without detainers/warrants (Cells III, VI, and VII). Yet, for both of these subgroups (VI and VII), charge seriousness is clearly the attribute most highly predictive of pretrial status. This differential interplay of the effects of defendant attributes can be noted as well on subsequent partitionings.

For the defendants grouped in Cell X (those who had *no* detainers/warrants; who were *not* on probation, parole, or work release; *and* who were charged with offenses of greater seriousness) partitioning on the basis of whether or not defendants had open cases[15] occurs next ($d = -.28$). About three-tenths (32 percent) of those with the above specified attributes *and* with *no* open cases were detained (Cell XII); but, as many as six-tenths (60 percent) of those with the specified attributes *and with* open cases (Cell XIII) were detained.

For Cell XI defendants—those with no detainers/warrants; not on probation, parole, or work release; *and* charged with offenses of lesser seriousness—the most strongly associated attribute was not open cases, as it was for Cell X defendants, but whether or not defendants had prior criminal convictions ($d = -.16$). Specifically, very few of those with the specified attributes *and no* prior convictions (Cell XIV) were detained, only about 6 percent. A considerably greater proportion of defendants with the previously specified attributes *and with* prior convictions were detained, about 22 percent (Cell XV).

Further partitioning—the fifth and last permitted—can occur in the case of only two cells (Cells XV and XII), because the rule precluding subdivisions that would result in less than 200 cases was observed in all the rest. Cell XV isolates defendants with no detainers/warrants; not on probation, parole, or work release; with charges of lesser seriousness; *and with* prior criminal convictions. For these defendants, the strongest association ($d = .17$) is shown between the income variable (lower income/higher income) and pretrial status.[16] That is, a greater proportion (28 percent) of defendants with the above specifications and with lower incomes were detained (Cell XVI), than defendants with those specifications *and* comparatively higher incomes, about 12 percent (Cell XVII).

The last partition occurs in Cell XII, consisting of defendants with no detainers/warrants; not on probation, parole, or work release; with charges of greater seriousness; *and* with no open cases. For these defendants race/ethnicity (dichotomized as nonwhite/white) is most strongly associated with pretrial status (d = .26). (See Cells XVIII and XIX.) It is striking that of defendants with the above specified attributes *but* who were nonwhites, nearly four-tenths were detained (39 percent), while those with the same specified attributes *but* who were white, only 12 percent were detained.

Summary: Construction of a Defendant/ Detention Typology with PAA

With a handful of independent variables, the foregoing description of successive partitionings has demonstrated that classes of defendants characterized by widely varying rates of detention may be devolved. At the same time, it has been learned that some independent variables may figure importantly in the formation of certain subgroups of defendants but not in the formation of others. Table 8–5 arrays the final classes or types of defendants that were generated in the predictive attribute analysis, according to the magnitude of their measures on the criterion variable—that is, the proportion of defendants detained or the rate of detention.

Reviewing Table 8–5, it can first be remarked that the proportions detained in the ten final classes vary considerably from a low of 6 percent to a high of 95 percent. This suggests that the analysis has been rather successful in creating classes or types that discriminate well among defendants in terms of detention rates, based on the relationships of their attributes with the determination of pretrial custody. Examination of these classes, however, should be grounded in the knowledge that the base rate of detention for all defendants in the sample was about 24 percent. It can then be noted first that a rather large number of defendants (nearly half of the total) fell into the class showing the lowest rate of detention. Class 1 defendants may best be characterized as those with no prior involvement in the criminal process (no detainers/warrants; not on probation, parole, work release; no prior convictions) and with the least serious of criminal charges. The low rate of detention (6 percent) for these defendants is not surprising, since earlier regression analysis of the bail decision suggests that, given their attributes, it is probably Class 1 defendants who are most likely to have been released on ROR.

Class 2 and 3 defendants, however, also show relatively low rates of detention, given that 24 percent is the overall norm. Specifically, only 12 percent of defendants with no detainers/warrants; not on probation, parole, or work release; not seriously charged; with prior

Table 8–5. Defendant Classes Using Predictive Attribute Analysis, by Rates of Detention

		Percent Detained	*Total in Class*
Class 1 (Cell XIV)	No detainers-warrants/not on probation, parole, work release/ charge: lesser seriousness/no prior convictions	5.5	4,036
Class 2 (Cell XVII)	No detainers-warrants/not on probation, parole, work release/ charge: lesser seriousness/prior convictions/upper income	11.8	204
Class 3 (Cell XIX)	No detainers-warrants/not on probation, parole, work release/ charge: greater seriousness/no open cases/white	12.3	575
Class 4 (Cell XVI)	No detainers-warrants/not on probation, parole, work release/ charge: lesser seriousness/lower income	27.5	364
Class 5 (Cell IX)	No detainers—warrants/on probation, parole, work release/charge: lesser seriousness	38.4	279
Class 6 (Cell XVIII)	No detainers-warrants/not on probation, parole, work release/ charge: greater seriousness/no open cases/nonwhite	38.5	1,742
Class 7 (Cell XIII)	No detainers-warrants/not on probation, parole, work release/ charge: greater seriousness/open cases	59.9	269
Class 8 (Cell VIII)	No detainers-warrants/on probation, parole, work release/charge: greater seriousness	66.9	387
Class 9 (Cell V)	Detainers-warrants/charge: lesser seriouness	73.3	195
Class 10 (Cell IV)	Detainers-warrants/charge: greater seriousness	95.4	259
Total Philadelphia defendants		24.1	8,316

convictions and higher incomes (Class 2) were detained. Similarly, only 12 percent of defendants with no detainers/warrants; who were not on probation, parole, or work release; who were seriously charged; who had no open cases; but who were white (Class 3) were detained after preliminary arraignment.

The highest rates of detention were experienced by defendants in Classes 7 through 10. At the upper extreme, nearly all defendants (95 percent) with detainers/warrants and serious charges were detained (Class 10). Also, a majority of defendants (73 percent) with detainers/warrants but with charges of lesser seriousness were detained (Class 9). Being on probation, parole, or work release and being seriously charged appear to have been contributors to the high detention rate of defendants in Class 8 (67 percent), just as being seriously charged and having open cases appeared central to the high rate of detention in Class 7 (60 percent).

Overall, it can be said that the same variables that accounted for the major share of the variance in the regression analysis of pretrial status also figured dominantly in PAA. The more seriously charged a defendant is and the greater indications of prior or pending involvement with the criminal process, the greater the likelihood of pretrial detention. Absent again are any indicators, such as residence, family ties, or employment history, that could be linked to a community-ties explanation of the determination of pretrial custody.

For a sizeable number of defendants, however, demographic factors (race/ethnicity and income) *do* enter as significant, though comparatively secondary predictors. For example, among the sizeable number of defendants who had no detainers/warrants; who were not on probation, parole, or work release; who were seriously charged; and who had no open cases, nonwhites were detained at the rate of *39 percent* (Class 6), but whites were detained at the rate of *12 percent* (Class 3). In the second example, among defendants with no detainers/warrants; who were not on probation, parole, or work release; who were charged with crimes of lesser seriousness, and who had prior convictions, lower income defendants showed a substantially higher rate of detention (*28 percent*) than higher income defendants (*12 percent*). It is important to add that these partitions (based on income and race/ethnicity) involve approximately 35 percent of all Philadelphia defendants. *These last findings ought to be viewed with particular dismay, for they indicate that minority and lower income status are to some extent concommitants of high rates of detention.*

In sum, these results might be viewed as demonstrating that the determinants of detention or release are to some extent appropriate or understandable (*i.e.*, where the "unfinished business" syndrome indicated by detainers, warrants, probation, parole violations, open cases, etc., is concerned), to some extent questionable (when the charge seriousness indicator is seen to figure so importantly in the absence of an explicit rationale), and to a certain extent unacceptable and inappropriate (when it is learned that race/ethnicity and income are discriminators of detention rates).

To a certain extent, it is inevitable that minority and low-income defendants will be discriminated against in the use of pretrial detention as long as the determination of pretrial custody continues to be framed in terms of dollars for a large number of defendants. This is not a new or earth-shaking insight; more than two decades ago Professor Caleb Foote announced this "fact of life" concerning the American way of bail when he wrote that "the ultimate abolition of the bail system is the only solution for the prejudice to jail defendants which results from their low economic status." (Foote, 1954: 1073).

NOTES

1. Critics have long argued that unfettered discretion to set cash bail at any amount has allowed bail judges to engage in a sub rosa form of preventive detention.

2. Custody was recorded after an initial twenty-four hour period in order to avoid inaccuracies that might derive from slow paperwork or persons who secured release several hours after the bail decision. Although many defendants were released immediately (on ROR or cash bail they were able to post at first appearance), a considerable number with cash bail set gained release after a wait of several hours. To simplify the custody question, it was considered more meaningful to record release after an initial twenty-four-hour period so that delayed releases could be included.

3. This figure was obtained from interviews with officials at the Philadelphia Detention Center.

4. Because even small differences in percentages between groups would be statistically significant (but not very meaningful to discuss), tests of significance are not presented but differences of ten percentage points or more are considered substantial.

5. "Upper" income is used loosely in this context; it refers to defendants earning projected annual incomes of $7,500 or more. Approximately 8 percent of all defendants reported earnings between $7,500 and $9,999 annually, and another 8 percent earned $10,000 or more. In short, very few Philadelphia defendants (probably much less than 8 percent) were in an upper income category, in the ordinary sense of that adjective. Defendants referred to as upper were upper income only in comparison with the other defendants, most of whom reported exceedingly low incomes.

6. See Kerlinger and Pedhazur (1973) for the rationale for use of multiple regression with a dichotomous dependent variable as comparable to simple discriminant function analysis.

7. For descriptions of the statistics employed in multiple regression analysis, see the notes in Chapter 7.

8. Recall from the Chapter 7 analysis of bail decisions that employment history differs somewhat from the measure referred to as employment status. Employment status simply indicates whether a defendant was employed at the time of arrest or not. Employment history is a community-ties score derived from information obtained in the Pretrial Services interview before first appearance. Employment history adds to knowledge of employment status the length of employment or unemployment and assigns points on that basis (*i.e.*, ranging from 0 for long-term unemployed to 4 for long-term employed).

9. The order of entry of independent variables in the stepwise solution is determined on the first step by the relative size of the product moment correlations of independent variables with the dependent variable. Correlations are sample estimates, surrounded by margins of error; thus, when two correlations are so similar, it is entirely conceivable that in another sample the other important variable, detainers/warrants, would have entered first.

10. Because of the size of the table and the lack of meaningful interaction effects, the results are reported but not presented in tabular form.

11. If variables were not naturally dichotomous, they were converted by either choosing a natural cutting point or one based on knowledge of their distributions. The pretrial status variable was naturally dichotomous: detention (0), release (1).

12. In both analytic techniques variables are chosen for inclusion on a given step based on the magnitude of their respective coefficients (*i.e.*, Somer's *d* in PAA, Pearson's correlation in regression). Since the difference between variables showing coefficients of comparable magnitude may be due to the error associated with them as sample estimates, an analytic procedure that is based on choosing the largest estimate may be capitalizing on the error factor. In both procedures, estimates of explained variance will be biased upwards as the selection of variables on successive steps may capitalize on the margin of error associated with sample statistics.

13. See Gottfredson (1976:131).

14. Note that this partition—resulting in only 195 cases in one cell—constitutes a minor violation of the 200-case stopping rule.

15. Recall that the term "open cases" refers to the fact that a defendant held on a current charge—the one that qualified him or her for inclusion in the present sample—may have been on pretrial release for an earlier charge not yet adjudicated.

16. Income was dichotomized as upper ($7,500 or more annually) and lower (less than $7,500 annually). See Note 5 above.

Chapter 9

Pretrial Custody and Later Judicial Outcomes

In the rhetoric of bail reform and in studies of bail, it has often been claimed that whether or not a defendant is detained before trial greatly affects his or her chances at later judicial decisions, such as adjudication and sentencing. Since the first mention of differential case outcomes for detained and released defendants (Morse and Beattie, 1932), nearly every subsequent study has included findings showing that greater proportions of released defendants received favorable dispositions—with respect to dismissal, conviction/nonconviction, and sentencing—than detained defendants (Foote, 1954; Alexander et al., 1958; Ares et al., 1963; Attorney General's Committee on Poverty and Federal Criminal Justice, 1963; Rankin, 1964; Single, 1972; Brockett, 1973; Landes, 1974). Examination of these findings and interpretation of the relationship perceived have become a central issue in the study of bail and detention.

INTERPRETATIONS OF THE RELATIONSHIP AND THEIR IMPLICATIONS

Two principal hypotheses are offered to explain the differential case outcomes that typify the two classes of accused (see Figure 9-1). A first hypothesis contends that pretrial detention exerts a strong negative bias against the defendant's prospects at adjudication and sentencing (see Model 1, Figure 9-1). Proponents of this hypothesis explain the apparent negative influence of pretrial detention in different ways. Some suggest that the detained defendant is placed at a distinct disadvantage in terms of accessibility to counsel and preparation of his or her defense in general. In the same vein, it is argued that the association between detention and negative judicial dispositions can be explained by the fact that detained defendants are pressured by the stress of confinement to plead guilty and to submit to sentencing, whereas those on pretrial release are compelled by no such motivation and, consequently, may feel free to take their chances in court.[1] Other supporters of the first hypothesis have maintained that the court's perceptions of a defendant's worthiness may be adversely affected by the spectacle of the defendant arriving as a prisoner in custody rather than as a free person arriving under his or her own volition.[2] It has also been implied that the mere knowledge of whether a defendant was in jail or on pretrial release will bias a judge's and/or jury's attitude toward the case under consideration (Koza and Doob, 1975).

In sharp contrast, a second hypothesis characterizes the perceived relationship between pretrial custody and later judicial dispositions as essentially spurious (see Model 2, Figure 9-1). While it would appear that pretrial detention "causes" more negative outcomes for defendants (all other factors being equal), the relationship can be explained in quite another fashion: Both pretrial custody and case dispositions may be strongly related to a common antecedent variable (or variables). The factors weighed in the bail decision and influential in determining pretrial status also serve as the basis for adjudicatory and sentencing decisions. This interpretation of the relationship has been summarized by its principal proponent in the following manner:

> At the initial stages of the criminal proceedings, judges are setting bond, in part, according to forecasts of the defendant's sentence. Thus, defendants likely to receive major penalties because they are accused of severe offenses or have lengthy prior records will have relatively high bonds and tend to be detained. In contrast, offenders likely to receive minor sentences if convicted will have relatively low bonds and tend to be released. . . . In these circumstances the determination of bond becomes the vehicle for effecting punishment because if the accused is released at this time, punishment becomes a remote possibility (Landes, 1974:333).

Because of methodological difficulties that seem to characterize the only studies to date to have focused specially on the perceived relationship between pretrial custody and later outcomes (Rankin, 1964; Single, 1972; Landes, 1974), no verdict may yet be reached concerning the nature of that relationship. (For a detailed methodological critique of the studies, see Goldkamp, 1977.) More specifically, two studies purported to present evidence supporting the causal

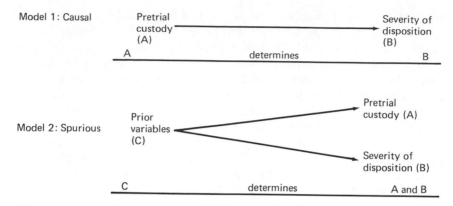

Figure 9-1. Models Explaining the Relationship Between Pretrial Custody and Disposition

interpretation (Model 1): Both Rankin (1964) and Single (1972) interpreted their respective findings as providing a strong case for the supposition that defendants who were detained were being deprived of "equal justice" by the fact of their detention, and were, as a result, likely to be found guilty and to receive severe sentences more often than released defendants. However, both studies suffered from important sampling biases and did not exercise sufficient controls. The methodological difficulties encountered in the studies (Rankin, 1964; Single, 1972) were substantive enough to render the strength of the conclusions drawn uncertain at best.

Landes (1974) carried out a more elaborate analysis of the pretrial custody/case outcomes relationship and claims to have demonstrated support for the spuriousness hypothesis (Model 2)—which states that final case outcomes and pretrial custody are related only because they are parallel decisions transacted from the same sources of information (*i.e.*, they share a common correlation with antecedent variables). However, Landes relied on the Single data base and—from the outset— his study suffered from the same injurious sampling restrictions as the Single study (*i.e.*, chiefly, that only cases from the Legal Aid Society files were employed). Use of the Single data base together with other methodological issues (pertaining to the exercise of controls) combine to qualify considerably the conclusions drawn by Landes.

Of research to date, it can be said that two studies favor the causal hypothesis and one favors the spuriousness explanation of the relationship between pretrial custody and later judicial outcomes, but all three studies, to varying degrees, suffer from methodological difficulties that could radically undermine their conclusions. Finding support for one hypothesis or the other is an undertaking of great importance, for if the first (Model 1) were true, for example, defendants who are detained before trial would not have access to the same kind of justice as defendants who are able to secure pretrial release. Not only would this development raise constitutional questions concerning equal protection and due process, but it would also dramatically underscore the implications of the bail decision that determines who is to be released and detained before adjudication.

If, on the other hand, support for the spuriousness hypothesis (Model 2) were found, different but equally important implications must be confronted. Specifically, support for the spuriousness hypothesis would suggest that pretrial custody is related to later judicial outcomes (*e.g.*, guilty/acquitted, severe/nonsevere sentences) because the different judicial decisions operate on the basis of the same information and similar concerns. This might imply, for one, that the bail decision (which so heavily influences whether or not a defendant will secure pretrial release) involves preliminary assessments of guilt and punishment, inappropriately, at a stage that occurs long before adjudication and sentencing. If this were the case, it would be necessary to question the propriety of such pretrial decisionmaking.

THE PHILADELPHIA DATA

The Philadelphia data was collected in such a way as to avoid the sampling biases that characterized previous studies. That is, the sample was drawn at a point early enough in criminal processing to include the cases of all defendants for whom bail decisionmaking and later judicial decisions were relevant concerns. Thus, for example, the Philadelphia data dealt with all defendants entering the process during a specified period (August 1 through November 2, 1975), rather than just those released on cash bail, or on ROR, or just those represented by Legal Aid. Data concerning final case outcomes were obtained during March of 1977 to allow a sufficient period of time for the cases of the defendants in the sample to reach their conclusions in the Court of Common Pleas and Municipal Court of Philadelphia.

In addition to utilizing a more representative sample than has previously been available, a second aim in this chapter is to clarify analysis of the relationship by subdividing the final resolution of defendants' cases into two components: final adjudication and sentencing. In this fashion, it is possible to specify the applicability of the relationship to particular stages of the criminal process, rather than treating final outcomes of cases undynamically, as an indistinguishable mix of dissimilar dispositions.

ADJUDICATION AND PRETRIAL CUSTODY

For the purposes of the present analysis, adjudicatory dispositions have been defined as four possible case outcomes:

1. A defendant may have had all charges *dropped*, or dismissed; or his or her case may have been discharged.[3]
2. A defendant may have been cleared of all charges through *acquittal*.[4]
3. A defendant may have received a *diversion* disposition, resembling probation, except that conviction is not required and, in fact, in most cases is avoided.
4. A defendant may have been *convicted* of one or more charges.[5]

The final adjudication of the cases of defendants in the Philadelphia cohort are shown in Table 9–1. Fully one-third (34 percent) of the Philadelphia defendants had all charges dropped, dismissed, or otherwise discharged. In addition, nearly one-tenth (9 percent) of the defendants were acquitted of all charges. Together, dismissals and acquittals account for more than four-tenths of the final dispositions of the cases of defendants in the Philadelphia sample. Another three-tenths (31 percent) overall were neither acquitted nor dismissed nor convicted of any crime; instead, they were granted pretrial diversion dispositions that had the effect of placing them in a preconviction "probationary" status. Finally, only about 26 percent of all defendants were convicted of one or more criminal charges.

Table 9–1 presents the relationship between adjudicatory dispositions and pretrial custody, using three categories of custody status: released by twenty-four hours, released sometime after twenty-four hours but before final disposition, and detained until adjudication. It is first apparent that dismissals varied little by custody status; defendants who were released immediately, who were released subsequently, or who were detained throughout the preadjudicatory period had their cases dropped, discharged, or dismissed at roughly the same rate (from 33 to 36 percent). The rates of acquittal for Philadelphia defendants also varied only slightly across custody statuses (from 8 percent of those released immediately to 14 percent of those released subsequently to 11 percent of those detained throughout). However, substantial differences among custody statuses can be noted when the use of pretrial diversion is considered: Thirty-nine percent of those released immediately were granted diversion, but only 12 percent of those released subsequently and 2 percent of those never released were able to dispose of their cases in that fashion. Finally,

Table 9-1. Estimated Number of Defendants Appearing at Preliminary Arraignment, by Final Case Disposition, by Pretrial Custody, Philadelphia: August to November, 1975

| | Total[a] | | Final Dispositions | | | | | | | |
| | | | Dropped/Dismissed | | Acquitted | | Diverted | | Convicted | |
	Num-ber	Per-cent	Num-ber	Per-cent	Num-ber	Per-cent	Num-ber	Per-cent	Num-ber	Per-cent
All Philadelphia defendants	8,171	100.0	2,776	34.0	724	8.9	2,533	31.0	2,138	26.2
Pretrial custody										
Released within twenty-four hours	6,216	100.0	2,108	33.9	484	7.8	2,400	38.6	1,224	19.7
Released after twenty-four hours but before final disposition	995	100.0	353	35.5	138	13.9	116	11.7	388	39.0
Detained until final disposition	960	100.0	315	32.8	102	10.6	17	1.8	526	54.8

[a]Subcategories may not sum to total due to rounding.

remarkable differences in the conviction rates of Philadelphia defendants were found when custody statuses were compared: Fifty-five
percent of defendants detained throughout the pretrial period were
convicted, compared to only 40 percent of those released part-way
through the pretrial period and *only 20 percent of those who gained
immediate pretrial release.* (It is worth noting one more finding: as
many as four-tenths of the defendants who were *detained* in Philadelphia later had all charges dropped or received acquittals.)

Multivariate Analysis of the Relationship
Between Custody and Adjudication:
Adjudication as a Trifurcated Process

As a result of the foregoing analysis of the relationship between
pretrial custody and adjudicatory outcomes in Philadelphia, a major
qualification of the meaning of that relationship needs to be made:
Although pretrial custody *does* appear to be strongly associated with
rates of conviction and diversion, it has *no* apparent bearing on the
final dispositions of the cases of more than four-tenths of all defendants (those receiving dismissals or acquittals). And, even though the
relationship in question does appear to be relevant in the remaining
cases, no judgments concerning the appropriateness of the "causal"
or "spurious" hypotheses postulated in Figure 9-1, of course, may
be ventured without a more elaborate multivariate analysis.

To facilitate such an analysis, the adjudication of the cases of Philadelphia defendants may be constructively viewed with the aid of a
three-step model.[6] (See Figure 9-2.) The principal advantage derived
from use of a contingent, trifurcated model is that it permits step-by-
step analysis of the relationship between pretrial custody and adjudicatory alternatives—based on the appropriate numbers of defendants.
Thus, for example, defendants whose charges were dropped are not
considered when the task is to assess the relationship as it pertains to
acquittal/conviction; only the relevant cases are considered.

To illustrate briefly, the decision process that results in the adjudication of defendants' cases may be viewed as trifurcated in the following fashion:

- *Step One:* For any number of reasons, cases may be dismissed or
  discharged or charges may be dropped at a point early in processing. Thus, the first decision stage consists of sorting defendants
  into those whose charges are dismissed and those whose cases will
  continue to be processed. As indicated in Figure 9-2, the final disposition in approximately one-third of all Philadelphia cases was
  dismissal, dropped charges, or discharges.

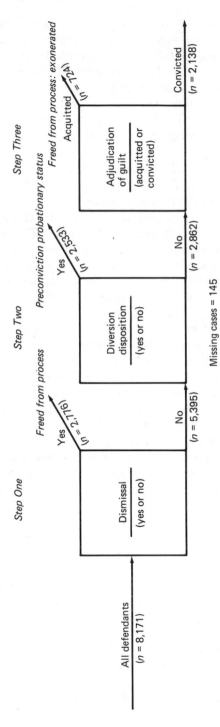

Figure 9–2.   The Adjudication of Defendants' Cases Viewed as a Trifurcated Decision Process

- *Step Two:* For 5,395 of the original 8,316 defendants, it was de-termined (on Step One) that charges were not to be dismissed. The decision on Step Two facing these "survivor" defendants is whether or not their cases may be resolved short of formal adjudication of guilt or innocence—through some program of diversion. Nearly half (47 percent) of Step Two defendants were granted diversion dispo-sitions.
- *Step Three:* Only 35 percent of the original cohort of Philadelphia defendants reached a third adjudicatory stage. The 2,862 defen-dants surviving to Step Three did not have their charges dropped on Step One and were not granted diversion on Step Two. For Step Three defendants, final adjudication could be framed only in terms of guilt or innocence. Only 25 percent were acquitted; as shown in Figure 9-2, 75 percent were convicted of one or more criminal charges.

By employing a trifurcated conceptualization of the adjudication of criminal cases, it is possible to evaluate the relationship between pretrial custody and outcomes at each decision stage. In the analyses that follow, once the existence of such a relationship has been estab-lished, the task will be to assess its robustness after appropriate con-trols are exercised. The relationship between pretrial custody and adjudication may be interpreted as spurious if, after the effects of control variables are discounted, knowledge of pretrial custody is not able to explain a meaningful amount of variance in the final outcomes of interest.

The Effect of Custody on Dismissal:
Step One
According to the analytic model posited in Figure 9-2, as a first step all defendants are separated into those whose cases can be dropped entirely—about one-third of all defendants—and those who must continue further with criminal processing. Table 9-1 revealed es-sentially no variation among custody groups in terms of dismissal or drop rates. Multivariate analysis (not presented here) was conducted as a cautionary measure and served only to confirm the earlier finding.

About 65 percent of the original sample of defendants were not freed from criminal processing on Step One through dismissals or dropped charges. However, nearly half (47 percent) of these 5,395 defendants were still able to have their cases disposed of through less formal means than adjudication of guilt or innocence—that is, through some form of pretrial diversion.

The Effect of Custody on Diversion:
Step Two

Contrary to the findings pertaining to dismissals and custody, where no relationship was found, there appears to be a pronounced relationship between custody and diversion outcomes. Nearly six-tenths (58 percent) of all defendants on Step Two who received immediate pretrial release had their cases disposed of through diversion. Only two-tenths of defendants who were detained for some interval prior to final disposition and only three percent of those detained for the duration were diverted.

For use in regression analysis, the subcategories of the pretrial custody measure employed in Table 9-1 were dummy-coded and two vectors produced. These vectors measure pretrial custody as release versus detention after twenty-four hours (Pretrial custody 1) and release versus detention throughout the pretrial period (Pretrial custody 2). (Together they incorporated more information than either when used separately.) The product moment correlations for these two detention measures with diversion (not diverted/diverted) are shown at the top of Table 9-2.[7] Both exhibit moderately strong relationships with diversion: release versus detention after twenty-four hours ($r = -.41$); release versus detention until final disposition ($r = -.33$).

Six control variables were chosen from among the principal contributors to the explanation of variance in the multivariate analysis of custody outcomes presented in Chapter 8. Logically, these were variables that were appropriately related to both pretrial custody and later outcomes—as posited in Model 2. They included charge seriousness, the existence of detainers/warrants; the number of prior arrests; probationary, parole, or work release status; the existence of open cases, and the number of different offenses originally charged. Their correlations with the granting of diversion—ranging from moderate to moderately strong—are displayed in Table 9-2. The seriousness of the criminal charge ($r = -.43$) and the number of prior arrests ($r = -.41$) showed the strongest relationships with diversion. The less serious the charge or the smaller the number of prior arrests, the greater the chances of diversion.

Multiple regression was employed as an effective means of controlling for the common correlations of these six initial control candidates. The strategy involved entering these variables on a first step in the regression of diversion (not diverted/diverted). Then, by entering the two dummied custody vectors on a second and last step, it would be possible to ascertain whether knowledge of pretrial custody in itself could still contribute meaningfully to the explanation of variance in diversion outcomes. (This amounts to calculating the squared semi-

Table 9–2. Product Moment Correlations between Pretrial Custody Vectors and Six Control Variables[a] with Diversion for Philadelphia Defendants with Step Two Dispositions

Dependent Variable: Diversion Outcomes (Not Diverted/Diverted)		
	Pearson's r	*Number*
Pretrial custody 1 (immediate release/detained after twenty-four hours)	–.41	(5,395)
Pretrial custody 2 (released before final disposition/detained until final disposition)	–.33	(5,395)
Control variables		
Charge seriousness	–.43	(5,389)
Detainers/warrants	–.20	(5,395)
Number of prior arrests	–.41	(5,395)
On probation, parole, work release	–.24	(5,395)
Open cases	–.24	(5,395)
Number of different offenses charged	–.30	(5,337)

[a]Control variables were selected from among the most significant contributors in the multiple regression of pretrial custody on independent variables presented in Appendix C.

partial correlation for custody with diversion.) If after the effects of the six control variables are held constant, custody adds little to the overall R^2, then the relationship between pretrial custody and diversion may be fairly characterized as spurious.

The results of this exercise are presented in Table 9–3. First, it can be seen that the six control variables entered on the first step in the regression solution were able to account for approximately 32 percent of the variance in the diversion variable—the largest contributions being made by charge seriousness and number of prior arrests. Holding the effects of these variables constant, pretrial custody vectors are entered on a second step. Knowledge of pretrial custody increases the R^2 by an inconsequential amount, only about 1 percent. This suggests that when appropriate controls are exercised simultaneously, the perceived relationship between custody and diversion outcomes is stripped of its explanatory power. Pretrial custody apparently wields no unique effect on the diversion decision as it pertains to Philadelphia defendants reaching that stage in the criminal process (Step Two in the trifurcated adjudication model). Because of its inability to survive the exercise of controls, one may reasonably con-

Table 9-3. Testing the Relationship Between Pretrial Custody and Diversion Outcomes: Multiple Regression of Diversion Outcomes on Six Control Variables (Entered on First Step) and Vectors Representing Pretrial Custody (Entered on Last Step) for Philadelphia Defendants with Step Two Dispositions

Dependent Variable: Diversion Outcomes (Not Diverted/Diverted)
(Total = 5,337)

Independent Variables	r	Beta	Multiple R	R^2	R^2 Change [b]
Entering first: control variables					
Charge seriousness	-.42	-.25	.42	.18	.18
Detainer/warrants	-.20	-.01	.45	.20	.02 (N.S.)
Number of prior arrests	-.42	-.27	.55	.30	.10
On probation, parole, work release	-.24	-.02	.55	.30	<.01
Open cases	-.24	-.08	.56	.31	.01
Number of different offenses charged	-.30	-.11	.57	.32	.01
Entering second: custody vectors [a]					
Pretrial custody 1	.40	.13	.58	.33	.01
Pretrial custody 2	.32	.00	.58	.33	<.01 (N.S.)

[a]Squared semipartial correlation (pretrial custody with diversion outcomes) = .01.

[b]All contributions were significant at the .001 level, unless indicated by N.S.

clude that the relationship between pretrial custody and diversion is generally spurious, explained by the common correlations of custody and diversion to antecedent variables—such as charge seriousness and prior arrests—rather than by some direct impact on diversion decisions deriving from the defendant's pretrial custody status.

The Effect of Custody on the Adjudication of Guilt or Innocence: Step Three

Of the more than an estimated 8,300 defendants who originally appeared for preliminary arraignment between August and November, 1975, only 34 percent were ever formally adjudicated. Of the 2,862 defendants who survived in criminal processing to the last adjudicatory decision stage, approximately 25 percent were acquitted and 75 percent were convicted of some charge. Table 9-1 suggested a rather weak relationship between pretrial custody and the adjudication of guilt or innocence. It may be generally observed that, regardless of custody status, the vast majority of defendants whose cases are formally adjudicated on Step Three find themselves convicted. Almost no difference exists between the proportions of defendants who

Table 9-4. Product Moment Correlations between Pretrial Custody Vectors and Six Control Variables[a] with Subsequent Adjudication for Philadelphia Defendants with Step Three Dispositions

Dependent Variable: Adjudication (Acquitted/Convicted)		
	Pearson's r[b]	*Number*
Pretrial custody 1 (released within 24 hours/ detained after 24 hours)	.08	(2,862)
Pretrial custody 2 (released before final disposition/ detained until final disposition)	.11	(2,862)
Control variables		
Charge seriousness	.04 N.S.	(2,858)
Detainers/warrants	.02 N.S.	(2,862)
Number of prior arrests	−.04 N.S.	(2,862)
On probation, parole, work release	.00 N.S.	(2,862)
Open cases	.03 N.S.	(2,862)
Number of different offenses charged	.04 N.S.	(2,862)

[a]Control variables were selected from among the most significant contributors in the multiple regression of pretrial custody on independent variables presented in Appendix C.
[b]Nonsignificance is indicated by N.S.

gained immediate release and those who were released sometime prior to final disposition. But, a noticeably larger proportion of defendants detained until formal adjudication (84 percent) than short-term detainees or defendants gaining immediate release (74 and 72 percent, respectively) were found guilty.

When considered in terms of product moment correlations, pretrial custody vectors show rather weak correlations with formal adjudication (acquittal versus guilt): for Pretrial custody 1, $r = .08$; for Pretrial custody 2, $r = .11$. (See Table 9-4.) Moreover, the control variables demonstrate relative independence from adjudication outcomes: None of the correlations were statistically significant at the specified level (*i.e.*, $p < .001$). Although the reported correlations were not large enough to warrant the conclusion that pretrial custody was related to adjudication of guilt or innocence, the same controlling procedure carried out for the Step Two analysis was carried out for Step Three. The results (presented in Table 9-5) were that together pretrial custody vectors explained about one percent of the variance in adjudication outcomes–an inconsequential amount–both before and after controls.

Table 9-5. Testing the Relationship Between Pretrial Custody and Adjudication: Multiple Regression of Formal Adjudication on Six Control Variables (Entered on First Step) and Vectors Representing Pretrial Custody (Entered on Last Step) for Philadelphia Defendants with Step Three Dispositions

Dependent Variable: Adjudication (Acquitted/Convicted)
(Total = 2,807)

Independent Variables	r	Beta	Multiple R	R^2	R^2 Change
Entering first: control variables					
Charge seriousness	.04	.00	.04	.00	.00
Detainer/warrants	.02	-.01	.05	.00	<.01
Number of prior arrests	-.04	-.07	.06	.00	<.01
On probation, parole, work release	-.00	-.01	.06	.00	<.01
Open cases	.03	-.04	.07	.00	<.01
Number of different offenses charged	.04	-.00	.07	.01	<.01
Entering second: custody vectors[a]					
Pretrial custody 1	.08	.04	.11	.01	<.01
Pretrial custody 2	.11	.11	.14	.02	<.01

[a]Squared semipartial correlation (pretrial custody with adjudication) = .01

Summary: The Effects of Pretrial Custody on Adjudication

In the foregoing analysis, an attempt was made to explore the possible relationship between custody and adjudication by employing a trifurcated analytic model to help specify its applicability. When all defendants were considered in terms of dismissal or nondismissal of all charges (on Step One), the rate of dismissals appeared to be unaffected by pretrial custody status. When nondismissed defendants were examined on a diverted/nondiverted dimension (Step Two), a moderately strong bivariate relationship with pretrial custody was found. But when six control variables were entered first in multiple regression, pretrial custody was stripped entirely of its ability to affect or explain variance in diversion decision outcomes. It was concluded from this that the relationship was spurious, explained by the common correlation of both custody and diversion to such variables as charge seriousness and prior arrests. Finally, a weak relationship of little consequence was found between pretrial custody and findings of guilt or innocence for defendants who had not been dismissed or diverted. It was concluded that pretrial custody had no noticeable effect on a defendant's prospective innocence or guilt.

PRETRIAL CUSTODY AND THE SENTENCING OF PHILADELPHIA DEFENDANTS

The sentencing decision is examined separately because of its special role in the criminal process. At sentencing guilt is assumed and the judicial function shifts to the assignment of an appropriate penalty. In addition, factors considered by judges at sentencing are not, as a rule, as restricted as those influential at adjudication. Sentencing decisions may involve a considerable amount of judicial discretion and may be governed to a large extent by the personal philosophy of the sentencing judge.

Sentencing and Pretrial Custody: Overview

For the relatively few defendants who reached the sentencing stage—only about 26 percent of the original cohort—a variety of sanctions were employed by Philadelphia sentencing judges. Table 9–6 shows, for example, that about one-tenth (11 percent) of the convicted defendants either had sentences suspended or were required only to pay fines or court costs or to make restitution.[8] By far the majority of sentenced defendants—about six-tenths (60 percent)— were placed on probation for varying periods.[9] The remaining three-tenths of the convicted defendants were sentenced to incarceration for varying lengths of time: a small proportion (6 percent) for minimum periods of less than one year, about 17 percent for minimum terms of one year, and about 6 percent for minimum terms of two years or more.

A rather pronounced relationship between defendants' pretrial statuses and their sentences is revealed in Table 9–6. For example, when contrasting custody groups of defendants in terms of incarcerative or nonincarcerative sanctions received at sentencing, it is apparent that nearly nine-tenths of those who were released within twenty-four hours received nonincarcerative terms. Slightly more than seven-tenths (72 percent) of defendants who were detained more than twenty-four hours but who gained release prior to final disposition of their cases received nonincarcerative sanctions. But, only about one-fourth (26 percent) of the defendants who were detained until conviction were not sentenced to terms of incarceration. Noticeably smaller proportions of the detained defendants (in either detention group) received suspended sentences or were required to pay costs or fines or to make restitution than those who had secured immediate release. Substantially greater proportions of both the immediate releasees and the short-term detainees were sentenced to probation than the long-term detainees. At the same time, noticeably larger propor-

Table 9-6. Estimated Number of Defendants Appearing at Preliminary Arraignment, by Sentences, by Pretrial Custody, Philadelphia: August to November, 1975

							Sentencing Outcomes					
	Total[a]		Cost, Fines Restitution, or Suspended Sentence		Probation		Incarceration: Less Than One Year		Incarceration: One Year		Incarceration: Two or More Years	
Pretrial Custody	Num-ber	Per-cent	Num-ber	Per-cent	Num-ber	Per-cent	Num-ber	Per-cent	Num-ber	Per-cent	Num-ber	Per-cent
All convicted Philadelphia defendants	2,135	100.0	228	10.7	1,284	60.1	119	5.6	371	17.4	133	6.2
Released within twenty-four hours	1,224	100.0	184	15.0	912	74.5	48	3.9	68	5.6	12	1.0
Released after twenty-four hours and before final disposition	388	100.0	23	5.9	258	66.5	17	4.4	73	18.8	17	4.4
Detained until final disposition	523	100.0	21	4.0	144	21.8	54	10.3	230	44.0	104	19.9

[a]Subcategories may not sum to total due to rounding.

tions of convicted defendants who had been detained until final disposition were sentenced to terms of incarceration of one year or
longer.

Multivariate Analysis of the Relationship Between Custody and Sentencing: Sentencing as a Bifurcated Process

Following the procedure employed for adjudication, it will be of
heuristic value in the analysis of the relationship between custody and
sentencing to employ an analytic model that subdivides sentencing
into two contingent decision components[10] (see Figure 9-3):

- *Step One:* On the first decision step, the sentencing question is
  whether defendants should be incarcerated or sentenced under a
  variety of possible nonincarcerative sanctions. Of all the defendants
  in the original sample cohort that were convicted, approximately
  seven-tenths (71 percent) were sentenced to probation or one of
  the other options not requiring incarceration. Only a relatively
  small proportion—three-tenths of those convicted—were sentenced
  to incarceration.
- *Step Two:* Very few defendants—three-tenths of those convicted—
  were sentenced to terms of incarceration. On their second decision step, the sentencing task involves specifying the length of
  incarceration. Nearly two-tenths (19 percent) of those sentenced
  to incarceration received terms of less than one year; approxi-

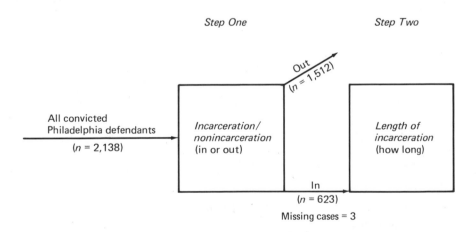

Figure 9-3. Sentencing of Philadelphia Defendants Viewed as a Bifurcated Decision Process

mately six-tenths (59 percent) received sentences with one year minimums; and the remaining two-tenths were given sentences with minimum terms of two years or more.

Using this conceptualization of the sentencing decision, it will be possible to assess the "effects of detention" on the in-or-out and the length of incarceration decision components separately. In the analyses that follow, the strength of the relationship between pretrial custody and sentencing will be described and then tested for spuriousness by exercising appropriate controls. Once again, the task will be to establish whether, after controlling for the effects of variables commonly correlated with both pretrial custody and sentencing, knowledge of pretrial custody still contributes meaningfully to the explanation of variance in sentencing outcomes.

The In-or-Out Sentencing Decision

As can be seen in Table 9-7, of all convicted defendants who submitted to sentencing, only about three-tenths were sentenced to terms of incarceration: Fully seven-tenths (71 percent) received less severe, nonincarcerative sentences. As noted above, pretrial custody appears to have been strongly related to the in-or-out decision—at least at the bivariate level: Nearly all (90 percent) of the Step One defendants who were released immediately after preliminary arraignment were

Table 9-7. Step One Sentencing Outcomes for Convicted Philadelphia Defendants: The Relationship Between Pretrial Custody and Nonincarceration/ Incarceration

Pretrial Custody	Total[a]		Nonincarceration Sentences		Incarceration Sentences	
	Number	Percent	Number	Percent	Number	Percent
All convicted Philadelphia defendants	2,135	100.0	1,512	70.8	623	29.2
Released within twenty-four hours	1,224	100.0	1,096	89.5	128	10.5
Released after twenty-four hours and before final disposition	388	100.0	281	72.4	107	27.6
Detained until final disposition	523	100.0	135	25.8	388	74.2

[a]Subcategories may not sum to total due to rounding.

not sentenced to incarceration, compared to about seven-tenths (72 percent) of those temporarily detained and only 26 percent of those detained through final disposition. This relationship translates into moderately strong product moment correlations (shown in Table 9–8): Pretrial custody 1 with nonincarceration/incarceration, $r = .48$; Pretrial custody 2 with nonincarceration/incarceration, $r = .56$.

As a first attempt to test for the possible spuriousness of the relatively strong relationship between custody status and the in-or-out sentencing decision, the six variables selected for use in the analysis of adjudication were again entered as controls. These variables were originally selected because they were among the most highly correlated with the determination of pretrial custody and/or were among the principal contributors to the explanation of variance in the multivariate analysis of custody status. In Table 9–8 each demonstrates a moderate correlation with the out/in sentencing determination—with the exception of the open cases indicator, which showed a relatively weak product moment correlation.

The strategy employed for assessing the possible spuriousness of the custody out/in relationship is the same as used in earlier analyses. The control variables are entered together on a first step in multiple

Table 9–8. Product Moment Correlations Between Pretrial Custody Vectors and Six Control Variables[a] With Nonincarceration/Incarceration Sentencing for Convicted Philadelphia Defendants

Dependent Variable: Nonincarceration/Incarceration		
	Pearson's r[b]	*Number*
Pretrial custody 1 (released within twenty-four hours/ detained after twenty-four hours)	.48	(2,135)
Pretrial custody 2 (released before final disposition/ detained until final disposition)	.56	(2,135)
Control variables		
Charge seriousness	.33	(2,132)
Detainers/warrants	.22	(2,091)
Number of prior arrests	.29	(2,135)
On probation, parole, work release	.23	(2,135)
Open cases	.12	(2,135)
Number of different offenses charged	.23	(2,135)

[a]Control variables were selected from among the most significant contributors in the multiple regression of pretrial custody on independent variables presented in Appendix C.

[b]All correlations were significant at the .001 level.

regression and the vectors representing pretrial custody are entered together on the last step. If the relationship is not wholly spurious—a product of the common correlation of the control variables with pretrial custody and the in-or-out determination—the pretrial custody vectors will contribute a meaningful amount to the explanation of variance after the effects of the controls are taken into account.

The results displayed in Table 9-9 suggest that the relationship between pretrial custody and the nonincarceration/incarceration decision outcomes is *not* wholly spurious. When the control variables are entered on the first step, an R^2 of .24 is produced—indicating that these variables explain a moderate amount of variance in the out/in determinations. If pretrial custody vectors had been entered first, alone, over 30 percent of the variance in the out/in criterion variable would have been explained. When these vectors are in fact entered last—after the six control variables—the custody vectors are still able to raise the R^2 from .24 to .38, an increment of .14 in explained variance. In short, although the strength of the relationship between custody and the dependent variable is diminished—by about half of the power it displayed when considered alone—a substantial relationship survives.

Table 9-9. Testing the Relationship Between Pretrial Custody and Sentencing: Multiple Regression of Nonincarceration/Incarceration on Six Control Variables (Entered on First Step) and Vectors Representing Pretrial Custody (Entered on Last Step) for Convicted Philadelphia Defendants

Dependent Variable: Nonincarceration/Incarceration (Total = 2,091)				
Independent Variables	*r*	*Multi-ple R*	R^2	R^2 *Change*[b]
Entering first: control variables				
Charge seriousness	.32	.32	.10	.10
Number of different offenses charged	.22	.34	.11	.01
Number of prior arrests	.30	.46	.21	.10
Detainers/warrants	.23	.48	.23	.02
Open cases	.12	.48	.23	<.01 (N.S.)
On probation, parole, work release	.23	.49	.24	.01 (N.S.)
Entering second: custody vectors[a]				
Pretrial custody 2	.56	.61	.38	.14
Pretrial custody 1	.47	.62	.38	<.01 (N.S.)

[a]Squared semipartial correlation (pretrial custody with nonincarceration/incarceration) = .14.

[b]All contributions are significant at .001, unless indicated by N.S.

In a further attempt to exercise controls (not presented here) several other variables were chosen from among those originally found to be influential in the determination of pretrial custody. (See Chapter 8.) These included, in a second regression analysis, an additional arrest indicator (seriousness of prior arrests) and two indicators of prior convictions (number and seriousness of prior convictions). The results were identical in impact to those (concerning the increment in R^2) in Table 9-9.

Although in this analysis one has not been able to dismiss the relationship between pretrial custody and outcomes on the first sentencing decision component as wholly spurious, it is not reasonable to conclude, therefore, that pretrial detention definitely biases the chances of convicted defendants regarding prospects for incarceration versus other sentencing alternatives. For one may be as justified in concluding that the proper controls may not have been exercised—that is, that variables influential both in pretrial custody and in out/in sentencing determinations still might explain the perceived relationship. Conceivably, these would be variables that were not recorded or properly measured in the present study.[11] Nevertheless, it is concluded that, although the relationship in question was noticeably diminished once controls were exercised, *this analysis has been unable to "write off" the entire relationship as wholly an artifact of spuriousness.* The contention that pretrial detention "causes" a greater likelihood of incarceration as a sentencing outcome—though unproven here—cannot in fairness be wholly rejected.

Pretrial Custody and Length of Incarceration

As both Figure 9-3 and Table 9-6 have already indicated, relatively few defendants have survived to the last stage of criminal processing treated in this investigation. Only 7 percent of the original group, or about three-tenths of all convicted Philadelphia defendants were convicted and sentenced to incarceration for varying lengths of time. More than six-tenths of these were detained from preliminary arraignment through to final disposition. Table 9-10 summarizes the relationship between pretrial custody and length of sentence for defendants who were convicted and sentenced to incarceration.[12]

It is first seen from Table 9-10 that a greater proportion (38 percent) of defendants originally released within twenty-four hours of preliminary arraignment than of defendants in the two detention groups received the shortest minimum terms of incarceration (less than one year). Roughly similar proportions of custody groups were given terms with minimums of one year[13]—although defendants who had been detained short-term showed the largest proportion (68 per-

Table 9-10. Step Two Sentencing Outcomes for Convicted Philadelphia Defendants Sentenced to Incarceration: The Relationship Between Pretrial Custody and Length of Incarceration

Pretrial Custody	Total[a]		Length of Minimum Sentences					
			Minimum Terms: Less Than One Year		Minimum Terms: One Year		Minimum Terms: Two Years or More	
	Number	Percent	Number	Percent	Number	Percent	Number	Percent
All convicted Philadelphia defendants sentenced to incarceration	623	100.0	119	19.1	371	59.6	133	21.3
Released within twenty-four hours	128	100.0	48	37.5	68	53.1	12	9.4
Released after twenty-four hours and before final disposition	107	100.0	17	15.9	73	68.2	17	15.9
Detained until final disposition	388	100.0	54	13.9	230	59.3	104	26.8

[a]Subcategories may not sum to total due to rounding.

cent) in this sentence category. And, finally, with a caveat concerning the reliability of estimates based on small numbers in mind, it appears that a larger proportion of long-term detainees than of short-term detainees and immediate releasees were sentenced to terms with minimums of two years or more.

Product moment correlations between sentence length and pretrial custody are shown in Table 9-11. Keeping in mind that sentence length was measured for this analysis as either the amount of "flat" time or the minimum sentence specified if indeterminate, it is seen that only rather weak correlations between sentence length and pretrial custody vectors are produced (Pretrial custody 1 with sentence length, r = .16; Pretrial custody 2 with sentence length, r = .20). Among the six control variables, four were not significantly correlated with sentence length. Charge seriousness showed a correlation, r = .34—as might be expected (the more serious the crime, the longer the sentence). Prior arrests showed a weak, but statistically significant correlation with sentence length (r = .13).[14]

Table 9-11. Product Moment Correlations Between Pretrial Custody Vectors and Six Control Variables[a] with Length of Sentences for Convicted Philadelphia Defendants Sentenced to Incarceration

Dependent Variable: Length of Sentence[b]		
	Pearson's r[c]	*Number*
Pretrial custody 1 (released within twenty-four hours/ detained after twenty-four hours)	.16	(623)
Pretrial custody 2 (released before final disposition/ detained until final disposition)	.20	(623)
Control variables:		
Charge seriousness	.34	(621)
Detainers/warrants	–.03 N.S.	(623)
Number of prior arrests	.13	(623)
On probation, parole or work release	–.10 N.S.	(623)
Open cases	–.10 N.S.	(623)
Number of different offenses charged	.08 N.S.	(588)

[a]Control variables were selected from among the most significant contributors in the multiple regression of pretrial custody on independent variables presented in Appendix C.
[b]Sentence length was defined as a decimal for parts of a year and as whole numbers for years—using either sentence minimums or length of flat sentences.
[c]Nonsignificance is indicated by N.S. Otherwise correlations were significant at the .001 level.

Although there appears to have been only a rather weak relationship evident between custody and sentence length—and mindful of the difficulties of exercising controls with small numbers of cases—the two-step regression control procedure described in earlier analysis was carried out for the sake of consistency. The results are reported in Table 9-12: When the controls were entered as a group on the first step, an R^2 of .12 was produced—due chiefly to the influence of charge seriousness on sentence length. When pretrial custody vectors entered together on a last step an increment of .03 can be noted. It may be concluded that (1) the relationship between pretrial custody and sentence length is relatively weak and that (2) when controls are exercised the relationship is relatively unaffected—that is, it remains inconsequential.[15]

Summary: The Effects of Pretrial Custody on Sentencing

In the analysis of the effects of detention on sentences for convicted Philadelphia defendants, the sentencing decision was viewed and subsequently examined as a contingent, two-step decision process. When the first decision component, the out-or-in decision, was considered, a moderately strong relationship with custody was de-

Table 9-12. Testing the Relationship Between Pretrial Custody and Sentence Length: Multiple Regression of Sentence Length on Six Control Variables (Entered on First Step) and Vectors Representing Pretrial Custody (Entered on Last Step) for Convicted Philadelphia Defendants Sentenced to Incarceration

Dependent Variable: Sentence Length (Flat Time or Minimum Terms)
(Total = 588)

Independent Variables	r	Beta	Multiple R	R^2	R^2 Change[b]
Entering first: control variables					
Charge seriousness	.33	.31	.33	.11	.11
Number of different offenses charged	.08	-.07	.34	.11	<.01
Number of prior arrests	.12	.04	.34	.11	<.01 (N.S.)
Detainers/warrants	-.03	.00	.34	.12	<.01 (N.S.)
Open cases	-.10	-.08	.35	.22	<.01
On probation, parole, work release	-.10	-.06	.35	.12	<.01
Entering second: custody vectors					
Pretrial custody 2	.19	-.18	.39	.15	.03
Pretrial custody 1	.16	.01	.39	.15	<.01 (N.S.)

[a]All contributions are significant at .001, unless indicated by N.S.

tected. When controls were exercised, the impact of pretrial custody on the nonincarceration versus incarceration decision was somewhat diminished, but certainly not "robbed" of all its power. It was concluded that the relationship was not shown to be totally spurious, thus leaving open the possibility that pretrial detention may have negatively biased defendants' chances for nonincarcerative sentences.

A rather slight relationship with pretrial custody was discerned in analysis of sentence length. The relationship was unaffected by the exercise of controls, most of which also showed very weak correlations with sentence length. In the sense that this last analysis may have suffered from inadequate controls (it was not possible to find commonly correlated independent variables) or from the small number of cases (it dealt with only 7 percent of the original cohort), its results may be considered less than conclusive. Yet, the general finding of a rather weak relationship between custody and sentence length in the first place ought to render those qualifications less important.

THE EFFECTS OF DETENTION: THE
VERDICT IN PHILADELPHIA AND
ITS IMPLICATIONS

In the Introduction, it was noted that findings of differential judicial outcomes for defendants who were released versus those who were detained before trial have been reported since the 1930s. The contention that pretrial detention unfairly prejudices a defendant's chances— in terms of adjudication and sentencing—has been a common bail reform argument for nearly two decades. However, as was pointed out earlier, of the three studies that specifically focused on this question, two (Rankin, 1964; Single, 1972) concluded that a defendant's pretrial status was, in some fashion, determinative of the final resolution of his or her case. The third (Landes, 1974) asserted, rather, that the relationship was spurious—that the apparent relationship could be explained by the fact that both bail decisionmaking and later judicial decisions not only operated on the basis of the same information (thus, the common antecedent correlations) but also were in fact decisions very similar in nature. That is, bail and custody decisions— according to the author of the third study—involved preliminary assessment of guilt and assignment of punishment (in terms of money-bail or likely detention). However, in a separate work (Goldkamp, 1977) several important methodological criticisms of these studies were lodged. Two of the most potentially damaging questions concerned the appropriateness of the samples employed and the adequacy of the exercise of multivariate controls. These two issues—as well as others—figured importantly in the design of the present inquiry.

Yet, sampling and statistical concerns aside, another major difficulty with the conclusions drawn by the earlier studies was their "either-or" character. *Either* the relationship existed globally and was causal (two "for"), *or* the relationship existed globally and was spurious (one "against"). The predilection in these studies for generalization can be traced to the method in which their analyses were framed—that is, by considering all final case outcomes together, unidimensionally. Step-by-step analytic models were utilized in the present study to reflect better the nature of the criminal process and to allow for a more detailed appraisal of the effects-of-detention question. The results of the analyses presented demonstrate the advantages of such a method. In short, the "verdict" concerning the relationship of pretrial custody to final case outcomes in Philadelphia is far from an either-or proposition, but varies according to the decision and/or decision component under study.

Using a trifurcated model for the process that resulted in the adjudication of cases, it was shown that for Philadelphia defendants no apparent relationship was discernible between pretrial custody and the dismissal or nondismissal of cases. One immediate implication of this finding is that for one-third of all Philadelphia defendants (those with cases dismissed) the effects of detention had no impact. Yet, a moderately strong relationship between pretrial custody and the diversion or nondiversion of defendants before trial was found when the remaining two-thirds were examined. When controls were exercised, however, this relationship was reduced to nothing and declared spurious (see Figure 9-1, Model 2). The next stage in the analysis called for eliminating defendants who received diversion as a final disposition. This left approximately one-third of the defendant cohort to reach the third and final disposition decision stage: the adjudication of guilt or innocence. Pretrial custody did not appear to be related to the acquittal or conviction of those defendants.

The verdict, then, as it applies to the final dispositions of the cases of Philadelphia defendants is that, regarding dismissal/nondismissal and acquittal/conviction, *no* relationship with pretrial custody was found to exist. But, pretrial custody *was* found to relate—spuriously—to the granting of pretrial diversion. This last result has some interesting ramifications, if the finding of spuriousness suggests that pretrial custody and pretrial diversion were parallel decisions operating on the same kinds of concerns and information. It is suggested here that the diversion/nondiversion decision closely resembles the ROR/not ROR decision that, after all, had such an impact on determining pretrial custody.[16] That is, just as those who were not seriously charged and had no prior criminal records were most likely to be granted ROR at preliminary arraignment, those same kinds of defendants were also likely to be granted pretrial diversion, obviating the requirement for formal adjudication. This contention is supported by the fact that diversion rates diminished markedly across custody categories, from a very high proportion of those immediately released (roughly 70 percent), to a considerably smaller proportion of those detained short-term (roughly 20 percent), to almost none of the defendants who were detained until final disposition of their cases (only 2 percent).

Fortunately, no relationship between a defendant's custody status before trial and his or her adjudication as guilty or innocent was found, implying that other factors—such as findings of fact—may have been more relevant in that determination. It is interesting, however, that among convicted defendants the custody relationship resurfaces in powerful form in the sentencing decision component where incarceration or nonincarceration is decided. Furthermore, although the relatively strong relationship found there diminished noticeably when controls were exercised, a substantial relationship between custody and the in-or-out sentencing decision remained (lending support to Model 1 in Figure 9-1). To the extent that the relationship was not found to be spurious at that stage, it is reasonable to contemplate the possibility that pretrial status may have had a role to play in enhancing or hampering defendants' prospects for nonincarcerative penalties. The finding of a weak custody relationship with sentence length may merely mean that compared to the decision to incarcerate, determination of the length of incarceration was of little import—that is, little variability among defendants sentenced to incarceration remained.

In summary, it has been shown that an either-or characterization of "the" relationship between pretrial custody status and later judicial outcomes is, in the case of this study of Philadelphia defendants at least, a considerable oversimplification. The analyses presented here serve to demonstrate that the relationship in question may or may not exist and may or may not be shown to be spurious, depending on the kind of decision and the place of that decision in the criminal process. The verdict, then, must be "it depends."

NOTES

1. This position was taken in a class action suit brought by a group of inmates awaiting trial in the Brooklyn House of Detention for Men (*Wallace v. Kern* 481 F. 2d 621, 1973).

2. In *Estelle v. Williams* 19 Cr. L. 3061 (1976), the Supreme Court reflected this concern when it ruled that the constitutionally guaranteed presumption of innocence may be impaired when detained defendants are forced to face a jury in jail garb. The Court noted that equal protection may be denied, since it is usually the poor who are detained and who rely on state clothing in jail. Responding to a similar fear that knowledge of a defendant's detention in itself might exert a negative influence on the processing of his or her case, the ABA's *Standards Relating to Pretrial Release* (1968) state under Standard 5.11: "The fact that a defendant has been detained pending trial should not be allowed to prejudice him at the time of trial or sentencing. Care should be taken to ensure that the trial jury is unaware of the defendant's detention."

3. These three terms are variations on the same occurrence. Only a judge may dismiss charges, but discharges and dropped charges may be heavily prosecutor-influenced.

4. Obviously, acquittal differs from dismissal because it is exoneration on a certain charge or charges after formal adjudication.

5. These four types of final disposition are conceived of as ranking from least to most serious. Acquittals are more serious than dismissals because, generally, acquitted defendants have had to struggle against a guilty determination by undergoing formal adjudication. Diversion is considered more serious than acquittal but less serious than conviction because it involves a "penalty" of sorts that by implication belies innocence: defendants must live up to some agreement in order to avoid the stigma of a formal conviction.

6. The principal value of this model lies in its heuristic properties, not in its accurate depiction of reality.

7. Technically, it would be more appropriate to summarize the relationship in a 2 × 2 table by using the *phi* coefficient. As a matter of practicality, Pearson's *r* is employed. It should be noted, however, that both values are identical.

8. In organizing sentence options for coding, a seriousness scheme was again employed. According to this scheme a suspended sentence only was considered least serious; payment of court costs only next; of restitution only next; and of fines only next in seriousness. (Restitution and fines were differentiated on the basis of the actual amounts recorded.) Probation in itself was considered a more serious sentence than any of the preceding sanctions, although it may have been combined with any one of them. In tabular form in the present analysis, the first sentencing category refers to suspended sentences, costs, restitution, or fines only. The probation cells refer to probation only and possible combinations of probation and sanctions of lesser seriousness. Lengths of probationary sentences were disregarded in the present analysis. After probation, incarcerative sentences ranked next in seriousness, ranging from sentences of a few days to life (arbitrarily coded as twenty years). In Philadelphia the possible incarcerative sentences were in two forms: flat terms and indeterminate sentences with minimums and maximums specified. After consultation with Philadelphia prison officials, it was decided to code indeterminate sentences—not by the midpoint of their time spans, which was one possible approach—but by the specified minimum terms, since these reportedly more nearly reflect the usual amounts of time served. For defendants with more than one sentence, the most serious single sentence was selected for use in the analysis.

9. Probationary sentences could range from one to ten years.

10. The author is not original in employing this conceptualization of sentencing. Elaborate precedent has been set by Wilkins et al. (1976).

11. Out of a concern that insufficient controls may have been exercised, yet a third effort, employing fifteen control variables simultaneously, was carried out. In addition to those originally described, such variables as race/ethnicity, sex, prior FTAs, and demographic measures were added to the list of those entered at the first group in regression. Once again, knowledge of both custody vectors was still able to increase the overall R^2 by .11.

12. It should be noted that in this part of the sentencing analysis the number of cases has become rather small and that estimates based on very small numbers may be of questionable reliability. As the number of cases on which the estimates are based becomes smaller, the associated standard error becomes larger. Estimates based on 10 percent of the cases had 95 percent confidence intervals spanning approximately three percentage points. Estimates based on even fewer cases may tend to be much larger. Still, it is worthwhile to examine the relationship, at least in general terms.

13. It is conceivable that, had sentences been coded differently—that is, based on the midpoints of their minimum to maximum terms—greater variability in sentence length may have resulted. This in turn may have allowed for a greater relationship between pretrial custody and sentence length to emerge.

14. One would expect that greater records of prior arrests would be associated with longer terms, other factors being equal.

15. When extra controls were added in subsequent regressions—after the fashion of the in-or-out decision analysis—the results were unchanged.

16. Roughly three-fourths of all those who were released within twenty-four hours of preliminary arraignment secured their release through ROR.

✳ *Part III*

Conclusion

Chapter 10

Bail and Detention in American Justice: Unresolved Issues

Overall, the results of the investigation of bail and detention set forth in this book ought to be viewed with particular pessimism, for they portray a segment of the criminal justice system that appears to be foundering in ideological ambiguity and in operational self-contradiction. To a great extent the bail decision defies open scrutiny because it is conducted securely from within the realm of judicial discretion. This research has demonstrated that the goals of the bail decision are not clearly or authoritatively articulated. The criteria relied on in the bail decision have been characterized as absent, poorly defined, confusing or, even, largely ineffective. Its outcomes may be frequently inadvertent—especially to the extent that release or detention is determined by the defendant's ability to raise cash. And yet, this is the crucial juncture in the early processing of criminal cases where fundamental defendant rights or interests (such as to pretrial liberty and the presumption of innocence) are pitted against those of the state (to guarantee appearance and to protect the community and the integrity of the judicial process). Important advances of bail reform notwithstanding, it may be fair to ask whether in the thousands of bail decisions that occur on a given day in the United States the interests of either party are effectively represented.

THE SEARCH FOR BAIL POLICY

In the early chapters of the book, the evolution of two bail ideologies were traced. Rationales supporting the legitimacy and legality of

217

each view were found. One ideology viewed bail and detention strictly as means to assure the appearance of defendants in court; the other was premised on the much more volatile concern for potential defendant dangerousness, defined in terms of harm to self or to the community and interference with court processes. These concerns were seen to merge in a confusing fashion in some of the guidelines examined. Adding considerably to the vagueness that seemed to confront analysis of the purpose behind the bail decision was the manner in which decision criteria were suggested for consideration in the guidelines. Often no instructions as to how the decision should be made were included; yet in some guidelines many criteria were listed for judicial consideration. When criteria were specified, they were seldom defined; neither were decisionmakers instructed as to their relative importance.

Proponents of both kinds of operational ideologies have been in evidence for a long while: Beeley, for example, was contending in 1927 that bail was only for guaranteeing appearance, and this was a cry often raised by bail reform activists during the 1950s and 1960s. But others have pointed out that denial of bail based on a concern for defendant dangerousness has a long history in the practice of American justice (*e.g.*, Mitchell, 1969; Hess, 1971). It is instructive that the chief arguments raised in support of each position hark back to two cases heard in the same term by the U.S. Supreme Court, (*Stack v. Boyle* and *Carlson v. Landon*) in 1951. Neither variety of bail ideology is able to point to a definitive ruling by the Supreme Court to "prove" its case incontestably; rather each has formulated a tradition of interpretation of its own based on a combination of common-law history, dicta from cases dealing with bail, and/or holdings that do not bear directly on bail practices in the states since they pertain to special circumstances (*e.g.*, *Carlson v. Landon* dealt with detention in a deportation proceeding). Moreover, interpretation has been plagued by the reality that cases dealing with unconvicted defendants have been extremely rare—bail questions are easily mooted by the time appeals can be heard. The analysis presented in the early chapters of this book, then, demonstrates how difficult it is to christen one ideology or the other as *the* constitutionally appropriate one, based on consideration of diverse sources of legal authority.

The two schools of bail thought have not simply existed side-by-side as alternative decision ideologies. It may be more accurate to view them dynamically as two competing ideologies locked in a dialectic relationship. Each has enjoyed greater and lesser degrees of acceptance over time, and it appears that a synthesis or hybrid has begun to appear (NAC, 1973; NAPSA, 1978).

Before the heyday of bail reform during the mid-1960s, for example, bail judges were substantially free to manipulate cash bail for the purposes of dangerousness-oriented preventive detention. The Bail Reform Act and the ABA Standards, however, were high points of bail activism and signaled the dominance of the appearance orientation; danger as a bail concern was carefully restricted. In retrospect, the dominance of the "liberal" appearance view—occuring as it did during the years of social action in many other areas—was tenuous. The American Bar Association, in fact, had narrowly avoided adoption of preventive detention standards in 1968. By 1970, a remarkable shift in the ideological balance had occurred. Under the tutelage of the Nixon-Mitchell administration, Congress passed the so-called Preventive Detention Code for the District of Columbia. With that act, after nearly a decade of increasing legislative disfavor, the danger ideology reemerged in powerful form in legal guidelines, as at least a coequal orientation. Just as the Bail Reform Act had served as a model for the appearance view of bail, the D.C. Code symbolized the legitimization of preventive detention based on defendant dangerousness.

The last decade has not produced a renunciation of preventive detention for danger. Rather, its appeal—political and emotional—has grown stronger, nourished in part by the law-and-order themes of the early 1970s and the same environment that has fostered fear of crime and popular support for capital punishment. NAPSA, an organization whose roots may be traced to the early reform movement, has clearly accommodated the detention-for-danger ideology in its 1978 Standards. Senate Bill 1437 (1978), the Michigan constitutional amendment of the 1978 election, and preventive detention proposals before state legislatures further testify that the ideology is not moribund. Moreover, the way has now been paved for outright (preventive) detention based on risk of flight (NAC, 1973; NAPSA, 1978).

The NAPSA Standards now recognize that bringing detention into the open can only be accomplished by abrogating the use of cash bail entirely. That is, the detention or release decision ought to be explicit and safeguarded by due process protections. Although constitutional questions remain to be tested, even with such safeguards, history will show whether the NAPSA Standards will be remembered for its belated call for abolition of cash bail and the installation of due process at bail *or* for its extension of the preventive detention concept into a new arena—open detention of defendants based on risk of flight. Although prevention of flight is certainly a noncontroversial use of bail, outright detention based on flight is certain to be—as long as it is impossible to predict who will abscond.

Whether one chooses to view the dangerousness ideology as acceptable or not, the results of the study of legal guidelines suggest, perhaps controversially, that it *may* be a constitutionally permissible use of bail. At least, the ambiguity that characterizes sources of legal authority on this question may foster interpretations supportive of both bail ideologies. Clearly, the danger ideology lurks potently behind the scenes of all bail decisionmaking, unaffected by arguments concerning its legality, appropriateness, or definition. It is a bail decision function that has so far proven impossible to regulate through legislation or to "reform" through innovative procedures. Because of the easy political mileage that can be gained from preventive detention proposals, it is certain that the danger issue in bail and detention poses a major dilemma—with overtones that are not only constitutional and judicial but also social and moral.

LESSONS FROM PREVIOUS RESEARCH

In Chapter 5 the aim was to assess the present state of knowledge in the area of bail and detention as reflected by empirical research. A number of descriptive studies—dating from 1927 and characterizing the administration of bail in a variety of jurisdictions—raised issues that remain troublesome to the present day. Common themes in the findings generated by these studies included the following: an excessive reliance on cash bail by bailsetting officials, a mechanical consideration of the nature of the criminal charge as the chief decision criterion (from which detention-for-danger motives were inferred), an unnecessary use of pretrial detention regardless of the apparent rationale, an inappropriate role for bondsmen in mitigating the prospects of release for defendants with cash bail set, and implications that bail decisions might influence the later resolution of defendants' cases. From findings produced in early descriptive studies, it was concluded that much had been amiss with the institutions of bail and detention in the American system of justice. Apart from the descriptive value of these studies, their major contribution was in providing the impetus for the movement toward reform of the bail system that flourished in the 1960s.

Most of the research in the 1960s was closely linked to interest in bail reform. In fact, most of the studies produced in the 1960s were premised on the notion that a great many defendants were detained merely because they could not afford cash bail or the bondsman's fee and that greater use of nonfinancial forms of release ought to be implemented to remedy this injustice. Vera pioneered a fact-gathering procedure that evaluated defendants "objectively" on the basis of community-ties scores as an alternative to the traditional, exclusive reliance on the seriousness of the criminal charge to encourage greater use of ROR at initial appearance. A number of the studies reviewed lent support to the idea that greater use of ROR would not mean an increase in failure-to-appear rates over traditional methods of pretrial release (*i.e.*, cash bail). It has never been demonstrated, however, (1) that use of any criteria, such as community-ties scores or criminal charge, can *effectively* discriminate between defendants who would or would not appear in court or who would or would not commit serious crimes while on pretrial release or (2) that those receiving ROR were defendants who would not have secured release on cash bail. (This last point is important if the aim of ROR programs is to release defendants who would not have been able to afford release on cash bail.) There is, in fact, cause to believe that performance on pretrial release cannot be predicted with reasonable accuracy using community-ties or any other criteria and that indigents needlessly detained under unaffordable cash bail in a traditional system might not gain release on ROR in a more reform-oriented jurisdiction.

When these Chapter 5 findings are tied in with those evolved in earlier chapters, an important implication is the following: *Whichever bail ideology may be operative, no decision criteria—including community ties, charge seriousness, or any others promulgated in the legal guidelines reviewed—have been found to do what presumably they are employed to do; that is, they cannot predict risk of flight or pretrial dangerousness.* Thus, even if there existed unanimity in the matter of bail decision ideology and in the kinds of criteria that ought to be weighed in the bail decision (which clearly there does not), it is impossible that the bail decision could pursue its predictive goals with a reasonable degree of effectiveness, based on any of the data currently available.

It is important to note that in the National Bail Study, Thomas (1976) reported that the use of pretrial detention appeared to have diminished noticeably over the decade surveyed. There are other indications that suggest the length of pretrial confinement may also be decreasing for detained defendants, as court procedures are improved. But weighing against these positive developments are the findings reported in the Survey of Inmates of Local Jails study (Goldkamp, 1977). More precisely, the characteristics of defendants detained in the nation's jails in 1972 closely resembled descriptions of the pretrial confined published in the earliest of bail studies (*e.g.*, Beeley, 1927; Foote. 1954; Alexander et al., 1958)—detainees were still disproportionately young, male, low income or unemployed, and black. If bail reform was indeed initially motivated by concern for jail conditions and by the realization that detention seemed exclusively the lot of the economically disadvantaged, the discouraging implication is that bail reform may not have changed that phenomenon. (This should be understood, of course, in the context of the finding that defendants overall—regardless of pretrial status—may be described in a similar fashion.)

BAIL AND DETENTION IN PHILADELPHIA: THE CHARGE STANDARD

To move from the generalities of the analyses conducted in the early chapters of this book, a case study of bail decisionmaking was undertaken in Philadelphia. Philadelphia was chosen not only because it was an important urban jurisdiction, but also because it had (and has) a national reputation as being a model of bail reform and pretrial services. Thus, rather than examining bail and detention in an "unreformed" jurisdiction and rediscovering the issues highlighted in early bail studies, Philadelphia offered the opportunity to study the bail process "at its best."

Given this characterization of Philadelphia bail procedures and defendant services, it is somewhat surprising to find that factors used in judicial decisionmaking there resembled what might have been expected in a more traditional jurisdiction. More specifically, from empirical analysis of bail decisions and the determination of pretrial custody in Philadelphia, it was learned that the charge-seriousness criterion predominated. By far, the largest shares of variance in both bail and custody analyses were explained by charge indicators. Judges may contend that there is an eminently logical basis for consideration of the seriousness of a defendant's charges in bail determinations: The more seriously a defendant is charged, the more he or she has to fear from conviction and from sentencing by the judge. The longer the possible sentence, bail judges might argue, the greater the incentive to flee and the greater the need for restraint. A supplemental role for prior convictions in bail determinations can be similarly defended: Defendants with prior convictions may have violated probation or parole with the new charges, and may be facing considerable "back time" on old convictions in addition to incarceration that could result from a new conviction.

Although such logic is compelling in that it represents the probable reasoning of many judges who set bail, it raises serious questions concerning the process that determines the release or detention of defendants before trial. First, this rationale for using criminal charge to assess defendants' propensities toward pretrial flight or pretrial crime is not supported by recent empirical research. In fact, studies that have sought statistically to predict pretrial flight or serious pretrial crime based on criteria such as criminal charge, prior record, or community ties have been notably unsuccessful; and where prediction has been shown to be very poor statistically, it is highly unlikely that it would be any more successful intuitively.

Second, it is very likely that such a rationale as the one described above for using the criminal charge criterion (where the seriousness of charges translates into differential probabilities of detention) assumes the guilt of defendants rather than presuming innocence as due process demands. Judgments about defendants' propensities to commit crime on release or to abscond based on consideration of the seriousness of charges necessarily involve judicial projections or assumptions of guilt. That is, high bail is set for seriously charged defendants because it is assumed that they have committed the alleged crimes and that, consequently, (1) they are more likely than other defendants to commit such acts again, and/or (2) they are more likely than other defendants to flee the jurisdiction to avoid conviction and sentencing. Once guilt is assumed from the seriousness of the charge for the purposes of bail, there can be no guarantee that pretrial punishment does not also enter into the use of pretrial detention.

A third problem with judicial reliance on the charge-seriousness criterion is that in a bail system where the cash option is frequently employed—and, it should be noted, cash bail was used in less than half of all cases in Philadelphia—release or detention may be determined by defendants' financial resources rather than more appropriate standards, such as likelihood of flight, thus raising serious equal protection issues. What would appear to be highly equitable on the surface—that similarly charged defendants have similar amounts of cash bail set—proves to be inequitable in practice. Where cash bail is frequently employed, release or detention before trial hinges largely on the differential ability of defendants to afford bail and not on some explicit judicial determination about who should or should not be detained.

Finally, the present system of bail and detention—dependent as it is on the criminal charge criterion and linked as it is with cash bail—has been found by many critics to be objectionable because it engages in preventive-detention decisionmaking without affording a mechanism for review of its custody decisions or the reasoning that led to them. In short, when bail decisionmaking is based chiefly on the seriousness of the charge and detention or release is determined in addition by the defendant's ability to pay, the determination of pretrial custody becomes a rather murky process about which one cannot be certain of the operating judicial concerns—even in a jurisdiction as developed as Philadelphia's. To the extent that the objectives of the decision process that "sorts" defendants into pretrial custody statuses are not clearly articulated, nor the reasoning behind the process and decisions made evident, it is difficult to question the appropriateness of outcomes. It is quite impossible to contest them.

THE EFFECT OF COMMUNITY TIES ON PRETRIAL CUSTODY

Since the early days of bail reform, many projects were instituted and laws enacted on the basis of the belief that data about defendants' community ties could facilitate the release of greater numbers on ROR rather than on cash bail. Knowledge of community ties (family, residence, and employment), it was reasoned, could better enable judges to discern among all defendants entering the criminal process those most likely to flee the jurisdiction or to commit serious crime while on pretrial release. Most bail reform projects operationalized during the last decade and a half have been structured around the tasks of interviewing defendants soon after arrest, compiling summaries of their community ties, and forwarding recommendations for ROR to bail judges. Legislation in the federal jurisdiction and in many states incorporated provisions specifying that judges consider community ties during the bail decision. In some states, like Pennsylvania, judicial consideration of community ties is mandated in court rules. In short, it is no understatement to conclude that the community-ties rationale has been at the heart of bail reform activity for many years. It is surprising, certainly, to find in this study that *in Philadelphia*, a jurisdiction known as a model of bail reform, *interview scores theoretically intended to measure defendants' community ties (along family, residence, and employment dimensions) did not appear to be influential in determining pretrial custody* at either the bivariate or multivariate levels of analysis.

One interpretation of this finding is that, in spite of the elaborate efforts of a model bail reform program, bail judges continue to ignore community-ties information out of preference for the traditional decision criteria: criminal charge, prior criminal record, and indications that defendants have warrants or detainers outstanding. *Apparently, judicial decisionmaking practices are not readily reformed by the mere addition of alternative kinds of data to the process.*

It is quite possible, in fact, that community-ties data have been among the least interesting items of information of which bail judges were made aware in defendant summaries they have been given. In fact, findings of this study suggest that judges may have been selecting out information on charges, prior arrests, and convictions that (in Philadelphia) accompanied summaries of defendants' community ties. Thus, through selective use of the background information provided at first appearance, bail judges in Philadelphia may have inadvertently deflected a reform mechanism from its original goal and used it instead to preserve the very decisionmaking practices that were the target of that reform.

The finding that community ties in Philadelphia did not play a statistically convincing role either in bail decisionmaking or in the determination of pretrial custody poses a difficult dilemma. If it is believed, for example, that community ties ought to play a meaningful role in bail decisionmaking, then questions must be asked about methods for assuring their use in judicial decisionmaking. If, on the other hand, it is no longer believed as it once was that community ties have a meaningful part to play in bail and pretrial custody decisionmaking, serious thought must be given to the relevance of the defendant-interviewing functions of bail reform projects that operate in many jurisdictions in the United States.

THE EFFECTS-OF-DETENTION QUESTION

In Chapter 9 the emphasis shifted from analysis of the bail decision and the determination of pretrial custody to consideration of the possible implications pretrial status might have had for the later resolution of the cases of Philadelphia defendants. It was concluded there that hitherto prevalent generalizations concerning the existence of a relationship between pretrial custody and later case outcomes may have unnecessarily oversimplified the phenomena under investigation. For, in the case of Philadelphia, it was learned that by subdividing final adjudicatory dispositions and sentencing into their respective decision components, the relationship might be seen to apply at certain junctures but clearly not at others. At the two decision points where it was found to exist—for the diversion/nondiversion dichotomy and in the incarceration versus probation sentencing choice—one of the relationships was spurious and one was not. In the case of the spurious relationship, future research might focus on questions about the apparent parallel nature of the determination of pretrial custody (chiefly, of ROR) and the prosecution decision to grant preadjudicatory diversion. Why do both respond similarly to the same decision factors, granting positive outcomes, for example, to those not seriously charged and having no prior records? In the case of the relationship of custody to sentencing—where those who were detained before trial were much more likely to receive incarcerative sentences—spuriousness did not serve as an adequate explanation. *The implications of that finding are more grave, for the possibility remains that the fact of detention before trial may somehow operate to deny convicted defendants equal justice at sentencing.*

TWO CLASSES OF ACCUSED: AN EQUAL PROTECTION ASSESSMENT OF THE FINDINGS

The bail decision process has been viewed—albeit somewhat impersonally—as a sorting mechanism, one that classifies defendants into two classes of accused before trial. The interest of defendants in pretrial release has been described as a "fundamental right" by some courts.[1] According to the U.S. Supreme Court, the constitutionality of a classification where a fundamental right is at issue may be judged by the manner in which the "distinctions made" in creating the classification have relevance to the purpose for which it was made.[2] It may be worthwhile to consider briefly the findings generated in the present study in the light of this equal protection/classification perspective.

The initial analytic task, undertaken in Chapters 2 through 4, involved an attempt to define a state interest or purpose behind the bail decision and the use of pretrial detention by examining a wide variety of legal guidelines. As noted above, two such interests were discerned: the interest in assuring that defendants will appear in court as required and the interest in protecting the community and the judicial process from defendants deemed to be dangerous. The question of whether the classification of defendants promotes these two interests is difficult to answer, for it must be tied to consideration of the standard concerning the nature of the classification (the distinctions made) and also weighed against the emerging defendant right to pretrial release. That is, does a classification based on charge relate to prediction of flight or danger? And, how strong a relationship must be demonstrated to legitimate the classification of some defendants as detainees in the face of their interest or right to pretrial release? Without considering these questions together, it would be difficult to counter the claim that detention of *all* defendants before trial would promote prevention of pretrial flight and pretrial danger quite effectively.

Inquiry into the distinctions made among defendants was carried out in the study from two perspectives. First, legal guidelines were scrutinized nationally for any instructions to bail decisionmakers that might serve as *prescriptions* for the proper classification of defendants in light of the two state interests outlined. Second, the bail decision and the determination of pretrial custody were analyzed empirically to learn what kinds of decision criteria (defendant characteristics) *actually* determined pretrial custody status in the case of one major urban jurisdiction. From the first investigation, it was found that a decisionmaker who relied on the prescriptive decision criteria set forth in many legal guidelines examined would probably become quite confused. Either no instructions pertaining to the evaluation of defendants were found, or just a few were in evidence, or a uselessly large list of recommended criteria was encountered. If poor definition of classification criteria was grounds for a finding of unconstitutionality, present legal guidelines in many states relating to bail and detention would surely be suspect.

But, from the analysis of bail decisionmaking and pretrial custody status in Philadelphia, it cannot be claimed that definition of the actual distinctions or classifying criteria remained mysterious or vague. Clearly, the principal distinction drawn by judges at bailsetting in Philadelphia was the nature of the defendant's charge: A nonserious charge usually meant ROR; a very serious charge meant comparatively high bail or, in the case of murder defendants, detention without bail. Custody outcomes were also heavily influenced by charge (the more seriously charged defendants were more likely to be detained) but were determined as well by such concerns as whether or not detainers or warrants were outstanding; whether other cases were already being processed involving the same defendants; or whether a defendant was on probation, parole, or work release. To a marginal but nevertheless disturbing extent, race/ethnicity and several indicators related to a defendant's socioeconomic status (*e.g.*, income, having a telephone, owning a motor vehicle) were factors in the classification of defendants as detained or released before trial.

But with these findings reported, the following question must be posed: Does the formulation of the pretrial classification of defendants (*i.e.*, the distinctions made) demonstrate "some relevance" to the purpose(s) for which it is made? The response is difficult, for it depends on the level of proof required. According to the purposes discerned in the analysis of legal guidelines, the chief business of the pretrial classification of defendants should be the prediction of likely absconders and dangerous defendants. Thus, whether the classification had relevance to the state interests delineated would require a strong showing that such predictive aims were served rather well. In the critical review of research presented in Chapter 5, it was emphasized that no such ability has yet been demonstrated—based either on community ties, charge seriousness, or any other available criteria. So, if the burden fell to the state to show that—in the face of a defendant's right to pretrial release—the present operation of the bail decision is relevant to the causes of assuring appearance and protecting the community from dangerous defendants, in the strictest empirical sense it would fail. The state could not demonstrate that the bail decision and the use of detention in a given jurisdiction serve to keep failure-to-appear rates and rates of pretrial crime at a noticeably lower rate than if all defendants were released before trial.

It must be admitted, however, that part of the reason this has not been shown can be explained by the unfeasibility of (and the risk that would be involved in) the ideal experiment. It would be a rare judge who offered to release *all* defendants on his or her own responsibility just to learn what would happen. Short of such a showing—one based on rigorously derived empirical findings—how then can the classification of defendants before trial be evaluated from an equal protection point of view? Does the nature of the classification then need only to show a "logical" relationship to the function it is thought to serve? If so, it then becomes necessary to ask only, in the instance of Philadelphia, if it is logical to differentiate among defendants based on charge seriousness. (There is little doubt, as previously noted, that judges could describe a logical relationship between the charge criterion and flight and/or dangerousness.) Or, perhaps, it would be necessary to show that the basis of the classification was not only logical but also somehow ethically "fair." Thus, as long as the classification scheme did not rely on race/ethnicity, income, and/or sex, for example, it could be judged acceptable from an equal protection point of view—because, in spite of the fact that it could not be shown to "work" in predicting defendant flight or danger, the distinctions made among defendants would be *intended* logically to serve those purposes without unfairly discriminating against particular subgroups of defendants.

But, even lessening the level of proof required to meet the equal protection standard of constitutionality, it is still not very easy to assess the Philadelphia results. Certainly, any influential role for race/ethnicity, or having a telephone, or owning a motor vehicle might cause the Philadelphia pretrial classification of defendants to be found quite objectionable (if one were to assume, for example, that the last two factors were tied to socioeconomic status). The roles of such indicators as detainers/warrants, open cases, probationary or parole status would, however, seem to meet the "logical" as well as the "fairness" standard.

The major question, however, would revolve around the dominant role of the nature of the criminal charge. Available research does not convincingly support the notion that the more serious a defendant's charge, the greater the likelihood that he or she will flee or commit serious crimes if released. It must be recognized, however, that as the level of proof moves away from the realm of empirical demonstration and into the realm of the subjective, the final judgment concerning the appropriateness of an almost exclusive reliance on criminal charge moves beyond the province of the researcher and becomes the responsibility of the legislature or the judiciary.

Chapter 9's findings also have weighty equal protection implications. There, a relationship between pretrial custody and sentencing outcomes was found when convicted defendants were studied. It appeared that defendants who had been released before trial were much more likely than defendants who had been detained to receive non-incarcerative sentences, even after controls were exercised. The relationship between pretrial custody and sentencing certainly requires more study, but the fact that pretrial detention would negatively influence a defendant's chances at sentencing certainly suggests that the pretrial classification of defendants in Philadelphia may in some respect act to deny equal justice to detained defendants.

DISPARITY IN BAIL AND DETENTION

The multivariate approaches presented in Chapters 7 and 8 were undertaken in part with the equal protection/classification framework in mind. That is, by searching for the factors most influential in bail decisions and custody outcomes, the real aim was to learn about the distinctions made among defendants entering the criminal process. The logic implicit in that analysis was that if defendants were classified according to certain discernible patterns, variance would of course be explained. It would only be necessary next to ascertain whether or not these decision criteria, or distinctions, had relevance to the purposes of the pretrial classification process (predicting flight or danger).

Although the multivariate analyses reported were moderately successful in isolating the dominant decision criteria (mainly criminal charge), a considerable amount of variance was left unexplained in each case. This finding raises an equal protection issue of another sort: disparity or "unwarranted variation"[3] in bail decisions. Simply stated, the large amount of variance left unexplained in the multivariate analyses suggests that to a significant degree no patterns or discernible distinctions systematically organized the Philadelphia bail and custody decisions. Certainly, it is conceivable that had other recorded data been available (*e.g.*, data relating to judge characteristics, defendant demeanor, or system variables), more variance might have been explained. But is is also highly plausible that the bail decisions studied were not more consistent than portrayed in these data. (Refer to the R^2 statistics in the analyses in Chapters 7 and 8.) In fact, it may be true that for the sample of Philadelphia defendants studied, the granting of ROR and cash bail and the determination of custody status for "similarly situated" defendants were *not* comparable. Disparity in bail decisions, therefore, may be as important an equal protection issue as it is in sentencing (Gottfredson et al., 1978). Yet disparity is not an unexpected result, given the ambiguous definition of goals and prescriptive criteria in guidelines across the United States.

CONCLUSION: MORE QUESTIONS

Although a number of useful findings may have been generated in the present study, it is not easy to conclude—for it is not clear that a conclusion is at all fitting. Much has been learned about bail decision-making, the role of pretrial detention, and the obscure theoretical framework from within which they operate. For instance, in this book the nature and impact of two competing bail ideologies have been documented. But, it has not been learned whether the perceived dialectic between the danger and appearance orientations toward bail is to be viewed as intentional and constructive—or as an inadvertent artifact of legal history. Legal analysis aside, are both orientations in fact equally acceptable? Why or why not?

In addition, it was discovered in the study of decision criteria recommended in a wide variety of guidelines that the sought-after "concrete" instructions resembled a forest into which prospective bail decisionmakers should not enter with much hope of finding clear, operational bearings. In fact, such a decisionmaker would probably find only enough insight there to confirm his or her original ideological stance. The confused state of prescriptive guidelines in the area of bail may stem from the fact that the purposes of the bail decision and the use of detention are not authoritatively or clearly set forth, much less well understood. For, given clear purposes for the bail decision, how could there be such an incredible variety of ways to accomplish them?

When bail and detention were studied in one jurisdiction—one with all the progressive features of an ROR/community-ties/appearance-oriented system—it was found that community ties had little to do with either the bail decision or the determination of pretrial custody. Rather, the seriousness of a defendant's criminal charge played the major (though not sole) role in those decisions. It was not learned, however, whether reliance on charge was entirely reprehensible or, to the contrary, perhaps almost as acceptable as any other criterion when faced with the realization that no criteria have been shown to predict flight-risk or dangerousness accurately. Without some evidence showing that certain criteria work well or poorly depending on the predictive aim (appearance or dangerousness), there are few empirical grounds for favoring or rejecting community ties or charge seriousness, for example. And if the proof cannot be acquired through empirical demonstration, on what grounds is the acceptability of the classification of defendants before trial determined?

Further, it was found in Chapter 9 that there may have been a negative impact on the prospects of defendants for nonincarcerative sanctions at sentencing, if they were detained before trial. The reason for this finding is not clear, but further investigation is clearly warranted. Why might a prejudicial effect from pretrial detention be experienced at sentencing but not in the adjudication of defendants' cases?

Hopefully, this inquiry has in its various facets contributed to the understanding of pretrial detention and bail decisionmaking—and their perplexing places in the American criminal process. Perhaps the most striking consequence of this investigation, however, is the realization that, in spite of the herculean efforts of reformers during the last decade, there has been little impact on a number of what by now are certainly very old issues. Rather, these issues may only have been sharpened, and new questions may have been raised that make their eventual resolution even more difficult.

NOTES

1. A Federal District Court in *Ackies v. Purdy* 322 F. Supp. 38, 41 (S.D. Fla., 1970) asserted that "the right to pretrial release under reasonable conditions is a fundamental right." More recently, a Federal Court of Appeals alluded to a right to release in its holding in *Pugh v. Rainwater*, 557 F.2d 1189 (5th Cir., 1977) as "the defendant's right to be free before trial, regardless of his financial status."

2. *Baxstrom v. Herold* 383 U.S. 107, 111 (1966).

3. This expression, "unwarranted variation," is borrowed from the discussion of disparity in sentencing outcomes by Gottfredson et al. (1978).

※ *Appendix A*

Directory of State Bail Guidelines

Alabama
Ala. Const. Art. I, §16
Ala. Code tit. 12, §4-5; tit. 15, §7-
22, tit. 15, §§13-1 to 13-8;
tit. 15, §13-40; tit. 15, §13-80;
Ala. Rules Jud. Admin. 2

Alaska
Alaska Const. Art. I, §§11,12
Alaska Stat. §12.30.010-080

Arizona
Ariz. Const. Art. II, §§15,22
Ariz. Rev. Stat. §§13:1571-1577
Ariz. Rules Crim. Pro. 7.1-7.6

Arkansas
Ark. Const. Art. II, §§8,9
Ark. Stat. Ann. §§43:609;613;622;
701-724
Ark. Rules Crim. Pro. 8.3-8.5;9.1-9.3

California
Cal. Const. Art. I, §12
Cal. [Penal] Code §§815a;985;1268-
1309;1318;1318.4(West)

Colorado
Colo. Const. Art. II, §§19,20
Colo. Rev. Stat. §§16-4-101 to 111

Connecticut
Conn. Const. Art. I, §§8,13,14
Conn. Gen. Stat. §§54:1-b;53;63;69

Delaware
Del. Const. Art. I, §§11,12
Del. Code tit. 11, §§2101-2115
Del. Common Pleas Court Crim. Rule
46

District of Columbia
D.C. Code §§23:1321-1332

Florida
Fla. Const. Art. I, §14
Fla. Stat. Ann. §§903.02 *et seq.*
Fla. Rules Crim. Pro. 3.130

Georgia
Ga. Const. Art. I, §8
Ga. Code §§27-901 to 915;1402

Hawaii
Haw. Const. Art. I, §9
Haw. Rev. Stat. §§660-30;660-31;
804-1 to 804-19

Idaho
Idaho Const. Art. I, §6
Idaho Code §§19-2901 to 2937

Illinois
Ill. Const. Art. I, §9
Ill. Rev. Stat. Ch. 38, §§102-6;
110-1 to 110-15

Indiana
Ind. Const. Art. I, §§16,17
Ind. Code §35-1-18-1

Iowa
Iowa Const. Art. I, §§12,17
Iowa Code §§811.1-811.9

Kansas
Kan. Const. Bill of Rights, §9
Kan. Stat. §22:2801-2905

Kentucky
Ky. Const. Bill of Rights, §§16,17
Ky. Rev. Stat. §§431:510-530
Ky. Rules Crim. Pro. 3.06;4.00-4.30

Louisiana
La. Const. Art. I, §12
La. Code Crim. Pro. Ann. Art. 311-
322;330;336(West)

Maine
Me. Const. Art. I, §§9,10
Me. Rev. Stat. tit. 15, §942
Me. Rules Crim. Pro. 46

Maryland
Md. Const. Dec. of Rights, Art. 25
Md. Ann. Code, Art. 27, §§638A;
638B

Massachusetts
Mass. Const. Part I, Art. 26
Mass. Gen. Laws Ann. Ch. 276,
§§42,58

Michigan
Mich. Const. Art. I, §§15,16
Mich. Comp. Laws §§765.1-765.31;
780.61-780.69(West)

Minnesota
Minn. Const. Art. I, §§5,7
Minn. Stat. §629.01-629.72
Minn. Rules Crim. Pro. 6.02

Mississippi
Miss. Const. Art. III, §29
Miss. Code Ann. §§99-5-1 to 99-
5-35

Missouri
Mo. Const. Art. I, §§20,21
Mo. Rev. Stat. §§544.040;455
Mo. Sup. Ct. Rules 21.12;21.14;
32.01-32.18

Montana
Mont. Const. Art. II, §§21,22
Mont. Rev. Codes Ann. §§95-1101 to
95-1123

Nebraska
Neb. Const. Art. I, §9
Neb. Rev. Stat. §§29:901-910

Nevada

Nev. Const. Art. I, §§6,7
Nev. Rev. Stat. §§173.175;178.484–
178.546

New Hampshire

N.H. Const. Part I, Art. 33
N.H. Rev. Stat. Ann. §§597:1–42

New Jersey

N.J. Const. Art. I, ¶¶11,12
N.J. Rules Crim. Pro. 3.26.1 to 3.26.7

New Mexico

N.M. Const. Art. II, §13
N.M. Stat. Ann. §§41–23–21 to 41–
23–26 (N.M. Crim. Pro. Rules
21–26)

New York

N.Y. Const. Art. I, §5
N.Y. [Crim. Pro.] Law, §§500.10;
510.30(McKinney)

North Carolina

N.C. Const. Art. I, §27
N.C. Gen. Stat. §§15A–531 to 534

North Dakota

N.D. Const. Art. I, §6
N.D. Rules Crim. Pro. 46§
29–08–26

Ohio

Ohio Const. Art. I, §9
Ohio Rules Crim. Pro. 46

Oklahoma

Okla. Const. Art. II, §§8,9
Okla. Stat. tit. 22, §§1101–1109

Oregon

Or. Const. Art. I, §§14,16
Or. Rev. Stat. §§135:230–295

Pennsylvania

Pa. Const. Art. I, §§ 13, 14, 19
Pa. Const. Stat. §§ 51–95
Pa. Rules Crim. Pro. 4001–4018
Philadelphia Schedule 5:16

Rhode Island

R.I. Const. Art. I, §§8,9
R.I. Gen. Laws, §§12–13–1 to 12–
13–20

South Carolina

S.C. Const. Art. I, §15
S.C. Code, §§17–15–10 to 17–15–220

South Dakota

S.D. Const. Art. VI, §§8,23
S.D. Comp. Laws Ann. §§23A–43–1
to 23A–43–32

Tennessee

Tenn. Const. Art. I, §§15,16
Tenn. Code Ann. §§40–1201 to 1247

Texas

Tex. Const. Art. I, §§11,11a,13
Tex. [Crim. Pro.] Code Ann. Tit. 17,
§§01–38

Utah

Utah Const. Art. I, §§8,9
Utah Code Ann. §§77–43–1 to
77–43–30

Vermont

Vt. Const. Ch. II, §40
Vt. Stat. Ann. tit. 13, §§7551–7573

Virginia

Va. Const. Art. I, §9
Va. Code §§19.1-109 to 19.1-124

Washington

Wash. Const. Art. I, §§14,20
Wash. Rev. Code §§10.19.010-
  10.19.130

West Virginia

W.Va. Const. Art. III, §§5,8
W.Va. Code §§62-1c-1 to 62-1c-19

Wisconsin

Wis. Const. Art. I, §§6,8
Wis. Stat. §§969:01-14

Wyoming

Wyo. Const. Art. I, §14
Wyo. Stat. §§7-10-101 to 7-10-121
Wyo. Rules Crim. Pro. 8

Pennsylvania Rules of Criminal Procedure—4001,4003,4004

Rule 4001. Setting of Bail Prior to Trial
(a) Pretrial bail shall be set:

1. by any issuing authority in all cases as provided by law;
2. by a judge of court of common pleas,
   (i)   when the issuing authority has no jurisdiction to set bail; and
   (ii) upon application by the defendant or his attorney, when bail has been denied or excessive bail has been set.

(b) A defendant may be admitted to bail on any day and at any time.

Note: Adopted July 23, 1973, effective sixty days hence, replacing prior Rule 4002.

Comment: The effect of this Rule is to permit justices of the peace, Pittsburgh police magistrates, and non-law judges of the Municipal Court of Philadelphia to set bail in all cases except those in which murder or voluntary manslaughter is charged. This is a change from prior Rule 4002, which permitted members of the minor judiciary to set bail for defendants charged with arson, rape, mayhem, sodomy, burglary, robbery or involuntary manslaughter only if the attorney for the Commonwealth approved. The instant Rule eliminates the requirement of such approval.

It is important to note that the Act of March 31, 1860, P.L. 427, §7, as amended through the Act of October 18, 1972, P.L.—No. 226, 19 P.S. §51, is suspended by Rule 4018(a) only insofar as it is inconsistent with the Rules of Chapter 4000. The inconsistency is two-fold. First, the said Act precludes members of the minor judiciary from setting bail in the offenses specified in the preceding paragraph. Second, the Act requires all bailed defendants to have one or more sureties. This is inconsistent with Rule 4003, which requires a defendant to be released on his own recognizance, without a surety, under circumstances specified herein.

Aside from these inconsistencies the Act remains in effect, including the extension of bail-setting authority to law judges of the Municipal Court of Philadelphia in murder and manslaughter cases.

Rule 4003. Release of Defendant on Defendant's own Recognizance or on Nominal Bail

(a) The issuing authority or the court shall release a defendant on his own recognizance (R.O.R.) or on nominal bail when:

1. the most serious offense charged is punishable by a maximum sentence of imprisonment of not more than three years, and
2. the defendant is a resident of the Commonwealth, and
3. the defendant poses no threat of immediate physical harm to himself or to others, and
4. the issuing authority or the court has reasonable grounds to believe that a defendant will appear as required.

(b) In court cases when the most serious offense charged is punishable by a sentence of imprisonment of more than three years, the issuing authority or the court may release a defendant on his own recognizance (R.O.R.) or on nominal bail.

(c) A defendant released on his own recognizance (R.O.R.) or on nominal bail shall execute a bond as set forth in Rule 4014.

Rule 4007 adopted November 22, 1965, effective June 1, 1966; amended, effective March 18, 1972; renumbered as Rule 4003 and amended July 23, 1973, effective in 60 days.

Comment: Section (a) is designed to facilitate the release of persons charged with minor crimes. Many justices of the peace have been releasing defendants on nominal bail as a matter of course when the criteria set out in Section (a) were met, and the Philadelphia Municipal Court, in such cases, has released defendants on their own recognizance (R.O.R.) with the assistance of a special R.O.R. program. The intention of this Section is to make such policy uniform throughout the Commonwealth.

Section (b) is intended to continue the policy of permitting release on defendant's own recognizance or on nominal bail in any appropriate case in which the issuing authority or the court has the power to set bail.

Nominal bail may be used as an alternative to the system of releasing a defendant on his own recognizance when it is desirable to have a surety. The purpose of the surety is to facilitate interstate apprehension of any defendant who absconds by allowing the nominal surety the right to arrest defendant without the necessity of extradition proceedings. See Frisbie v. Collins, 72 S.Ct. 509, 342 U.S. 519, 96 L.Ed. 541 (1952), rehearing denied 72 S.Ct. 768, 343 U.S. 937, 96 L.Ed. 1344. R.O.R. should be used when a defendant has a family and economic ties with the community, is not likely to flee the jurisdiction, and does not appear to need a third party to assure his appearance.

For suspension of Act of Assembly, see Rule 4018(c).

Rule 4004. Standards for Setting Bail

In setting pre-verdict bail, bail shall be such as to insure the presence of the defendant as required by the bond and shall be determined according to the following standards:

- (i) the nature of the offense charged and any mitigating or aggravating factor that may bear upon the likelihood of conviction and possible penalty;
- (ii) the defendant's employment status and history and his financial condition;
- (iii) the nature of his family relationships;
- (iv) his past and present residences;
- (v) his age, character, reputation, mental condition, record of relevant convictions, and whether addicted to alcohol or drugs;
- (vi) if he has previously been released on bail, whether he appeared as required; and
- (vii) any other facts relevant to whether the defendant has strong ties with the community or is likely to flee the jurisdiction.

Note: Adopted July 23, 1973, effective sixty days hence, replacing prior Rule 4005.

Comment: "Pre-verdict" means all stages from the initiation of criminal proceedings up to and including trial, until a finding of guilt. For standards following a guilty verdict, see Rule 4010.

Bail shall not be set solely according to the designation of the offense, but must be based on the standards set forth in this Rule.

For suspension of Acts of Assembly, see Rule 4018(d).

✳ *Appendix C*

List of Variables in the Philadelphia Data

I. From Court preliminary arraignment listings:
   Philadelphia photo number (individual identification number)
   Case (Municipal Court) identification number
   Date of preliminary arraignment of first appearance
   Criminal charges
   Number of transcripts
   Immediate bail outcome (detained, ROR, Ten Percent)
   Custody status after first appearance
II. From files of Pretrial Services Division:
   Age at preliminary arraignment
   Race/ethnicity (black, white, Hispanic/other)
   Sex
   Custody status
   Philadelphia photo number
   Case identification number
   Pays own utilities
   Relationship of complaining witness to defendant
   On public assistance
   Philadelphia resident
   Length of residence in Philadelphia
   Kind of residence in Philadelphia
   Has phone in residence
   Length of present residence
   Open cases (pending cases for which defendant was on pre- or post-
      adjudicatory release: no, yes)
   Defendant lives with (relationship_____)

Pays own rent or mortgage
Amount of rent or mortgage
Prior residence
Kind of prior residence
Length of prior residence
Family in Philadelphia not living with defendant
Marital status (never married, widowed, divorced, married/common-
  law marriage)
Presently separated
Does defendant support partner
How many children does defendant have
By whom (spouse, friend)
Children living with whom
Presently employed
Length of present employment
Type of present occupation
Weekly earnings
Prior employment
Length of prior employment
Type of prior occupation
Length of unemployment
Student (no/yes)
Highest grade completed
Military service
Owns motor vehicle
Outstanding loans
Health: physical disorder (no/yes)
Hospitalized: mental disorder (no/yes)
Narcotics use
How long
Last use
Kind of use
Treated for drug abuse
Alcohol abuse
Treated for alcoholism
Prior record (for misdemeanors and/or felonies)
Prior FTAs
Currently on probation, parole, or work release
References given (number of)
Attorney listed
Probable surety listed
Defendant requests court appointed counsel
Qualifies for Philadelphia court

Qualifies for TASC
Recommendation for ROR (no/yes)
Points: Philadelphia residence
Points: present/prior address
Points: family
Points: employment history
Points: total
If no recommendation for ROR, reason given:

    Nature of charge
    Prior record
    Prior FTAs
    Open cases
    Interview waived
    Address not verified
    Insufficient community ties/family ties
    On conditional release
    Other reasons given

Detainers or warrants outstanding
Is public defender listed
Shift when preliminary arraignment occurred
Judge at preliminary arraignment
Disposition of preliminary arraignment
Cash bail: amount
Criminal charges
Number of charges
Number of transcripts
Number of counts
Weapons charges
Attempt or conspiracy charges
Prostitution
III. Data Processing Unit of the Court of Common Pleas and the Municipal Court of Philadelphia:
Number of prior arrests
Most serious prior arrests
Mean seriousness of prior arrests
Number of prior convictions
Most serious prior convictions
Mean seriousness of prior convictions
Subsequent arrests
Subsequent convictions
Philadelphia photo number

Case identification number (Municipal Court and Court of Common
  Pleas)
Criminal charges
Number of transcripts
Representation by counsel
Type of surety
Pretrial custody final status
Preliminary arraignment outcomes

✳ *Appendix D*

Coding of Charge in the Philadelphia Study

Description of defendants in terms of the offenses with which they were charged is not necessarily a simple task. Charging may be a relatively complex phenomenon, and any attempt to simplify it to facilitate description may result in discarding potentially useful information. In Philadelphia as well as in most other jurisdictions, for example, a defendant may be charged with not one but a configuration of offenses seen by the police as the equivalent of a particular alleged criminal act. Thus, a defendant suspected of committing a burglary may be charged not only with burglary but also with possession of stolen property. In Philadelphia each "configuration" of charges is processed on paper as a single complaint or "transcript" and bail must be decided for each. It is true that most Philadelphia defendants (93 percent) were processed on the basis of only one transcript, but 5 percent were processed for two, and 2 percent for three or more. Each transcript could include up to nine individual charges.

Further complicating any attempt to describe defendants' charges simply is the fact that—as an artifact of configuration charging—many defendants were charged with more than one kind of offense—this apart from transcript considerations. For 38 percent of Philadelphia defendants, the task was simple; they were processed on the basis of only one kind of charge included on a single transcript. However, 16 percent were charged with two different offenses; 15 percent with three; and 32 percent with as many as four or more. And, as a final obstacle to descriptive simplicity, it should further be noted that not only can a defendant be charged with more than one kind of offense on more than one transcript but he or she may be charged with more than one "count" of a particular offense on one or more transcripts.

To begin to simplify criminal charges of Philadelphia defendants, it was necessary first to employ a scheme that ranked charges according to their relative seriousness. Because there is no "universal" seriousness-ranking scheme available to solve this problem, a seriousness-ranking scheme first adapted by the U.S. Bureau of the Census from the Federal Bureau of Investigation's *Uniform Crime Reports* (see Goldkamp, 1977) was further adapted for use in this study. Using this ranking scheme, all the offenses charged for each individual defendant were ranked according to seriousness. (Example: A defendant charged with drunkenness, simple assault, and robbery would have the charge ranked in just that order, low to high.)

Then, the single most serious offense (robbery, in the example) associated with the arrest of each defendant was selected. (Attempts were coded as equivalent to completed acts.)

Approximately 180 different criminal charges were grouped and ranked according to the following scheme (from *least* to *most* serious):

1. Traffic-related offenses—especially driving while under the influence of alcohol or drugs
2. Drunkenness, vagrancy, disorderly conduct, loitering and prowling, failure to disperse, defiant trespass
3. Petty larceny, retail theft, shoplifting
4. Possession of drugs (knowing and intentional possession of a controlled substance)
5. Other offenses/not included elsewhere
6. Other offenses/public order: liquor, cigarette tax violations, gambling, gaming, lotteries
7. Other offenses/property: receiving stolen property, criminal mischief, malicious mischief, vandalism, bad checks
8. Other offenses/sex: indecent assault, lewd and lascivious behavior, incest, sodomy, prostitution
9. Weapons violations
10. Forgery, fraud, credit cards
11. Simple assault, assault and battery, reckless endangerment, terroristic threats
12. Auto theft, unauthorized use of an auto
13. Grand theft, grand larceny
14. Burglary
15. Drug sales, or manufacture of, possession with intent to deliver or delivery of a controlled substance

16. Aggravated assault, motor vehicle manslaughter, involuntary manslaughter
17. Arson
18. Robbery
19. Forcible rape, involuntary deviate sexual intercourse, statutory rape
20. Murder, willful killing, kidnapping, voluntary manslaughter

This classification scheme was based on expected charge patterns. But as actual charges were compared with the expected, a need for revision became evident. For instance, it was expected that a sizeable number of persons would have been arrested for auto theft—hence, the ninth category was devoted only to that crime. In reality, so few of the sample defendants were charged with that offense (as their "most serious") that it formed a category so small that it would have been of little analytic value. It was also thought that arson, because of its unique character, would constitute a separate offense category (17). However, not only were arson arrests very infrequent, but they were not of the serious type. Consequently the need for an arson category was reexamined.

In addition, because analysis of charge based on twenty subcategories would still be unwieldy, the classification was further consolidated into only twelve subcategories. This entailed combining the following subcategories from the above classification: rape (19) with murder/kidnapping (20) to form a "violent personal crimes" category; drug sales (15) with drug possession (4) to form a "drugs-combined" category; weapons (9) with simple assaults (11); arson (17) with auto theft (12), forgery/fraud (10), other offense/property (7), and petty larceny (3) to form a "lesser property offenses" category; and other offenses/sex (8) with other offenses/public order (6) to form a "public nuisance/public order" category. The following simplified classification scheme resulted (ranked from least to most serious):

1. Other—miscellaneous
2. Traffic/Driving while intoxicated
3. Drunkenness/disorderly
4. Public nuisance/public order
5. Lesser property offenses
6. Simple assaults/weapons
7. Theft/larceny
8. Burglary

9.   Drugs-combined
10.   Aggravated assaults
11.   Robbery
12.   Violent personal crimes

In the analyses, "offense" or "charge" will refer to the single most serious offense charged as determined by the procedures outlined above.

References

1951   *Black's Law Dictionary.* St. Paul, Minn.: West Publishing Co.

Alexander, George; M. Glass; P. Kind; J. Palermo; J. Roberts; and A. Schurz

1958   "A Study of the Administration of Bail in New York City." 106 *University of Pennsylvania Law Review* 685.

American Bar Association

1968   *Standards Relating to Pretrial Release.* Approved draft.

1978   *Standards Relating to the Administration of Criminal Justice: Pretrial Release.* 2d ed., tentative draft.

American Law Institute

1965   *Model Code of Pre-arraignment Procedure.* Philadelphia: American Law Institute.

Angel, Arthur; E. Green; H. Kaufman; and E. Van Loon

1971   "Preventive Detention: An Empirical Analysis." 6 *Harvard Civil Rights—Civil Liberties Law Review* 301.

Ares, Charles; A. Rankin; and H. Sturz

1963   "The Manhattan Bail Project: An Interim Report on the Use of Pretrial Parole." 38 *New York University Law Review* 67.

Attorney General's Committee on Poverty and the Administration of Federal Criminal Justice

1963   *Poverty and the Administration of Federal Criminal Justice.* Washington, D.C.: U.S. Government Printing Office.

Barnes, Harry E. and Teeters, Negley K.

1959   *New Horizons in Criminology.* New York: Prentice-Hall.

Bases, Nan C. and McDonald, William F.

1975   *Preventive Detention in the District of Columbia: The First Ten Months.* Washington, D.C.: Georgetown Institute of Criminal Law and Procedure; New York: Vera Institute of Justice.

249

Beaudin, Bruce
 1970–1971 "Bail in the District—What It Was; Is; and Will be." 20 *American Law Review* 432.
Beeley, Arthur
 1927   *The Bail System in Chicago.* University of Chicago Press; reprint ed., Chicago: University of Chicago Press, 1966.
Bogomolney, Robert and W. Gau
 1972   "An Evaluation of the Dallas Pre-Trial Release Project." 26 *Southwestern Law Journal* 510.
Borman, Paul
 1971   "The Selling of Preventive Detention." 65/6 *Northwestern Law Review* 879.
Bowman, Charles H.
 1965   "The Illinois Ten Percent Bail Deposit Provision." 1965 *University of Illinois Law Forum* 35.
Brockett, William
 1973   "Presumed Guilty: The Pretrial Detainee." 1 *Yale Review of Law and Social Action* 10.
Burns, Henry
 1971   "The American Jail in Perspective." 17 *Crime and Delinquency* 446.
Chicago Community Trust
 1922   *Survey of the Cook County Jail.* Chicago: Chicago Community Trust.
Clarke, Stevens; J. Freeman; and G. Koch
 1976   *The Effectiveness of Bail Systems: An Analysis of Failure-to-Appear in Court and Rearrest While on Bail.* Chapel Hill: Institute of Government, University of North Carolina at Chapel Hill.
Dershowitz, Alan
 1970   "The Law of Dangerousness: Some Fictions About Prediction." 23 *Journal of Legal Education* 24.
Dill, Forrest
 1972   "Bail and Bail Reform: A Sociological Study." Ph.D. dissertation, University of California at Berkeley.
Ervin, Sam
 1971   "Foreword: Preventive Detention—A Step Backward for Criminal Justice." 6 *Harvard Civil Rights—Civil Liberties Law Review* 290.
Fabricant, Neil
 1968–1969 "Bail As a Preferred Freedom and the Failures of New York's Revision." 18/1 *Buffalo Law Review* 303.
Feeley, Malcolm and J. McNaughton
 1974   "The Pretrial Process in the Sixth Circuit: A Qualitative and Legal Analysis." Mimeographed. New Haven.
Feeney, Floyd
 1972   "Citation in Lieu of Arrest: The New California Law." 25 *Vanderbilt Law Review* 367.
Foote, Caleb
 1954   "Compelling Appearance in Court: Administration of Bail in Philadelphia." 102 *University of Pennsylvania Law Review* 1031.

1965a "The Coming Constitutional Crisis in Bail: I." 113 *University of Pennsylvania Law Review* 959.

1965b "The Coming Constitutional Crisis in Bail: II." 113 *University of Pennsylvania Law Review* 1125.

Foucault, Michel
1973 *Madness and Civilization.* New York: Vintage Books.

Freed, Daniel and P. Wald
1964 *Bail in the United States: 1964.* Working paper. National Conference on Bail and Criminal Justice; May, 1964.

Friedman, Lee
1976 "The Evolution of A Bail Reform." 7 *Policy Sciences* 281.

Gedney, Dewaine L.
1976 "Readings on the Bail System of the Court of Common Pleas and Municipal Court of Philadelphia." Philadelphia: Pretrial Services Division of Philadelphia Court of Common Pleas. Mimeographed.

Goldfarb, Ronald
1965 *Ransom: A Critique of the American Bail System.* New York: John Wiley and Sons.

Goldkamp, John S.
1977 "Bail Decisionmaking and the Role of Pretrial Detention in American Justice." Ph.D. dissertation, School of Criminal Justice, State University of New York at Albany.

1978 *Inmates of American Jails: A Descriptive Study.* Working Paper Number One. Albany: Criminal Justice Research Center.

1979a "American Jails: Characteristics and Legal Predicaments of Inmates." 15/3 *Criminal Law Bulletin* 223 (May-June).

1979b "Philadelphia Revisited: An Examination of Bail and Detention Two Decades After Foote." *Crime and Delinquency*, in press.

Gottfredson, Don M.; Leslie T. Wilkins; and Peter B. Hoffman
1978 *Guidelines for Parole and Sentencing.* Lexington, Mass.: D.C. Heath.

Gottfredson, Michael R.
1974 "An Empirical Analysis of Pretrial Release Decisions." 2 *Journal of Criminal Justice* 287.

1976 "The Classification of Crimes and Victims." Ph.D. dissertation, School of Criminal Justice, State University of New York at Albany.

Groege, James
1970 *First Annual Report of the Indianapolis Bail Project 1970.* Indianapolis: Indianapolis Bail Project, Indianapolis Law School.

Hawthorne, Jack and M. McCully
1970 "Release on Recognizance in Kalamazoo County." 49 *Michigan State Bar Journal* 23.

Hess, Frederick
1971 "Pretrial Detention and the 1970 D.C. Crime Act—The Next Step in Bail Reform." 37 *Brooklyn Law Review* 277.

Hindelang, Michael
1972 "On the Methodological Rigor of the Bellamy Memorandum." 8 *Criminal Law Bulletin* 507.

Hindelang, Michael; Michael R. Gottfredson and James Garofalo.
   1978   *Victims of Personal Crime: An Empirical Foundation for a Theory of Personal Victimization.* Cambridge: Ballinger Publishing Co.
Kennedy, Padraic
   1968   "Vista Volunteers Bring About Successful Bail Reform Project in Baltimore." 54 *American Bar Association Journal* 1093.
Kerlinger, Fred and E. Pedhazur
   1973   *Multiple Regression in Behavioral Research.* New York: Holt, Rinehart, and Winston.
Kirby, Michael P.
   1974   "An Evaluation of Pretrial Release and Bail Bond in Memphis and Shelby County." Mimeographed. Memphis: Policy Research Institute, Southwestern at Memphis.
Kish, Leslie
   1953   "Selection of the Sample," in L. Festinger and D. Katz, eds. *Research Methods in the Behavioral Sciences.* New York: Dryden Press.
Kituse, J. and A. Cicourel
   1963   "A Note on the Use of Official Statistics." 9 *Social Problems* 247.
Kuykendall, Jack L. and R.W. Deming
   1967   "Pretrial Release in Oakland, California: Final Research Report." Mimeographed. Oakland: Pretrial Release Agency.
Labovitz, Sanford
   1967   "Some Observations on Measurement and Statistics." 56 *Social Forces* 151–160.
Landes, William
   1973   "The Bail System: An Economic Approach." 2 *Journal of Legal Studies* 79.
   1974   "Legality and Reality: Some Evidence on Criminal Proceedings." 3 *Journal of Legal Studies* 287.
Lazarsfeld, Paul F.
   1974   "An Evaluation of the Pretrial Services Agency of the Vera Institute of Justice." N.Y.: Vera Institute. Unpublished report.
Lewin, Gerald
   1969   "The San Francisco Bail Project." 55 *American Bar Association Journal* 135.
Locke, J.W.; R. Penn; R. Rick; E. Bunten; and G. Hare
   1970   *Compilation and Use of Criminal Court Data in Relation to Pretrial Release of Defendants: Pilot Study.* Washington, D.C.: U.S. Government Printing Office.
Mattick, Hans
   1975   "The Contemporary Jails of the United States," in Daniel Glaser, ed. *Handbook of Criminology.* Chicago: Rand McNally.
MacNaughton-Smith, P.
   1963   "The Classification of Individuals By the Possession of Attributes Associated With a Criterion." 19 *Biometrics* 364.

McCarthy, David and J. Wahl
    1965   "The District of Columbia Bail Project: Illustration of Experimentation and a Brief for Change." 55(3) *The Georgetown Law Journal* 218.
Mitchell, John
    1969   "Bail Reform and the Constitutionality of Pretrial Detention." 55 *Virginia Law Review* 1223.
Morris, Norval
    1974   *The Future of Imprisonment.* Chicago: University of Chicago Press.
Morse, Wayne and R. Beattie
    1932   "Survey of the Administration of Criminal Justice in Oregon." *Oregon Law Review* (Supp. 1932)100; reprint ed., New York: Arno Press, 1974.
Mullen, Joan
    1974   *Pretrial Services: An Evaluation of Policy Related Research.* Cambridge, Mass.: ABT Associates.
National Advisory Commission on Criminal Justice Standards and Goals
    1973   *Corrections.* Washington, D.C.: U.S. Government Printing Office.
National Association of Pretrial Services Agencies
    1977   "Performance Standards and Goals for Pretrial Release." Unpublished draft. Washington, D.C.: National Association of Pretrial Services Agencies.
    1978   *Performance Standards and Goals for Pretrial Release and Diversion: Release.* Washington, D.C.: National Association of Pretrial Services Agencies.
National Center for State Courts
    1975   *An Evaluation of Policy-related Research on the Effectiveness of Pretrial Release Programs.* Denver: National Center for State Courts.
National Conference of Commissioners on Uniform State Laws
    1974   *Uniform Rules of Criminal Procedure.* St. Paul: West Publishing Co.
Obert, Ronald J.
    1973   *Pretrial Release Program in an Urban Area: Final Report.* Santa Clara: Santa Clara Pretrial Release Program.
O'Rourke, Thomas and R. Carter
    1970   "The Connecticut Bail Commission." 79 *Yale Law Review* 513.
Ozanne, Marq; R. Wilson; and D. Gedney
    1976   *Toward a Theory of Bail Risk. Wilmington: College of Urban Affairs,* University of Delaware.
Plato
    1960   *The Laws.* Translated by A.E. Taylor. London: J.M. Dent and Sons.
Pound, Roscoe and F. Frankfurter
    1922   *Criminal Justice in Cleveland.* Cleveland: The Cleveland Foundation; reprint ed., Montclair, N.J.: Patterson Smith, 1968.
President's Commission on Crime in the District of Columbia
    1966   *Report of the President's Commission on Crime in the District of Columbia.* Washington, D.C.: U.S. Government Printing Office.

President's Commission on Law Enforcement and Administration of Justice
  1967 *Task Force Report: Corrections.* Washington, D.C.: U.S. Government Printing Office.
Rankin, Anne
  1964 "The Effect of Pretrial Detention." 39 *New York University Law Review* 641.
Rothman, David J.
  1971 *The Discovery of the Asylum: Social Order and Disorder in the New Republic.* Boston: Little, Brown.
San Francisco Committee on Crime
  1971 *A Report on the Criminal Court of San Francisco: Part II, Bail and OR Release.* San Francisco: The San Francisco Committee on Crime.
Schaffer, Stephen
  1970 "Bail and Parole Jumping in Manhattan in 1967." Mimeographed. New York: Vera Institute of Justice.
Sellin, Thorsten
  1938 *Culture Conflict and Crime.* New York: Social Science Research Council.
Sellin, Thorsten and Marvin Wolfgang
  1964 *The Measurement of Delinquency.* New York: Wiley and Sons.
Silverstein, Lee
  1966 "Bail in the State Courts—A Field Study and Report." 50 *Minnesota Law Review* 621.
Single, Eric
  1972 "The Unconstitutional Administration of Bail: Bellamy v. The Judges of New York City." 8 *Criminal Law Bulletin* 459.
Steadman, Henry
  1973 "Some Evidence on the Inadequacy of the Concept and Determination of Dangerousness in Law and Psychiatry." 13 *Journal of Psychiatry and the Law* 409.
Steadman, Henry and Cocozza, Joseph
  1974 *Careers of the Criminally Insane.* Lexington, Mass.: Lexington Books, D.C. Heath.
Stochastic Systems Research Corporation
  1972 *An Evaluation of Monroe County (New York) Pretrial Release, Inc.* Rochester, N.Y.: Stochastic Systems Research Corporation.
Sykes, Gresham
  1958 *Society of Captives.* Princeton: Princeton University Press, 1958.
Teague, H.
  1965 "The Administration of Bail and Pretrial Freedom in Texas." 43 *Texas Law Review* 356.
Thomas, Wayne
  1976 *Bail Reform in America.* Berkeley: University of California Press.
Tribe, Laurence
  1970 "An Ounce of Detention: Preventive Justice in the Works of John Mitchell." 56 *Virginia Law Review* 371.

Turk, Austin
1969   *Criminality and Legal Order.* Chicago: Rand-McNally.
U.S. Department of Justice, Law Enforcement Assistance Administration, National Criminal Justice Statistics Service
1974a   *National Jail Census, 1970.* Series SC–No. 1. Washington, D.C.: U.S. Department of Justice, Law Enforcement Assistance Administration, National Criminal Justice Statistics Service.
1974b   "Survey of Inmates of Local Jails, 1972: Advance Report." Washington, D.C.: U.S. Department of Justice, Law Enforcement Assistance Administration.
1975   "The Nation's Jails: A Report on the Census of Jails from the 1972 Survey of Inmates of Local Jails." Washington, D.C.: U.S. Department of Justice, Law Enforcement Assistance Administration.
Vera Institute of Justice
1965   *National Conference on Bail and Criminal Justice: Proceedings and Interim Report,* Washington, D.C. and N.Y.: The Vera Foundation.
von Hirsch, Andrew
1972   "Prediction of Criminal Conduct and Preventive Confinement of Convicted Persons." 21(3) *Buffalo Law Review* 717.
Wald, Patricia
1972   "The Right to Bail Revisited: A Decade of Promise Without Fulfillment." In Stuart S. Nagel (ed.), "The Rights of the Accused." 1 *Sage Criminal Justice Annuals* 175.
Welsh, J. Daniel
1977   "The Pretrial Offender in the District of Columbia: A Report on the Characteristics and Processing of 1975 Defendants." Washington, D.C.: District of Columbia Bail Agency, Statistical Analysis Center, Office of Criminal Justice Planning and Analysis.
Wice, Paul
1970   *Bail and Its Reform: A Summary Report.* U.S. Department of Justice, Law Enforcement Assistance Administration. Washington, D.C.: U.S. Government Printing Office.
1973   "Bail Reform in American Cities." 9 *Criminal Law Bulletin* 770.
1974   *Freedom for Sale.* Lexington, Mass.: Lexington Books, D.C. Heath.
Wilkins, Leslie; Kress, Jack; Gottfredson, Don; Calpin, Joseph; Gelman, Arthur
1976   *Sentencing Guidelines: Structuring Judicial Discretion.* Albany: Criminal Justice Research Center.
Wilson, Robert
1975   "A Practical Procedure For Developing and Updating Release on Recognizance Criteria." Wilmington: College of Urban Affairs, University of Delaware.

Author Index

Alexander, Glass, Kind, Palermo,
    Roberts and Schurz, 13n, 83,
    84, 105n 221
Angel, Green, Kaufman and Vanloon,
    95, 98-100
Ares, Rankin and Sturz, 4, 84, 88,
    106n, 108n
Barnes and Teeters, 4
Bases and McDonald, 53n
Beaudin, 53n
Beeley, 13n, 18, 36n, 78-79, 81, 87,
    103, 104n, 218, 221
Bogomolney, 107n
Borman, 32n
Brockett, 185
Burns, 4
Clarke, Freeman and Koch, 107n
Dershowitz, 108n
Dill, 9
Ervin, 52n
Fabricant, 17
Feeley and McNaughton, 93, 97, 103,
    107n
Feeney, 9
Foote, 5, 13n, 16, 17, 18, 36n, 81-83,
    103, 104n, 182, 221
Foucault, 4
Freed and Wald, 5, 9, 88-89, 106n
Friedman, 6
Gedney, 119, 120, 134n, 135n
Goldfarb, 104n
Goldkamp, 13n, 53n, 86-87, 88,
    106n, 133, 134n, 186, 109, 221

Gottfredson (Don), Wilkins and
    Hoffman, 231n
Gottfredson (Michael), 93-94, 96, 104,
    107n, 108n, 130n, 174, 183n
Groege, 107n
Hawthorne and McCully, 107n
Hess, 16, 32n, 34, 218
Hindelang, Gottfredson (Michael) and
    Garofalo, 145-169
Kennedy, 106
Kerlinger and Redhazur, 145, 150n,
    160n, 183n
Kirby, 98
Kish, 135n
Kituse and Cicourel, 135n
Koza and Doob, 186
Kuykendall and and Deming, 107n
Labovitz, 145
Landes, 92, 93, 96, 97, 103, 108n,
    186, 187, 209
Lazarsfeld, 91, 93, 102
Lewin, 106n
Locke, Penn, Rick, Bunten and Hare,
    95-96, 97
Mattick, 4
MacNaughton-Smith, 92, 174
McCarthy and Wahl, 84-85, 106n
Mitchell, 16, 32n, 34, 218
Morris, 108n
Morse and Beattie, 18, 36n, 79-81,
    103, 104n
Mullen, 104n
Obert, 107n

O'Rourke, 107n
Ozanne, Wilson and Gedney, 92, 102
Plato, 4
Pound and Frankfurter, 79, 104
Rankin, 103, 186, 187, 209
Rothman, 4
Schaffer, 89, 92
Sellin, 135n
Sellin and Wolfgang, 135n
Silverstein, 105n
Single, 103, 108n, 186, 187, 209
Steadman and Cocozza, 108n

Sykes, 12
Teague, 105n
Thomas, 5, 6, 9, 13n, 85-86, 87, 91,
    105n, 106n, 108n, 221
Turk, 135n
von Hirsch, 108n
Wald, 6
Welsh, 92, 98
Wice, 90, 106n, 107n
Wilkins, Kress, Gottfredson (Don),
    Calpin and Gelman, 213
Wilson, 92

Subject Index

American Bar Association
  Standards 1968, 39-41
  1968 preventive detention proposal,
    51n-52n
  Standards 1978, 53n
Analytic models
  for bail decisionmaking, 143-145
  for effects of detention, 186-189
  for adjudication, 191-193
  for sentencing, 201-202
Bail
  definition, 6-7
  history, 4-5
  caselaw, 18-23, 25-31, 72
  denial of, 5, 16-17, 62
  excessive, 33n, 34
  right to, 16-18, 31-32n, 60
Bail decision
  as classification mechanism, 11-12
  capital cases, 16-17, 23, 31-32, 34
  criteria, 9, 15, 25, 25-30
  danger, 18-23, 27-31, 35n, 36n, 68,
    69, 70-73
  equal protection, 11-12, 226-230
  flight, 18-23, 26-27, 88-92
  gatekeeping mechanism for
    detention, 4, 7, 8,
  in Philadelphia, 81-83, 139-161
  noncapital cases, 23, 31-32n, 34n
Bail policy, 70-73, 217-221
Bail reform, 4-6, 224-225, 230-231
Chicago Study, 78-79
Classes of accused, 4, 12, 174-182,
  185, 226-227

Conditional release, 5, 114
Community ties, 5, 6, 68, 88-92, 93,
  101, 125
  in Philadelphia, 158, 224-225
  validity of, 92-95, 221
Criminal charge, 9, 13n, 67-68, 107n
  in Philadelphia, 157, 221-224,
    245-248
Criminal record, 68, 158
Disparity in bail, 229-230
District of Columbia Study, 84-85
Due Process, 3, 33n
Effects of detention, 8, 10, 80, 85,
  185-188, 209-211, 225-226
  in Philadelphia: on adjudication,
    189-209, on sentencing, 199-209
  Models explaining, 185-188
Equal protection, 11-12, 226-229
Failure to appear, 89-92, 106n
Federal Bail Reform Act of 1966,
  2, 3, 25, 35n, 61, 67, 72
Financial ability of defendants, 21,
  33n, 68
Harvard Preventive Detention Study,
  98-100
Michigan Amendment of 1978, 72,
  219
National Advisory Commission on
  Criminal Justice Standards and
  Goals, 43-45, 50
National Association of Pretrial
  Services Agencies, 46-49, 51, 219
National Bail Study, 85-86, 105n
New York Study, 83-84

Oregon Study, 79-81
Philadelphia
  characteristics of defendants,
    126-133
  community ties, 127-133
  description of the bail process,
    112-122
  legal guidelines for bail, 115-122,
    237-239
  variables in the study, 241-244
  bail decisions, 139-143
    by selected attributes, 142-143
    multivariate analysis, 145-157
    ROR, 145-151
    detention without bail, 151
    cash bail, 151-157
    Ten Percent bail, 114, 115
    criminal charge, 157, 222-224
    community ties, 158, 224-225
  Pretrial custody
    by selected attributes, 165-169
    multivariate analysis, 169-174
    predictive attribute analysis,
      174-182
    criminal charge, 222-224
    community ties, 224-225
  effects of detention, 185-211
Philadelphia Bail Study of 1954,
    81-83
Pretrial crime, 95-100
  prediction of, 97
Pretrial detention
  as classification, 12
  as punishment, 3, 11, 33n
  due process, 3, 33n
  due process, 3, 33n
  equal protection, 11-12, 226-230
  history, 4-5
  prediction of, 174-182
  reform, 5
Presumption of innocence, 3, 19

Preventive detention, 32n
  American Bar Association, 51n-52n,
    53n
  criticisms, 52n
  District of Columbia Code, 41-43,
    51
  NAC, 53n
  NAPSA, 47-48
  procedures, 52n
  URCP, 45-46
Previous research, 77-108, 220-222
Proof and presumption clause, 55-59
ROR, 5, 13n
  presumption favoring, 20, 21, 23,
    24, 88-92
ROR interview, 5, 9, 81, 84, 88, 91,
    93, 101
  in Philadelphia, 112-114, 117-122
Right to pretrial release, 11, 20, 21
Sample design and methodology
  previous research, 103-104, 105n,
    107n, 108n
  Philadelphia, 111-115, 122-126,
    133-137n
State bail laws, 55-75, 223-236
  bail schedules, 62
  directory, 233-236
  prescriptive criteria, 62-70
  provisions, 55-62
  purpose clauses, 61
  vagueness, 63-66
Survey of Inmates of Local Jails,
    86-87
Ten Percent bail, 5, 13n
  in Philadelphia, 114, 153
Uniform Crime Reports
  charge grading, 246
URCP, 45-46, 51
United States Constitution, 15-16, 72
Vera New York study, 84

About the Author

John S. Goldkamp is presently assistant professor and Acting Chairperson in the Department of Criminal Justice, Temple University. He earned his Ph.D. in criminal justice from the School of Criminal Justice, State University of New York at Albany, and worked at the Criminal Justice Research Center as a research analyst. Presently, he co-directs a project funded by the National Institute of Corrections to study the feasiblity of a guidelines approach to bail.